What People Are Saying About
Chicken Soup for the Unsinkable Soul . . .

"This is a very smart book. It understands that no obstacle in life is hardy enough to resist a strong character, a valiant heart and a ready sense of humor."

Eunice Shriver
founder, Special Olympics,
executive vice president, Joseph P. Kennedy Jr. Foundation

"It is known that nothing is more important than persistence and perseverance. *Unsinkable Soul* is a moving read."

James Redfield
author, *The Celestine Prophecy*

"Too many of us stuff our bodies and starve our souls. Now straight out of God's kitchen comes *Chicken Soup for the Unsinkable Soul*. I heartily recommend it for those who've learned that we cannot live by bread alone."

Jack Anderson
news correspondent

"The search for inspiring, uplifting and challenging illustrations for the Sunday sermon has been made extremely easy through the wonderful stories in *Chicken Soup for the Soul*. The congregation always wants to know the source of the stories. These true-life stories are great encouragement to hungry souls."

Dennis G. Wood
president, Purpose Ministries

"My dreams were dashed at age eighteen; I was completely paralyzed by polio. I eventually achieved my dreams because of encouragement from people like the ones in *Chicken Soup for the Unsinkable Soul*."

Dan Miller
motivational speaker and author,
Living, Laughing and Loving Life!

"*Chicken Soup for the Unsinkable Soul* is a wonderful selection of inspirational stories. They tell how you can achieve a meaningful life with belief in yourself, in the greatness of people and the goodness of God."

Ruth Stafford Peale
chairman, Guideposts, Inc.

"Each story in *Chicken Soup for the Unsinkable Soul* will be read with zest, pondered quietly, and used widely—a truly life-affirming accomplishment."

Rabbi Earl A. Grollman, DHC, D.D.
author, *Living When a Loved One Has Died*

"*Chicken Soup for the Unsinkable Soul* is a collection of short stories that are inspirational, heartwarming and profoundly meaningful. These anecdotes provide examples of the indomitable human spirit. Open your heart with this book and your life will be forever enriched."

Dr. Nilufer P. Medora
professor, child development and family studies

"Thank you for *Chicken Soup for the Unsinkable Soul*! Everybody goes through tough times sooner or later. This book shows how others made it and how you can too."

Harold H. LeCrone Jr., Ph.D.
psychologist and author, *Striking Out at Stress*

"The stories in *Chicken Soup for the Unsinkable Soul* are incredible! People need a well-balanced diet—this extraordinary *Chicken Soup* book meets that requirement resoundingly."

Ronnie Marroquin
president, Rutherford Publishing, Inc.

"Here is a book that can give hope to those in search of hope, courage to those who need courage, and fresh insight into how to live every day to its fullest."

Venita VanCaspel Harris
author, *Money Dynamics for the 1990s*
founder, VanCaspel & Company, Inc.

CHICKEN SOUP FOR THE UNSINKABLE SOUL

101 Inspirational Stories of Overcoming Life's Challenges

Jack Canfield
Mark Victor Hansen
Heather McNamara

Health Communications, Inc.
Deerfield Beach, Florida

www.hci-online.com
www.chickensoup.com

We would like to acknowledge the following publishers and individuals for permission to reprint the following material. (Note: The stories that were penned anonymously, that are in the public domain, or that were written by Jack Canfield, Mark Victor Hansen or Heather McNamara are not included in this listing.)

Growing Roots. Excerpted from *Front Porch Tales,* ©1997 by Philip Gulley. Used by permission of Multnomah Publishers, Inc.

A New Day for Dorothy. By Frances Leslie. Reprinted with permission from *Guideposts* magazine. Copyright ©1966 by *Guideposts,* Carmel, NY 10512.

My Mother's Greatest Gift. Reprinted by permission of Marie Ragghianti. ©1999 Marie Ragghianti.

Sensory Deprivation. Reprinted by permission of Deborah Hill. ©1999 Deborah Hill.

The Ugliest Cat in the World, The Flight of the Red-Tail, The Ludenschide Connection and *Cyclops Stole Our Hearts.* Reprinted by permission of Penny Porter. ©1999 Penny Porter.

(Continued on page 368)

Library of Congress Cataloging-in-Publication Data

Chicken soup for the unsinkable soul: 101 inspirational stories of overcoming life's challenges / [compiled by] Jack Canfield, Mark Victor Hansen, Heather McNamara.
    p.   cm.
    ISBN 1-55874-698-6
    1. Conduct of life.   2. Spiritual life.   I. Canfield, Jack.   II. Hansen, Mark Victor.
III. McNamara, Heather.
    BJ1597.C45   1999
    158.1'28—dc21   99-28465
                                          CIP

Publisher: Health Communications, Inc.
               3201 S.W. 15th Street
               Deerfield Beach, FL 33442-8190

Cover redesign by Lisa Camp
Book design by Lawna Patterson Oldfield

Contents

3. THE POWER OF LOVE

4. THE POWER OF SUPPORT

5. INSIGHTS AND LESSONS

6. ON COURAGE AND DETERMINATION

7. ON ATTITUDE

8. A MATTER OF PERSPECTIVE

9. ECLECTIC WISDOM

Acknowledgments

Chicken Soup for the Unsinkable Soul took more than three years to write, compile and edit. It has been a joyous— though often difficult—task, and we wish to thank the following people whose contributions have made it possible.

Our life partners, Inga, Patty and Rick, and our children, Christopher, Oran, Kyle, Elisabeth and Melanie, who have supported us for months through the process of compiling this book.

Georgia Noble, for being such a beautiful person and for sharing your heart with us.

Patty Aubery, who was always there when we needed her, as well as for keeping the whole *Chicken Soup for the Soul* central office up and running in the middle of what always feels like a tornado of activity.

Nancy Autio, our friend, thank you for your invaluable feedback and for your impeccable job researching and obtaining permissions.

Katy McNamara-Abatemarco, who read many of the stories, and who thought up the title that best befits the stories included in this book.

Cristi Leahs, who did an extraordinary job reading and researching stories. We deeply appreciate your support, your friendship and your loving attention to this project.

Leslie Forbes, for an outstanding job starting the permission process and assisting whenever and wherever needed. D'ette Corona, a new addition at Chicken Soup Enterprises, for diving in at the end of this project and doing what she could to help.

Peter Vegso at Health Communications, Inc., for his continuing vision of the direction and value of *Chicken Soup* books, and for his unflagging support in getting these stories out to people all over the world.

Veronica Valenzuela, Robin Yerian, Lisa Williams, Laurie Hartman and Deborah Hatchell for working to make sure everything ran smoothly during the production of this book.

Rosalie Miller, who kept all of the communication flowing efficiently throughout this project, all while triumphing over her own obstacles.

Teresa Esparza, who brilliantly coordinated all of Jack's speaking, travel, and radio and television appearances during this time.

Christine Belleris, Matthew Diener, Lisa Drucker and Allison Janse, our editors at Health Communications, Inc., for bringing this book to its high state of excellence. You bring such value to the *Chicken Soup* series. You also never falter in the support department; we thank you for that.

Erica and Maryanne Orloff, Ann Reeves and Eric Wing for their brilliant edits and input on the stories in this book.

Randee Feldman, *Chicken Soup for the Soul* manager at Health Communications, Inc., for her masterful coordination and support of all the *Chicken Soup* projects.

Terry Burke and the sales team, Kelly Maragni and the marketing team at Health Communications, Inc., for their wonderful sales and marketing efforts.

Lisa Camp at Health Communications, Inc., for working with us so patiently and cooperatively on the cover design of this book. And Lawna Oldfield and Dawn Grove for their skillful typesetting of the book.

We also want to thank the following people who completed the monumental task of reading the preliminary manuscript of the book, helped us make the final selections, and made invaluable comments on how to improve the book: Tamy Aberson, Willanne Ackerman, Jerry Acuña, Fred Angelis, Nancy Autio, Christine Belleris, Bonnie Block, Nora Bridges, Julie Brookhart, Dave and Marsha Carruthers, Diana Chapman, Linda Rohland Day, Mary Jane West Delgado, Eldon Edwards, Nancy Richard Guilford, Elinor Hall, Sandra Hutchins, Allison Janse, Bettie Kapiloff, Robin Kotok, Tom Krause, Lillian Lamb, Cristi Leahs, Audrey Lohr, Barbara LoMonaco, Robert MacPhee, Danny and Laura McNamara, Joan McVittie, Suzanne Ohler, Judie Sinclair, Milly VanDerpool, Danene Van Hecker and Dottie Walters.

To the more than five thousand "Daily Soup" subscribers who answered our call for a title with wonderful suggestions. You all played an integral part in deciding the title of this book!

Chicken Soup coauthors: Patty and Jeff Aubery, Nancy Autio, Marty Becker, Dan Clark, Tim Clauss, Barbara De Angelis, Mark and Chrissy Donnelly, Irene Dunlap, Patty Hansen, Jennifer Read Hawthorne, Kimberly Kirberger, Carol Kline, Hanoch and Meladee McCarty, Maida Rogerson, Martin Rutte, Marci Shimoff and Barry Spilchuk.

Larry and Linda Price, who, in addition to keeping Jack's Foundation for Self-Esteem operating smoothly, continue to administrate the Soup Kitchens for the Soul project, which distributes thousands of *Chicken Soup for the Soul* books free each year to prisoners, halfway houses, homeless shelters, battered women's shelters and inner-city schools.

To Kim Weiss, who is a pleasure, a great publicist and a great friend. And to Kim's diligent and conscientious staff, Larry Getlen and Ronni O'Brien.

Rick Frischman at Planned Television Arts and Newmann Communications, who continue to help us keep our books on the bestseller lists.

Claude Choquette and Tom Sand, who manage year after year to get each of our books translated into more than twenty languages around the world.

We also wish to thank the more than eight thousand people who took the time to submit stories, poems and other pieces for consideration. You all know who you are. While many of the stories submitted were wonderful, most did not fit into the overall structure of the book. However, many will be used in future volumes of the *Chicken Soup for the Soul* series.

Because of the immensity of this project, we may have left out names of some people who helped us along the way. If so, we are sorry. Please know that we really do appreciate all of you.

We are truly grateful for the many hands and hearts that made this book possible. We love you all!

Introduction

Un·sink·able Soul (un sink ā´bᴇl sōl) **noun. 1.** Person who faces any challenge with hope, humor and heart. See stick-to-it-ness. See perseverance. See pit bull. See also victory.

Since the first *Chicken Soup for the Soul* book was released, readers continue to tell us that their favorite chapter is Overcoming Obstacles.

It's no wonder. We all face obstacles—some are tiny hurdles that may trip us up for a time before we land on our feet; others loom like ominous clouds, sending even the bravest souls in search of shelter. How we handle these situations determines the course of our life; whether we will live with fear and anger or acceptance and joy.

We compiled *Chicken Soup for the Unsinkable Soul* to help readers overcome the obstacles in their daily lives, whether they're dealing with an emotional loss, battling an illness, experiencing the ups and downs of pursuing a lifelong dream, or trying to make themselves a better person.

From the humorous to the heroic, from the extraordinary to the everyday, each story emphasizes victory in spite of the odds. For instance, you'll share in the triumph of a determined climber who scaled one of the world's most challenging mountains despite being blind; a middle-aged woman who took a chance on a new career and became an award-winning columnist; a little girl with a stuttering problem who found her voice at a school pageant; and a young mother who was suddenly paralyzed but chose to embrace the positive over pity.

With each turn of the page in chapters like Taking the Challenge and Living Your Dream, you'll find yourself amazed at how others have taken risks and kept their faith even when others told them, "It can't be done!"

The chapters on Attitude and A Matter of Perspective will show you how to view life through hopeful eyes—to see a hurdle as a possible stepping stone to something great—and to appreciate the things you have.

You'll come to realize the priceless value of unconditional support by reading The Power of Love and The Power of Support. We hope these stories encourage you to reach out to others when you need help and to open your heart to someone who needs a shoulder on which to lean.

And finally, Eclectic Wisdom proves that many times obstacles are our best teachers: They shine a light on our strengths; remind us of the areas we need to improve; show us to have faith in ourselves; and force us to accept things that are beyond our control.

We offer this book as a gift to you. We hope you find it an instrument of strength and a constant reminder that you *do* have the power to achieve your dreams.

Share with Us

We would love to hear your reactions to this book. Please let us know what your favorite stories were and how they affected you. Tell us if you want to see more or less of something in the next book, and please tell us if a story resulted in you changing in any way.

We also invite you to send us items you would like to see published in future editions of *Chicken Soup for the Unsinkable Soul.* You can send us stories, poems and cartoons you have written or ones written by others (from the newspaper, newsletters, magazines, bulletin boards, refrigerator, etc.).

It is our belief that the next book will be even better because so many more of you will know about it and will submit your stories for consideration.

Write to us and send your submissions to:

Chicken Soup for the Unsinkable Soul
P.O. Box 30880-U
Santa Barbara, CA 93130
fax: 805-563-2945

You can also submit a story or send an e-mail by visiting our Web site at: *www.chickensoup.com.*

"CHICKEN SOUP FOR THE SOLE."

CALLAHAN

[EDITORS' NOTE: *John Callahan's sense of humor is shaped in part by his being a quadriplegic, but also by his being an adopted child, having been educated in Catholic schools, and being a recovered alcoholic.*]

Reprinted by permission of Levin Represents.

1

TAKING THE CHALLENGE

A ship in port is safe, but this is not what
ships are built for.

Grace Hopper

Growing Roots

Our strength grows out of our weakness.

Ralph Waldo Emerson

When I was growing up, I had an old neighbor named Dr. Gibbs. He didn't look like any doctor I'd ever known. Every time I saw him, he wore denim overalls and a straw hat, the front brim of which was green sunglass plastic. He smiled a lot, a smile that matched his hat—old and crinkly and well worn. He never yelled at us for playing in his yard. I remember him as someone who was a lot nicer than circumstances warranted.

When Dr. Gibbs wasn't saving lives, he was planting trees. His house sat on ten acres, and his life's goal was to make it a forest.

The good doctor had some interesting theories concerning plant husbandry. He came from the "no pain, no gain" school of horticulture. He never watered his new trees, which flew in the face of conventional wisdom. Once I asked why. He said that watering plants spoiled them, and that if you water them, each successive tree generation will grow weaker and weaker. So you have to make things rough for them and weed out the weenie trees early on.

He talked about how watering trees made for shallow roots, and how trees that weren't watered had to grow deep roots in search of moisture. I took him to mean that deep roots were to be treasured.

So he never watered his trees. He'd plant an oak and, instead of watering it every morning, he'd beat it with a rolled-up newspaper. Smack! Slap! Pow! I asked him why he did that, and he said it was to get the tree's attention.

Dr. Gibbs went to glory a couple of years after I left home. Every now and again, I walk by his house and look at the trees that I'd watched him plant some twenty-five years ago. They're granite strong now. Big and robust. Those trees wake up in the morning and beat their chests and drink their coffee black.

I planted a couple of trees a few years back. Carried water to them for a solid summer. Sprayed them. Prayed over them. The whole nine yards. Two years of coddling has resulted in trees that expect to be waited on hand and foot. Whenever a cold wind blows in, they tremble and chatter their branches. Sissy trees.

Funny thing about those trees of Dr. Gibbs's. Adversity and deprivation seemed to benefit them in ways comfort and ease never could.

Every night before I go to bed, I check on my two sons. I stand over them and watch their little bodies, the rising and falling of life within. I often pray for them. Mostly I pray that their lives will be easy. "Lord, spare them from hardship." But lately I've been thinking that it's time to change my prayer.

This change has to do with the inevitability of cold winds that hit us at the core. I know my children are going to encounter hardship, and my praying they won't is naive. There's always a cold wind blowing somewhere.

So I'm changing my eventide prayer. Because life is

tough, whether we want it to be or not. Instead, I'm going to pray that my sons' roots grow deep, so they can draw strength from the hidden sources of the eternal God.

Too many times we pray for ease, but that's a prayer seldom met. What we need to do is pray for roots that reach deep into the Eternal, so when the rains fall and the winds blow, we won't be swept asunder.

Philip Gulley

A New Day for Dorothy

As the lady talked, I tried to concentrate on the beautiful room around us instead of on her words. For she was telling me about Dorothy, her eight-year-old daughter, the middle one of her five children, a mentally retarded child.

"She's never spoken a single word," the mother repeated. "The doctors say it's hopeless. We took her up to Boston last year and. . . ."

I fixed my thoughts on the green damask draperies framing tall windows that looked out on Park Avenue. How handsome the whole room was, with its crystal chandeliers, its concert-grand piano, its fresh flowers everywhere. What a lovely woman the mother was, an opera singer whose name I had known even before her letter came asking me if I would consider a job with Dorothy.

Yes, a lovely woman—and especially her love for this little girl whom all the experts said should be put away. The love was the thing to concentrate on. And so while pretending to listen, I closed my ears to the results of reflex tests and encephalograms. In my years of working with retarded children I had discovered that my attention must not go to the lacks but to the special strengths of such children.

There was strength in each one of them, I was sure. I believe that a little of God lives in every one of us, and that to bring it out is the only job of any teacher.

Dorothy and I met the next weekend. With me it was love at first sight: this beautiful, blonde, blue-eyed child—surely a very lovely person lived in such a form. For her part, Dorothy only stared at me with inscrutable eyes.

"It's one of her quiet days, thank heaven," her mother said. "On her wild ones, there's no *controlling* her." My mind considered those wild days. I liked the sound of them. They told me there was a person here—trapped in whatever chemical or physical prison—but an individual struggling to be seen and recognized. I told her mother I would try the job for a month.

It was a hard one from the beginning. In the afternoons I would take Dorothy to a special class for retarded children. She just sat in a chair, staring straight ahead, making no effort to join in the activities.

"She's unreachable," her teacher told me. "I don't know why they keep sending her."

I gazed around the room at the other children, all engrossed in simple mechanical tasks, and I silently agreed with Dorothy. What was challenging about fitting a square peg into a square hole? With her parents' permission we stopped going there.

Dorothy's problem everywhere, it seemed to me, was the nonexpectation of everyone around her. I remember breakfast one morning when the other four children and their nurse had come into town. The others quickly finished their cereal but Dorothy, dazzled by the activity around her, hadn't touched hers.

"Just spoon it into her!" the nurse cried impatiently.

"She can eat by herself," I said. "I guess she's just too

interested in what's going on."

"Interested?" Nurse gave a snort of contempt. "She doesn't have any more idea what's happening than that canary! It's a shame she's allowed at the table. She just upsets the other children."

It wasn't true. Dorothy's brothers and sisters—especially her older sister Martha—seemed genuinely happy to be with her. But even Martha had fallen into Nurse's habit of talking *about* her ("Dorothy looks nice today." "Dorothy's hair needs combing. Shall I do it?") rather than *to* her. It was so easy to assume that because she had no words she had no understanding either.

I understood the problem. I felt it most during our daily walk in Central Park. It was October, warm sunny Indian summer, and Dorothy and I spent hours just walking. When the silence threatened to absorb us both, I sang.

I started with the hymns I remembered from my own childhood back in England. Dorothy seemed to like the songs, for her feet marched in time to the music and her head nodded rhythmically.

We also brought sketch pads and crayons to the park. I was fascinated by some drawings I had found in Dorothy's room, a pattern of graceful waving lines, drawn over and over again. What it meant I had no idea, but it certainly wasn't "scribble" as Nurse impatiently called it.

And so we would sit on a park bench and sketch. I drew trees and strolling people and the loft skyline beyond the park, and Dorothy drew pigeons. I saw the very first time what they were, not perhaps the outside of pigeons like other people draw, but the souls of the birds instead, the very way it feels to be a pigeon. Faster than my eyes could follow, her hand moved: the wings in flight, the thrust for the neck, the self-important walk.

The golden autumn passed too swiftly. Then a day dawned when the rain streamed down the tall windows and wind rattled the doors. So Dorothy sat on the piano bench beside me as I sang the songs I had sung in the park. I started off with one of Fenwicke Holme's "Songs of the Silence."

Halfway through this joyous song the miracle happened. One moment I was singing alone, the next Dorothy was singing with me, word for word in perfect tune. Electrified, I played on and on without a break, praying that the spell would not be broken. What a memory! How marvelously her mind had retained the words of song after song—far better than an average eight-year-old!

I heard someone sob. I turned and saw Dorothy's mother in the doorway, tears streaming down her cheeks, unable to do anything but hold out her arms to her child.

From that moment on, life was different for Dorothy. From singing, it was not far to speaking, although words with music always came first. We made up songs for everything.

"Water, a washcloth, see what I mean?
Knees that are dirty will soon be clean!"
"At the planetarium I can watch the stars;
There is Venus, here is Mars."

Other changes took place in Dorothy. Her tensions disappeared along with the frustrations of a spirit bottled up; so did her wildness. The nurse never adjusted to the difference in her and took another job.

As Dorothy continued to learn I lengthened my stay: just another month until she learned the alphabet. When I left, Dorothy was a poised, self-sufficient thirteen-year-old.

Normal? Not if normal means "average." All of us have strong points and weak points, and in Dorothy everything is extreme. But this means extremes of knowing and expressing that most of us never reach.

Those wavy lines, for instance, the ones she drew again

and again? When she had enough words she told me, "That's what the wind looks like."

Dorothy, your eyes see deep down, important things. Your ears hear silent things, your world is set to music. Oh, if God left something out of you, it was only to fill it with himself.

Frances E. Leslie

My Mother's Greatest Gift

Optimism is a cheerful frame of mind that enables a tea kettle to sing though it's in hot water up to its nose.

Anonymous

I was ten years old when my mother was left paralyzed by a spinal tumor. Prior to that, she had been a vital, vibrant woman—active to an extent most people found astonishing. Even as a small child, I was awed by her accomplishments and beauty. But at thirty-one, her life changed. And so did mine.

Overnight, it seemed, she was flat on her back, confined to a hospital bed. A benign tumor had incapacitated her, but I was too young to comprehend the irony of the word "benign," for she was never to be the same.

I still have vivid images of her before the paralysis. She had always been gregarious and entertained frequently. She often spent hours preparing hors d'oeuvres and filling the house with flowers, which we picked fresh from the gardens that she kept in the side yard. She would get out the popular music of that era and rearrange the furniture to make room for friends to abandon themselves to dance. In fact, it was Mother who loved to dance most of all. Mesmerized, I watched her dress for the evening's festivities. Even today, I remember our favorite dress, with its black skirt and midnight-lace bodice, the perfect foil for her blond hair. I was as thrilled as she the day she brought home black lace high-heeled pumps, and that night my mother surely was the most beautiful woman in the world.

She could do anything, I believed, whether it was play tennis (she won tournaments in college) or sew (she made all our clothes) or take photographs (she won a national contest) or write (she was a newspaper columnist) or cook (especially Spanish dishes for my father).

Now, although she could do none of these things, she faced her illness with the same enthusiasm she had brought to everything else.

Words like "handicapped" and "physical therapy" became part of a strange new world we entered together, and the child's rubber balls she struggled to squeeze assumed a mystique that they had never before possessed. Gradually, I began to help take care of the mother who had always taken care of me. I learned to care for my own hair—and hers. Eventually, it became routine to wheel her into the kitchen, where she instructed me in the art of peeling carrots and potatoes and how to rub down a good beef roast with fresh garlic and salt and chunks of butter.

When, for the first time, I heard talk of a cane, I objected: "I don't want my pretty mother to use a cane." But all she said was, "Wouldn't you rather have me walk with a cane than not walk at all?"

Every accomplishment was a milestone for us both: the electric typewriter, the car with power steering and brakes, her return to college, where she earned a master's degree in special education.

She learned everything she could about the disabled and eventually founded an activist support group called The Handicappers. One day, without saying much beforehand, she took me and my brothers to a Handicappers meeting. I had never seen so many people with so many disabilities. I returned home, silently introspective, thinking how fortunate we really were. She took us many other times after that and, eventually, the sight of a man or woman without legs or arms no longer shocked us. My mother also introduced us to victims of cerebral palsy, stressing that most of them were as bright as we were—maybe brighter. And she taught us to communicate with the mentally retarded, pointing our how much more affectionate they often were compared to "normal" people. Throughout all of this, my father remained loving and supportive.

When I was eleven, Mother told me she and Daddy were going to have a baby. Much later, I learned that her doctors had urged her to have a therapeutic abortion—an option she vehemently resisted. Soon, we were mothers together, as I became a surrogate mom to my sister, Mary Therese. In no time at all, I learned to change diapers, bathe and feed her. Though Mother maintained maternal discipline, for me it was a giant step beyond playing with dolls.

One moment stands out even today: the time Mary Therese, then two, fell and skinned her knee, burst into tears and ran past my mother's outstretched arms into mine. Too late, I glimpsed the flicker of hurt on Mother's face, but all she said was, "It's natural that she should run to you, because you take such good care of her."

Because my mother accepted her condition with such optimism, I rarely felt sad or resentful about it. But I will never forget the day my complacency was shattered. Long after the image of my mother in stiletto heels had receded from my consciousness, there was a party at our house. I was a teenager by then, and as I saw my smiling mother sitting on the sidelines, watching her friends dance, I was struck by the cruel irony of her physical limitations. Suddenly, I was transported back to the days of my early childhood, and the vision of my radiant, dancing mother was before me again.

I wondered whether Mother remembered, too. Spontaneously, I moved toward her, and then I saw that, though she was smiling, her eyes were brimming with tears. I rushed out of the room and into my bedroom, buried my face in my pillow and wept copious tears—all the tears she'd never shed. For the first time, I raged against God and at life and its injustices to my mother.

The memory of my mother's glistening smile stayed with me. From that moment, I viewed her ability to overcome the loss of so many former pursuits and her drive to look forward—things I had taken for granted—as a great mystery and a powerful inspiration.

When I was grown and entered the field of corrections, Mother became interested in working with prisoners. She called the penitentiary and asked to teach creative writing to inmates. I recall how they crowded around her whenever she arrived and seemed to cling to every word, as I had as a child.

Even when she no longer could go out to the prison, she corresponded frequently with several inmates.

One day, she asked me to mail a letter to one prisoner, Waymon. I asked if I could read it first, and she agreed, little realizing, I think, what a revelation it would be to me. It read:

Dear Waymon,

I want you to know that I have been thinking about you often since receiving your letter. You mentioned how difficult it is to be locked behind bars, and my heart goes out to you. But when you said that I couldn't imagine what it is like to be in prison, I felt impelled to tell you that you are mistaken.

There are different kinds of freedom, Waymon, different kinds of prison. Sometimes, our prisons are self-imposed.

When, at the age of thirty-one, I awoke one day to find that I was completely paralyzed, I felt trapped— overwhelmed by a sense of being imprisoned in a body that would no longer allow me to run through a meadow or dance or carry my child in my arms.

For a long time I lay there, struggling to come to terms with my infirmity, trying not to succumb to self-pity. I asked myself whether, in fact, life was worth living under such conditions, whether it might not be better to die.

I thought about this concept of imprisonment, because it seemed to me that I had lost everything in life that mattered. I was near despair.

But then, one day it occurred to me that, in fact, there were still some options open to me and that I had the freedom to choose among them. Would I smile when I saw my children again or would I weep? Would I rail against God—or would I ask Him to strengthen my faith?

In other words, what would I do with the free will He had given me—and which was still mine?

I made a decision to strive, as long as I was alive, to live as fully as I could, to seek to turn my seemingly negative experiences into positive experiences, to look for ways to transcend my physical limitations by expanding my mental and spiritual boundaries. I could choose to be a positive role model for my children, or I could wither and die, emotionally as well as physically.

There are many kinds of freedom, Waymon. When we lose one kind of freedom, we simply must look for another.

You and I are blessed with the freedom to choose among good books, which ones we'll read, which ones we'll set aside.

You can look at your bars, or you can look through them. You can be a role model for younger inmates, or you can mix with the troublemakers. You can love God and seek to know Him, or you can turn your back on Him.

To some extent, Waymon, we are in this thing together.

By the time I finished Waymon's letter, my vision was blurred by tears. Yet for the first time I saw my mother with greater clarity.

And I understood her.

Marie Ragghianti

Reprinted with permission from Parade *©1988.*

The Ugliest Cat in the World

Weakness of character is the only defect which cannot be amended.

Francóis de La Róchefoucald

The first time I ever saw Smoky, she was on fire! My three children and I had arrived at the dump outside our Arizona desert town to burn the weekly trash. As we approached the smoldering pit, we heard the most mournful cries of a cat entombed in the smoking rubble.

Suddenly a large cardboard box, which had been wired shut, burst into flames and exploded. With a long, piercing meow, the animal imprisoned within shot into the air like a flaming rocket and dropped into the ash-filled crater.

"Oh, Mama, do something!" three-year-old Jaymee cried as she and Becky, age six, leaned over the smoking hole.

"It can't possibly still be alive," said Scott, fourteen. But the ashes moved, and a tiny kitten, charred almost beyond recognition, miraculously struggled to the surface and crawled toward us in agony.

"I'll get her!" Scott yelled. As my son stood knee-deep in ashes and wrapped the kitten in my bandanna, I wondered why it didn't cry from the added pain. Later we learned we had heard its last meow only moments before.

Back at our ranch, we were doctoring the kitten when my husband, Bill, came in, weary from a long day of fence-mending.

"Daddy! We found a burned-up kitty," Jaymee announced.

When he saw our patient, that familiar "Oh, no, not again!" look crossed his face. This wasn't the first time we had greeted him with an injured animal. Though Bill always grumbled, he couldn't bear to see any living creature suffer. So he helped by building cages, perches, pens and splints for the skunks, rabbits and birds we brought home. This was different, however. This was a cat. And Bill, very definitely, did not like cats.

What's more, this was no ordinary cat. Where fur had been, blisters and a sticky black gum remained. Her ears were gone. Her tail was cooked to the bone. Gone were the claws that would have snatched some unsuspecting mouse. Gone were the little paw pads that would have left telltale tracks on the hoods of our dusty cars and trucks. Nothing that resembled a cat was left—except for two huge cobalt-blue eyes begging for help.

What could we do?

Suddenly I remembered our aloe vera plant and its supposed healing power on burns. So we peeled the leaves, swathed the kitten in slimy aloe strips and gauze bandages, and placed her in Jaymee's Easter basket. All we could see was her tiny face, like a butterfly waiting to emerge from its silk cocoon.

Her tongue was severely burned, and the inside of her mouth was so blistered that she couldn't lap, so we fed her milk and water with an eyedropper. After a while, she began eating by herself.

We named the kitten Smoky.

Three weeks later, the aloe plant was bare. Now we

coated Smoky with a salve that turned her body a curious shade of green. Her tail dropped off. Not a hair remained—but the children and I adored her.

Bill didn't. And Smoky despised him. The reason? He was a pipe smoker armed with matches and butane lighters that flashed and burned. Every time he lit up, Smoky panicked, knocking over his coffee cup and lamps before fleeing into the open air duct in the spare bedroom.

"Can't I have any peace around here?" he'd groan.

In time, Smoky became more tolerant of the pipe and its owner. She'd lie on the sofa and glare at Bill as he puffed away. One day he looked at me and chuckled, "Damn cat makes me feel guilty."

By the end of her first year, Smoky resembled a well-used welding glove. Scott was famous among his friends for owning the ugliest pet in the country—probably, the world.

Slowly, oddly, Bill became the one Smoky cared for the most. And before long, I noticed a change in him. He rarely smoked in the house now, and one winter night, to my astonishment, I found him sitting in his chair with the leathery little cat curled up on his lap. Before I could comment, he mumbled a curt, "She's probably cold—no fur, you know."

But Smoky, I reminded myself, liked the touch of cold. Didn't she sleep in front of air ducts and on the cold Mexican-tile floor?

Perhaps Bill was starting to like this strange-looking animal just a bit.

Not everyone shared our feelings for Smoky, especially those who had never seen her. Rumors reached a group of self-appointed animal protectors, and one day one of them arrived at our door.

"I've had numerous calls and letters from so many people," the woman said. "They are concerned about a poor little burned-up cat you have in your house. They say," her voice dropped an octave, "she's suffering. Perhaps it should be put out of its misery?"

I was furious. Bill was even more so. "Burned she was," he said, "but suffering? Look for yourself!"

"Here, kitty," I called. No Smoky. "She's probably hiding," I said, but our guest didn't answer. When I turned and looked at her, the woman's skin was gray, her mouth hung open and two fingers pointed.

Magnified tenfold in all her naked splendor, Smoky glowered at our visitor from her hiding place behind our 150-gallon aquarium. Instead of the "poor little burned-up suffering creature" the woman expected to see, tyrannosaurus Smoky leered at her through the green aquatic haze. Her open jaws exposed saber-like fangs that glinted menacingly in the neon light. Moments later the woman hurried out the door—smiling now, a little embarrassed and greatly relieved.

During Smoky's second year, a miraculous thing happened. She began growing fur. Tiny white hairs, softer and finer than the down on a chick, gradually grew over three inches long, transforming our ugly little cat into a wispy puff of smoke.

Bill continued to enjoy her company, though the two made an incongruous pair—the big weather-worn rancher driving around with an unlit pipe clenched between his teeth, accompanied by the tiny white ball of fluff. When he got out of the truck to check the cattle, he left the air conditioner on maximum-cold for her comfort. Her blue eyes watered, the pink nose ran, but she sat there, unblinking, in ecstasy. Other times, he picked her up, and holding her close against his denim jacket, took her along.

Smoky was three years old on the day she went with Bill to look for a missing calf. Searching for hours, he left the truck door open whenever he got out to look. The pastures were parched and crisp with dried grasses and tumbleweed. A storm loomed on the horizon, and still no calf. Discouraged, without thinking, Bill reached into his pocket for his lighter and spun the wheel. A spark shot to the ground and, in seconds, the field was on fire.

Frantic, Bill didn't think about the cat. Only after the fire was under control and the calf found did he return home and remember.

"Smoky!" he cried. "She must have jumped out of the truck! Did she come home?"

No. And we knew she'd never find her way home from two miles away. To make matters worse, it had started to rain—so hard we couldn't go out to look for her.

Bill was distraught, blaming himself. We spent the next day searching, wishing she could meow for help, and knowing she'd be helpless against predators. It was no use.

Two weeks later, Smoky still wasn't home. We were afraid she was dead by now, for the rainy season had begun, and the hawks, wolves and coyotes had families to feed.

Then came the biggest rainstorm our region had experienced in fifty years. By morning, flood waters stretched for miles, marooning wildlife and cattle on scattered islands of higher ground. Frightened rabbits, raccoons, squirrels and desert rats waited for the water to subside, while Bill and Scott waded knee-deep, carrying bawling calves back to their mamas and safety.

The girls and I were watching intently when suddenly Jaymee shouted, "Daddy! There's a poor little rabbit over there. Can you get it? "

Bill waded to the spot where the animal lay, but when he reached out to help the tiny creature, it seemed to shrink back in fear. "I don't believe it," Bill cried. "It's Smoky!" His voice broke. "Little Smoky!"

My eyes ached with tears when that pathetic little cat

crawled into the outstretched hands of the man she had grown to love. He pressed her shivering body to his chest, talked to her softly, and gently wiped the mud from her face. All the while her blue eyes fastened on his with unspoken understanding. He was forgiven.

Smoky came home again. The patience she showed as we shampooed her astounded us. We fed her scrambled eggs and ice cream, and to our joy she seemed to get well.

But Smoky had never really been strong. One morning when she was barely four years old, we found her limp in Bill's chair. Her heart had simply stopped.

As I wrapped her tiny body in one of Bill's red neckerchiefs and placed her in a child's shoe box, I thought about the many things our precious Smoky had taught us—things about trust, affection and struggling against the odds when everything says you can't win. She reminded us that it's not what's outside that counts—it's what's inside, deep in our hearts.

Penny Porter

Small Soldiers

I intended to move my troops to a better location, not into the line of fire. As a twenty-seven-year-old single mother of four children, I tended to think of myself as a fearless leader of my brood. And, in fact, our life often reflected the austere setting of boot camp. The five of us were crammed into close quarters—a two-bedroom apartment in New Jersey—and we lived a life of self-deprived discipline. I couldn't afford any of the niceties and luxuries other parents did, and aside from my mother, none of the rest of our family was involved in the kids' lives at all.

That left me as commander in chief. Many nights, I lay awake on my bed, planning strategies to get more things for my children. Though my children never complained about what they lacked and seemed to bask in my love, I was continually on the alert for ways to improve their simple lives. When I found a five-bedroom apartment in a three-story house—the second and third stories belonging completely to us—I leapt at the opportunity. At last, we could spread out. The home even had a big backyard.

The landlord promised to have everything fixed up for us in a month. I agreed on the repairs, paid her in cash for the first month's rent and the same in security, and hurried home to inform my troops we were moving out. They were excited, and we all camped on my bed that night, planning what we'd do to the new home. The next morning, I gave notice to my current landlord and started packing. We loaded our boxes with the precision of a well-oiled machine. It warmed my heart to see the troops in action.

And then I realized my strategic error. I had no keys to the new house in hand, and when day after day of unreturned phone calls and fruitless searches produced no access to the house, I began to panic. I did some espionage work and called the utility company. They told me someone else had just requested new service for the same address. I'd been duped.

With a heavy heart, I looked at my children's expectant faces and tried to find the words to tell them the bad news. They took it staunchly, though I fought back tears of disappointment.

Already feeling defeated, I faced even worse obstacles. Our lease was now up on our current apartment. I couldn't afford rent on a new place because I'd paid so much for the house. My mother wanted to help, but children were not allowed in her small apartment. Desperate, I asked a fellow veteran fighter to help: a single mother of five who was struggling as much as I. She tried her best to be hospitable, but nine kids in four rooms. . . . Well, you get the picture.

After three weeks, we were all mutinous. We had to get out. I had no options left, no new orders to follow. We were on the run. I stored our furniture, stuffed our winter clothes in the back of our yellow Escort, and informed my small soldiers that we had nowhere to camp for the present time except in our car.

My sons, six and ten, met my gaze and listened intently. "Why can't we stay at Grandma's?" my oldest asked. That question was followed by several suggestions of others we should be able to stay with. In each case, I had to tell them the harsh truth. "People have their own lives, Honey. We have to handle this on our own. We can do this." But if my bravado appeased them, it didn't fool me. I needed strength. Where could I get help?

Knowing it was time to turn in for the night, I gathered up my troops, and we marched to the car. The children were calm and compliant, but my thoughts were engaged in fierce warfare. Should I do this to them? What else *could* I do?

Unexpectedly, it was my own troops who gave me the strength I needed. As we lived in our car for the next four weeks, showering at my mother's in the mornings and eating at fast-food joints, the kids seemed to enjoy the odd routine. They never missed a day of school, never complained and never questioned my judgment. They were so certain of their commander's wisdom that even I began to feel courageous. We *could* manage this! We parked in a different spot each night, well-lighted areas near apartment buildings. When the nights grew cold, the kids cuddled in the back seat that folded down into a bed, sharing body heat and blankets. I sat in the front, keeping watch between dozes and starting the motor every so often to run the heat.

When I had earned enough to afford rent someplace, I couldn't find any apartments that would accept four children, so we checked into a hotel. It was like being on a fantastic furlough. We were thrilled, reveling in the heat, the beds, the safety. We sneaked in our rations to cook and learned to prepare savory meals with a two-burner hot plate. We cooled dairy items in the bathtub. (Hotels have lots of ice.)

Finally, many months later, the landlord of the promised house sent me a money order refunding all that was due me, with many apologies. I used the money to find us an apartment.

That was thirteen years ago. I'm sharing command now with a husband, and we keep our children in a wonderfully large house. Every morning, when I run the inspection on my troops—taller now, looking at me eye to eye—I think back on the horrible enemy of desperation that we fought and defeated together. And then I thank God for my small soldiers: a courageous, tough little crew who never stumbled in their frightening march. Their bravery was the stuff of the greatest of heroes.

Rachel Berry

CALVIN AND HOBBES By Bill Watterson

Journey Out of Silence

Nothing can stop the man with the right mental attitude from achieving his goal; and nothing on earth can help the man with the wrong mental attitude.

Thomas Jefferson

My adventure began in October 1966, when Miss Neff, my occupational therapist, took me into her stale, windowless room. She was a thirty-year-old woman barely above five feet tall, but she could make a student who was labeled as uncooperative at the Dr. J. P. Lord School for the Physically Handicapped tremble in his wheelchair with fear. As one of them, I was scared to death when she came to get me for an unscheduled visit.

Then, I was labeled a horrible little boy who wouldn't do what his therapist told him to do. I seemed rebellious because I was so uncoordinated: Even after years of physical, speech and occupational therapy, I still could not walk, talk or use my hands.

Sometimes I asked myself, *Why should I make the effort?* As Miss Neff told my parents, "We always try to do what we've done in other, similar situations, and if that doesn't work, we look for something new." But nothing—old or new—was working for me.

There I was, at any rate, being pushed by Miss Neff into her office when it wasn't even time for my therapy. I was petrified! What had I done wrong this time? Had they finally given up on me? Was I getting kicked out of school? I felt like Daniel wheeling into a stuffy lions' den.

Miss Neff parked me in front of her steel teacher's desk, then she sat in her armless chair behind it. Instead of scolding me, as I had anticipated, she showed me some mimeographed diagrams of what looked like a large but poorly shaped slingshot that was rounded at the fork. It looked ridiculous to me. Then she showed me another diagram of a kid typing with this contraption on his head.

During that year's teachers' convention, Miss Neff—along with the school's speech therapist, physical therapist and Mrs. Clanton, my new classroom teacher—attended another special school that was in Iowa City. At that school, they saw a student using a headstick to type his schoolwork.

"This is a headstick," she said sternly. "It is not a toy or a weapon. We think that you will be able to use it if you want to, but it will be very hard work. And if I ever see you using it to poke somebody, I'll take it away from you and set it on this desk. Understand?"

I nodded stiffly.

"Now," she continued, "at the next PTA meeting, I will give your mother some directions for exercises to strengthen your neck. I suggest that you do them at home every day. I also suggest that you do them in the morning when you are fresh. It will be tiresome work, but you just might be able to do it."

After Miss Neff lectured me, Mrs. Clanton who, unlike all my therapists, had not witnessed my many failures said simply, "I think you can do it. Do you?"

I nodded. My journey from solitary confinement had begun. Every day I did my neck exercises before going to school. After a family friend crafted me a homemade headstick to use, I practiced using it at school to turn the pages of a spiral-bound book; to point to words on an elaborate language board made by my speech therapist, and, of course, to do those lovely neck exercises. I cannot give you a day-by-day description of my first real taste of success. It was like a dream. Up until this adventure with the headstick, everything the therapist had tried on me had not worked because I was so uncoordinated that I gave up in frustration. But this was different.

Mrs. Clanton believed in me. If she'd said I could fly, I would have jumped off the Empire State Building without any reservations and flapped my spindly arms until I splattered on the sidewalk. She was a friend as well as a teacher. I still remember how she played baseball with my class to make up for an extremely dull recreation hour when we had to sit through an inaudible play. So I worked hard to please her, not minding the very few disappointments of this project.

My teacher and therapists thought that I was intelligent because they watched my eyes and facial expressions during my lessons. But as Mrs. Clanton told my parents, "We have no way of testing his knowledge of each of his subjects."

The climax of this successful adventure came when Miss Neff put me in a straight-backed wooden chair with arms. She tied me in because I couldn't balance on my own. She put the band with a stylus attached to it on my head. Then she pushed me up to an ancient black typewriter. I swear that typewriter was used by Thomas Edison. In fact, I thought then that he had made it himself, and still do!

Miss Neff told me to turn the old clunker on. To our surprise I did—quickly! She told me to type my name. I did. She told me to type the alphabet. I did! By this time, the speech therapist, the physical therapist and Mrs. Clanton had been called into the occupational therapy room to share in my victory over silence.

The people who were crowded into that stale, windowless OT room thought that my communication had gotten the best that it could have gotten. We were so wrong. Throughout the years my ability to communicate has been enriched and augmented by the computer age.

Although this adventure may be small compared with climbing Mount Everest or sailing the ocean on a raft, it was just as important. Through it God enabled me to conquer higher mountains and sail wider seas, now that he had helped me break the bounds of silence that held me for eleven years.

William L. Rush

READER/CUSTOMER CARE SURVEY

If you are enjoying this book, please help us serve you better and meet your changing needs by taking a few minutes to complete this survey. Please fold it and drop it in the mail.

NAME: _____ C8D

ADDRESS: _____

_____

TELEPHONE NUMBER: _____

FAX NUMBER: _____

E-MAIL: _____

WEBSITE: _____

(1) Gender: 1)_____Female 2)_____Male

(2) Age:

1)_____12 or under   5)_____30-39
2)_____13-15   6)_____40-49
3)_____16-19   7)_____50-59
4)_____20-29   8)_____60+

(3) Your Children's Age(s):
Check all that apply.

1)_____6 or Under   3)_____11-14
2)_____7-10   4)_____15-18

(7) Marital Status:

1)_____Married
2)_____Single
3)_____Divorced/Wid.

(8) Was this book

1)_____Purchased for yourself?
2)_____Received as a gift?

(9) How many Chicken Soup books have you bought or read?

1)_____1   3)_____3
2)_____2   4)_____4+

(10) How did you find out about this book?
Please check ONE.

1)_____Personal Recommendation
2)_____Store Display
3)_____TV/Radio Program
4)_____Bestseller List
5)_____Website
6)_____Advertisement/Article or Book Review
7)_____Catalog or mailing
6)_____Other_____

(11) What FIVE subject areas do you enjoy reading about most?
Rank: 1 (favorite) through 5 (least favorite)

A)_____ Self Development
B)_____ New Age/Alternative Healing
C)_____ Storytelling
D)_____ Spirituality/Inspiration
E)_____ Family and Relationships
F)_____ Health and Nutrition
G)_____ Recovery
H)_____ Business/Professional
I)_____ Entertainment
J)_____ Teen Issues
K)_____ Pets

(16) Where do you purchase most of your books?
Check the top TWO locations.

A)_____ General Bookstore
B)_____ Religious Bookstore
C)_____ Warehouse/Price Club
D)_____ Discount or Other Retail Store
E)_____ Website
F)_____ Book Club/Mail Order

(18) Did you enjoy the stories in this book?

1)_____Almost All
2)_____Few
3)_____Some

(19) What type of magazine do you SUBSCRIBE to?
Check up to FIVE subscription categories.

A)_____ General Inspiration
B)_____ Religious/Devotional
C)_____ Business/Professional
D)_____ World News/Current Events
E)_____ General Entertainment
F)_____ Homemaking, Cooking, Crafts
G)_____ Women's Issues
H)_____ Other (please specify) _____

(24) Please indicate your income level

1)_____Student/Retired-fixed income
2)_____Under $25,000
3)_____$25,000-$50,000
4)_____$50,001-$75,000
5)_____$75,001-$100,000
6)_____Over $100,000

TAPE HERE DO NOT STAPLE

BUSINESS REPLY MAIL
FIRST-CLASS MAIL PERMIT NO 45 DEERFIELD BEACH, FL

POSTAGE WILL BE PAID BY ADDRESSEE

CHICKEN SOUP FOR THE SOUL
HEALTH COMMUNICATIONS, INC.
3201 SW 15TH STREET
DEERFIELD BEACH FL 33442-9875

Ialllaalllalaladladaladallllaladaladlaaalalaladadal

FOLD HERE

(25) Do you attend seminars?

1)_____Yes   2)_____No

(26) If you answered yes, what type?

Check all that apply.

1)_____Business/Financial
2)_____Motivational
3)_____Religious/Spiritual
4)_____Job-related
5)_____Family/Relationship issues

(31) Are you:

1) A Parent?_____   2) A Grandparent?_____

Thank You!!

Do you have your own Chicken Soup story you would like to send us?

Please submit separately to: Chicken Soup for the Soul, P.O. Box 30880, Santa Barbara, CA 93130

Additional comments you would like to make:

_____

_____

_____

_____

CS-GEN   C8D

The Flight of the Red-Tail

*When faced with a challenge, look for a way,
not a way out.*

David L. Weatherford

The hawk hung from the sky as though suspended from an invisible web, its powerful wings outstretched and motionless. It was like watching a magic show until—suddenly—the spell was shattered by a shotgun blast from the car behind us.

Startled, I lost control of my pickup. It careened wildly, sliding sideways across the gravel shoulder until we stopped inches short of a barbed-wire fence. My heart pounded as a car raced past us, the steel muzzle of a gun sticking out the window, but I will never forget the gleeful smile on the face of the boy who'd pulled that trigger.

"Geez, Mom. That scared me!" Scott, fourteen, sat beside me. "I thought he was shooting at us! But look! He shot that hawk!"

While driving back to the ranch from Tucson along Arizona's Interstate 10, we had been marveling at a magnificent pair of red-tailed hawks swooping low over the

Sonoran Desert. Cavorting and diving at breathtaking speeds over the yucca and cholla cacti, the beautiful birds mirrored each other in flight.

Suddenly, one hawk changed its course and soared skyward, where it hovered for an instant over the interstate as though challenging its mate to join in the fun. But the blast from the gun put an end to their play, converting the moment into an explosion of feathers dashed against the red and orange sunset.

Horrified we watched the red-tail spiral earthward, jerking and spinning straight into the path of an oncoming eighteen-wheeler. Air brakes screeched. But it was too late. The truck struck the bird, hurling it onto the median strip.

Scott and I jumped from the pickup and ran to the spot where the stricken bird lay. Because of the hawk's size, we decided it was probably a male. He was on his back, a shattered wing doubled beneath him, the powerful beak open, and round, yellow eyes wide with pain and fear. The talons on his left leg had been ripped off. And where the brilliant fan of tail feathers had once gleamed like a kite of burnished copper against the southwestern sky, only one red feather remained.

"We gotta do something, Mom," said Scott.

"Yes," I murmured. "We've got to take him home."

For once I was glad Scott was in style with the black leather jacket he loved because when he reached for him, the terrified hawk lashed out with his one remaining weapon: a hooked beak as sharp as an ice pick. To protect himself, Scott threw the jacket over the bird, wrapped him firmly and carried him to the pickup. When I reached for the keys still hanging in the ignition, the sadness of the moment doubled. From somewhere high in the darkening sky, we heard the plaintive, high-pitched cries of the other hawk.

"What will that one do now, Mom?" Scott asked.

"I don't know," I answered softly. "I've always heard they mate for life."

At the ranch we tackled our first problem: restraining the flailing hawk without getting hurt ourselves. Wearing welding gloves, we laid him on some straw inside an orange crate and slid the slats over his back.

Once the bird was immobilized we removed splinters of bone from his shattered wing, and then tried bending the wing where the main joint had been. It would only fold halfway. Through all this pain, the hawk never moved. The only sign of life was an occasional rising of the third lid over the fear-glazed eyes.

Wondering what to do next, I telephoned the Arizona-Sonora Desert Museum. When I described the plight of the red-tail, the curator was sympathetic. "I know you mean well," he said, "but euthanasia is the kindest thing."

"You mean destroy him?" I asked, leaning down and gently stroking the auburn-feathered bird secured in the wooden crate on my kitchen floor.

"He'll never fly again with a wing that badly injured," he explained. "He'll starve to death. Hawks need their claws as well as their beaks to tear up food. I'm really sorry."

As I hung up, I knew he was right.

"But the hawk hasn't even had a chance to fight," Scott argued.

Fight for what? I wondered. To huddle in a cage? Never to fly again?

Suddenly, with the blind faith of youth, Scott made the decision for us. "Maybe, by some miracle, he'll fly again someday," he said. "Isn't it worth a try?"

For three weeks the bird never moved, ate or drank. We forced water into his beak with a hypodermic syringe, but the pathetic creature just lay there staring, unblinking, scarcely breathing. Then came the morning when the eyes of the red-tail were closed.

"Mom, he's . . . dead!" Scott pressed his fingers beneath the matted feathers. I knew he was searching, praying for a heartbeat, and the memory of a speeding car and a smiling boy with a gun in his hands returned to haunt me.

"Maybe some whiskey," I said. It was a last resort, a technique we had used before to coax an animal to breathe. We pried open the beak and poured a teaspoon of the liquid down the hawk's throat. Instantly his eyes flew open, and his head fell into the water bowl in the cage.

"Look at him, Mom! He's drinking!" Scott said, with tears sparkling in his eyes.

By nightfall the hawk had eaten several strips of roundsteak dredged in sand to ease digestion. The next day, his hands still shielded in welding gloves, Scott removed the bird from the crate and carefully wrapped his good claw around a fireplace log where he teetered and swayed until the talons locked in. As Scott let go of the bird, the good wing flexed slowly into flight position, but the other was rigid, protruding from its shoulder like a boomerang. We held our breath until the hawk stood erect.

The creature watched every move we made, but the look of fear was gone. He was going to live. Now, would he learn to trust us?

With Scott's permission, his three-year-old sister, Becky, named our visitor Hawkins. We put him in a chain-link dog-run ten feet high and open at the top. There he'd be safe from bobcats, coyotes, raccoons and lobos. In one corner of the pen, we mounted a manzanita limb four inches from the ground. A prisoner of his injuries, the crippled bird perched there day and night, staring at the sky, watching, listening, waiting.

As fall slipped into winter, Hawkins began molting. Despite a diet of meat, lettuce, cheese and eggs, he lost most of his neck feathers. More fell from his breast, back and wings, revealing scattered squares of soft down. Pretty soon he looked like a baldheaded old man huddled in a patchwork quilt.

"Maybe some vitamins will help," said Scott. "I'd hate to see him lose that one red tail feather. He looks kinda funny as it is."

The vitamins seemed to help. A luster appeared on the wing feathers, and we imagined a glimmer on that tail feather, too.

In time, Hawkins's growing trust blossomed into affection. We delighted in spoiling him with treats like bologna and beef jerky soaked in sugar water. Soon, the hawk—whose beak was powerful enough to snap the leg bone of a jackrabbit or crush the skull of a desert rat—had mastered the touch of a butterfly. Becky fed him with her bare fingers.

Hawkins loved playing games. His favorite was tug-of-war. With an old sock gripped tightly in his beak and one of us pulling on the other end, he always won, refusing to let go, even when Scott lifted him into the air and swung him around like a bolo. Becky's favorite game was ring-around-the-rosy. She and I held hands and circled Hawkins's pen, while his eyes followed until his head turned 180 degrees. He was actually looking at us backward!

We grew to love Hawkins. We talked to him. We stroked his satiny feathers. We had saved and tamed a wild creature. But *now what?* Shouldn't we return him to the sky, to the world where he belonged?

Scott must have been wondering the same thing, even as he carried his pet around on his wrist like a proud falconer. One day, he raised Hawkins's perch to twenty inches, just over the bird's head. "If he has to struggle to get up on it, he might get stronger," he said.

Noticing the height difference, Hawkins assessed the

change from every angle. He scolded and clacked his beak. Then, he jumped—and missed, landing on the concrete, hissing pitifully. He tried again and again with the same result. Just as we thought he'd give up, he flung himself up at the limb, grabbing first with his beak, then his claw, and pulled. At last he stood upright.

"Did you see that, Mom?" said Scott. "He was trying to use his crippled wing. Did you see?"

"No," I said. But I'd seen something else, the smile on my son's face. I knew he was still hoping for a miracle.

Each week after that, Scott raised the perch a little more, until Hawkins sat proudly at four feet. How pleased he looked—puffing himself up grandly and preening his ragged feathers. But four feet was his limit. He could jump no higher.

Spring brought warm weather and birds: doves, quail, roadrunners and cactus wrens. We thought Hawkins would enjoy all the chirping and trilling. Instead we sensed a sadness in our little hawk. He scarcely ate, ignoring invitations to play, preferring to sit with his head cocked, listening.

One morning, we found him perched with his good wing extended, the crippled one quivering helplessly. All day he remained in this position, a piteous rasping cry coming from his throat. Finally we saw what was troubling him: High in the sky over his pen, another red-tail hovered.

His mate? I wondered. *How could it be?* We were at least thirty miles from where we'd found Hawkins, far beyond a hawk's normal range. Had his mate somehow followed him here? Or through some secret of nature, far beyond our understanding, did she simply know where he was?

"What will she do when she realizes he can't fly?" Scott asked.

"I imagine she'll get discouraged and leave," I said sadly. "We'll just have to wait and see."

Our wait was brief. The next morning, Hawkins was gone. A few broken feathers and bits of down littered his pen—silent clues to a desperate struggle.

Questions tormented us. How did he get out? The only possibility was that he'd simply pulled himself six feet up the fence, grasping the wire first with his beak, then his one good claw. Next he must have fallen ten feet to the ground.

How would he survive? He couldn't hunt. Clinging to his perch and a strip of meat at the same time with one claw had proven nearly impossible. What about the coyotes and bobcats? Our crippled hawk would be easy prey. We were heartsick.

A week later, however, there was Hawkins perched on the log pile by our kitchen door. His eyes gleamed with a brightness I'd never seen before. And his beak was open! "He's hungry!" I shouted. The bird snatched a package of bologna from Scott's hand and ate greedily.

Finished, Hawkins hopped awkwardly to the ground and prepared to leave. We watched as he lunged, floated and crashed in short hops across the pasture, one wing flapping mightily, the other a useless burden. Journeying in front of him, his mate swooped back and forth, scolding and whistling her encouragement until he reached the temporary safety of a mesquite grove.

Hawkins returned to be fed throughout the spring. Then one day, instead of taking his food, he shrank back, an unfamiliar squawk coming from his throat. We talked to him softly like we used to do, but suddenly he struck out with his beak. The hawk that had trusted us for nearly a year was now afraid. I knew he was ready to return to the wild.

As the years passed, we occasionally saw a lone red-tail gliding across our pastures, and my heart would leap with hope. Had Hawkins somehow survived? And if he hadn't, was it worth the try to keep him alive as we did?

Nine years later, when Scott was twenty-three, he met

an old friend in Phoenix, who had lived near our ranch. "You won't believe this, Scott," he said, "but I think I saw your hawk roosting in a scrub oak down by the wash when I was home for Christmas. He was all beat up, broken wing just like Hawkins."

"You gotta go take a look, Mom."

The next day I drove north until the dirt roads became zigzagging cattle trails and finally no trails at all. When a barricade of thorny mesquite trees and wild rose bushes stopped me, it was time to walk. Finally an opening through the maze led me down to a twisting, sandy river bed; a paradise for lizards, toads, tarantulas, snakes and small rodents of the desert. It was also an ideal feeding ground for a hawk.

Flanked by the spiny overgrowth on the banks above, I walked for hours, but saw no trace of Hawkins. But hope plays such tricks on the eyes, ears and mind, I confess there were moments when the rustling of leaves, the clumps of mistletoe swaying on high branches and the shifting shadows against gnarled tree trunks both kindled my fantasies and snuffed them out in a single second. Finding him was too much to hope for.

It was getting cold when I sensed I was being watched. All of a sudden, I was looking straight into the eyes of a large female red-tail. Roosting in a mesquite less than fifteen feet away, she was perfectly camouflaged by the autumn foliage surrounding her.

Could this magnificent creature have been Hawkins's mate? I wondered. I wanted so much to believe she was, to tell Scott I had seen the bird that had cared for her mate, scavenged for his food and kept him safe. But how could I be sure?

Then I saw him!

On a low branch, beneath the great dark shadow of the larger bird, hunched a tattered little hawk. When I saw the crooked wing, the proud bald head and withered claw, my eyes welled with tears. This was a magic moment: a time to reflect on the power of hope. A time to pray for the boy with a gun. A time to bless the boy who had faith.

Alone in this wild, unaltered place, I learned the power of believing, for I had witnessed a miracle.

"Hawkins," I murmured, longing to stroke the ragged feathers, but daring only to circle around him. "Is it really you?"

Like a silent echo my answer came when the yellow eyes followed my footsteps until he was looking at me backward, and the last rays of sunlight danced on one red feather.

Then, finally, I knew—and, best of all, my son would know. It *had* been worth the try.

Penny Porter

Albert

I am only one, but still I am one; I cannot do everything; but still I can do something; and because I cannot do everything, I will not refuse to do the something that I can do.

Edward Everett Hale

Working in a hospital with recent stroke patients was an all-or-nothing proposition. They were usually so grateful to be alive or just wanted to die. A quick glance told all.

Albert taught me much about strokes.

One afternoon while making rounds I'd met him, curled in a fetal position. A pale, dried-up old man with a look of death, head half-buried under a blanket. He didn't budge when I introduced myself, and he said nothing when I referred to dinner "soon."

At the nurse's station, an attendant provided some history. He had no one. He'd lived too long. Wife of thirty years dead, five sons gone.

Well, maybe I could help. A chunky but pretty divorced nurse avoiding the male population outside of work, I could satisfy a need. I flirted.

The next day I wore a dress, not my usual nursing uniform but white. No lights on. Curtains drawn.

Albert hollered at the staff to get out. I pulled a chair close to his bed, crossing my shapely legs, head tilted. I gave him a perfect smile.

"Leave me. I want to die."

"What a crime, all us single women out there."

He looked annoyed. I rambled on about how I liked working "rehab" unit because I got to watch people reach their maximum potential. It was a place of possibilities. He said nothing.

Two days later during shift report, I learned that Albert had asked when I'd be "on." The charge nurse referred to him as my "boyfriend" and word got around. I never argued. Outside his room, I'd tell others not to bother "my Albert."

Soon he agreed to "dangle," sit on the side of the bed to build up sitting tolerance, energy and balance. He agreed to "work" with physical therapy if I'd return "to talk."

Two months later, Albert was on a walker. By the third month, he'd progressed to a cane. Fridays we celebrated discharges with a barbecue. Albert and I danced to Edith Piaf. He wasn't graceful, but he was leading. Tear-streaked cheeks touched as we bade our good-byes.

Periodically roses, mums and sweet peas would turn up. He was gardening again.

Then one afternoon, a lovely lavender-clad woman came on the unit demanding "that hussy."

My supervisor called; I was in the middle of giving a bed bath.

"So you're the one! The woman who reminded my Albert that he's a man!" Her head tilted in full smile as she handed me a wedding invitation.

Magi Hart

The Racking Horse

The first time Bart told me about his horse, Dude, I knew their bond had been something special. But I never suspected Dude would deliver a wonderful gift to me.

Growing up on a one-hundred-year-old family farm in Tennessee, Bart loved all animals. But Dude, the chestnut-colored quarter horse Bart received when he turned nine, became his favorite. Years later when Bart's father sold Dude, Bart grieved in secret.

Even before I met and married Bart, I knew all about grieving in secret, too. Because of my dad's job, our family relocated every year. Deep inside, I wished we could stay in one place, where I could have deep, lasting friendships. But I never said anything to my parents. I didn't want to hurt them. Yet sometimes I wondered if even God could keep track of us.

One summer evening in 1987, as Bart and I glided on our front porch swing, my husband suddenly blurted out, "Did I ever tell you that Dude won the World Racking Horse Championship?"

"Rocking horse championship?" I asked.

"Racking," Bart corrected, smiling gently. "It's a kind of dancing horses do. Takes lots of training. You use four reins. It's pretty hard." Bart gazed at the pasture. "Dude was the greatest racking horse ever."

"Then why'd you let your dad sell him?" I probed.

"I didn't know he was even thinking about it," Bart explained. "When I was seventeen, I'd started a short construction job down in Florida. I guess Dad figured I wouldn't be riding anymore, so he sold Dude without even asking me. Running a horse farm means you buy and sell horses all the time.

"I've always wondered if that horse missed me as much as I've missed him. I've never had the heart to try to find him. I couldn't stand knowing if something bad. . . ."

Bart's voice trailed off.

After that, few nights passed without Bart mentioning Dude. My heart ached for him. I didn't know what to do. Then one afternoon while I walked through the pasture, a strange thought came to me. In my heart, a quiet voice said, "Lori, find Dude for Bart."

How absurd! I thought. I knew nothing about horses, certainly not how to find and buy one. That was Bart's department.

The harder I tried to dismiss the thought, the stronger it grew. I did not dare mention it to anyone except God. Each day I asked him to guide me.

On a Saturday morning, three weeks after that first "find Dude" notion, a new meter reader, Mr. Parker, stopped by while I was working in the garden. We struck up a friendly conversation. When he mentioned he'd once bought a horse from Bart's dad, I interrupted.

"You remember the horse's name?" I asked.

"Sure do," Mr. Parker said. "Dude. Paid twenty-five hundred dollars for him."

I wiped the dirt from my hands and jumped up, barely catching my breath.

"Do you know what happened to him?" I asked.

"Yep. I sold him for a good profit."

"Where's Dude now?" I asked. "I need to find him."

"That'd be impossible," Mr. Parker explained. "I sold that horse years ago. He might even be dead by now."

"But could you . . . would you be willing to try to help me find him?" After I explained the situation, Mr. Parker stared at me for several seconds. Finally, he agreed to join the search for Dude, promising not to say anything to Bart.

Each Friday for almost a year, I phoned Mr. Parker to see if his sleuthing had turned up anything. Each week his answer was the same. "Sorry, nothing yet."

One Friday I called Mr. Parker with another idea. "Could you at least find one of Dude's babies for me?"

"Don't think so," he said, laughing. "Dude was a gelding."

"That's fine," I said. "I'll take a gelding baby."

"You really *do* need help." Mr. Parker explained that geldings are unable to sire. He seemed to double his efforts to help. Several weeks later, he phoned me on a Monday.

"I found him," he shouted. "I found Dude."

"Where?" I wanted to jump through the phone.

"On a farm in Georgia," Mr. Parker said. "A family bought Dude for their teenage son. But they can't do anything with the horse. In fact, they think Dude's crazy. Maybe dangerous. Bet you could get him back real easy."

Mr. Parker was right. I called the family in Rising Fawn, Georgia, and made arrangements to buy Dude back for three hundred dollars. I struggled to keep my secret until the weekend. On Friday, I met Bart at the front door after work.

"Will you go for a ride with me?" I asked in my most persuasive voice. "I have a surprise for you."

"Honey," Bart protested, "I'm tired."

"Please, Bart, I've packed a picnic supper. It'll be worth the ride. I promise."

Bart got into the Jeep. As I drove, my heart thumped so fast I thought it'd burst as I chatted about family matters.

"Where are we going?" Bart asked after thirty minutes. "Just a bit farther," I said.

Bart sighed. "Honey, I love you. But I can't believe I let you drag me off."

I didn't defend myself. I'd waited too long to ruin things now. However, by the time I steered off the main highway and onto a gravel road, Bart was so aggravated that he wasn't speaking to me. When I turned from the gravel road to a dirt trail, Bart glared.

"We're here," I said, stopping in front of the third fence post.

"Here where? Lori, have you lost your mind?" Bart barked.

"Stop yelling," I said. "Whistle."

"What?" Bart shouted.

"Whistle," I repeated. "Like you used to . . . for Dude . . . just whistle. You'll understand in a minute."

"Well . . . I . . . this is crazy," Bart sputtered as he got out of the Jeep.

Bart whistled. Nothing happened.

"Oh, God," I whispered, "don't let this be a mistake."

"Do it again," I prodded.

Bart whistled once more, and we heard a sound in the distance. What was it? I could barely breathe.

Bart whistled again. Suddenly, over the horizon, a horse came at a gallop. Before I could speak, Bart leapt over the fence.

"Dude!" he yelled, running towards his beloved friend. I watched the blur of horse and husband meet like one of those slow-motion reunion scenes on television. Bart hopped up on his pal, stroking his mane and patting his neck.

Immediately, a sandy-haired, tobacco-chewing teenage boy and his huffing parents crested the hill.

"Mister," the boy yelled. "What are you doing? That

horse is crazy. Can't nobody do nothing with 'im."

"No," Bart boomed. "He's not crazy. He's Dude."

To the amazement of everyone, at Bart's soft command to the unbridled horse, Dude threw his head high and began racking. As the horse pranced through the pasture, no one spoke. When Dude finished dancing for joy, Bart slid off of him.

"I want Dude home," he said.

"I know," I said with tears in my eyes. "All the arrangements have been made. We can come back and get him."

"Nope," Bart insisted. "He's coming home tonight."

I phoned my in-laws, and they arrived with a horse trailer. We paid for Dude and headed home.

Bart spent the night in the barn. I knew he and Dude had a lot of catching up to do. As I looked out of the bedroom window, the moon cast a warm glow over the farm. I smiled, knowing my husband and I now had a wonderful story to tell our future children and grandchildren.

"Thank you, Lord," I whispered. Then the truth hit me. I'd searched longer for Dude than I'd ever lived in one place. God had used the process of finding my husband's beloved horse to renew my trust in the friend who sticks closer than a brother.

"Thank you, Lord," I whispered again as I fell asleep. "Thank you for never losing track of Dude—or me."

Lori Bledsoe
As told to Rhonda Reese

Tina's Ten Points

She was seventeen years old and always wore a bright smile. This may not seem that unusual except that Tina suffered from cerebral palsy, a condition that left her muscles stiff and, for the most part, unmanageable. Because she had trouble speaking, it was this bright smile that reflected her true personality—a great kid. She used a walker most of the time to navigate through the crowded school hallways. A lot of times people didn't speak to her. Why? Who knows? Maybe it was because she looked different and the rest of the students didn't know how to approach her. Tina usually broke the ice with people she met in the halls (especially boys) with a big "Hi."

The assignment was to memorize three stanzas of the poem "Don't Quit." I only made the assignment worth ten points since I figured most of my students wouldn't do it anyway. When I was in school and a teacher assigned a ten-point homework assignment, I would probably have blown it off myself. So I wasn't expecting much from today's teenagers either. Tina was in the class, and I noticed a look on her face that was different from the normal bright smile. The look was one of worry. *Don't worry, Tina*, I thought to myself, *it's only ten points.*

The day the assignment came due arrived and as I went through my roster my expectations were met, as one by one each student failed to recite the poem. "Sorry, Mr. Krause," was the standard reply. "It's only worth ten points anyway . . . right?" Finally, in frustration and half kidding, I proclaimed that the next person who didn't recite the poem perfectly had to drop on the floor and give me ten push-ups. This was a leftover discipline technique from my days as a physical education teacher. To my surprise, Tina was next. Tina used her walker to move to the front of the class and, straining to form the words, began to try to recite the poem. She made it to the end of the first stanza when she made a mistake. Before I could say a word, she threw her walker to the side, fell to the floor and started doing push-ups. I was horrified and wanted to say, "Tina, I was just kidding!" But she crawled back up in her walker, stood in front of the class and continued the poem. She finished all three stanzas perfectly, one of only a handful of students who did, as it turned out.

When she finished, a fellow student spoke up and asked, "Tina, why did you do that? It's only worth ten points!"

Tina took her time forming the words and said, "Because I want to be like you guys—normal."

Silence fell on the whole room when another student exclaimed, "Tina, we're not normal—we're teenagers! We get in trouble all the time."

"I know," Tina said as a big smile spread across her face.

Tina got her ten points that day. She also got the love and respect of her classmates. To her, that was worth a whole lot more than ten points.

Tom Krause

Don't Quit

When things go wrong, as they sometimes will,
When the road you're trudging seems all uphill,
When the funds are low, and the debts are high,
and you want to smile, but you have to sigh.
When care is pressing you down a bit,
Rest if you must, but don't you quit.

Life is queer with its twist and turns
As every one of us sometimes learns,
And many a failure turns about,
When he might have won had he stuck it out;
Don't give up though the pace seems slow,
You may succeed with another blow.

Success is failure turned inside out,
the silver tint of the clouds of doubt,
and you never can tell how close you are,
It may be near when it seems so far;
So stick to the fight when you're hardest hit,
It's when things seem worst,
that you must not quit.

Clinton Howell

Beat the Drum

Troubles are like babies. They only grow bigger by nursing.

Old Postcard

Capuchin monkeys are being trained to help quadriplegics with household chores, fetching and carrying. As I watch the television special about their spritely service, I have a flash memory—a little monkey helped with my polio rehabilitation, too, more than forty years ago.

Age four and home from the hospital a few weeks, my days were pretty dull. The hospital bed my parents had rented had railing sides so I wouldn't fall out. It felt like an oversized crib. Morning and afternoon, Mom carried me to the tub for a hot soak and then back to the bed for tedious exercises as prescribed by the Kenny Method in favor with the local pediatrician. Still, there were long hours when Mom had to be cooking or cleaning, doing laundry or sewing. My big brother was in school, Dad at work and I was alone.

Cranks at the bottom of the bed allowed my parents to raise the head of the bed, or my knees or feet. The visiting nurse had instructed my folks not to leave me propped in a sitting position. The doctors feared my spine would settle in a curved position while my back and side muscles were too weak to support me upright. Nor was I allowed to lie on my tummy propped on my elbows. It would arch my back too much.

To strengthen my grip, they had given me a rubber ball to squeeze, but it was large for my hand. Squeezing it as hard as I could didn't seem to accomplish much, and I'd lay it aside in favor of a stuffed animal or a picture book. As often as not, my squirming would dislodge it from the bed covers. It would slip between the rails of the bed and go bouncing across the room to lie out of range until the next time Mom retrieved it.

During our formal exercise sessions, Mom would lay two of her fingers across my palm and tell me to squeeze as hard as I could, ten times. She was hoping to feel a little more pressure each day, but often she could feel only the first few attempts. She had no way of knowing if I was really trying or whether I had given up from boredom or frustration. I learned to show my effort on my face, scrunching my lips and brows to prove I was trying, as if one set of muscles could apologize for the others. But every day as she left to do other chores, it was still "Keep practicing with the ball, Honey."

One day Dad came home from work with a small paper bag from Woolworth's. From it he presented a mechanical monkey about four inches high. The monkey was smartly uniformed in a red felt suit with gold trim, and he carried a little snare drum on straps around his shoulders. The paws at the end of his furry arms held drumsticks, poised to strike. Coming out of the monkey's back was a rubber tube about the size of a drinking straw. At the end of the tube was a walnut-sized rubber bulb.

Dad showed me how it worked. If you squeezed the

bulb, the monkey's arms would . . . whump, whump . . .
beat the drum. Whump, whump . . . tap, tap.
"Now you try it, Carol." He put the bulb in my out-
stretched hand.
I squeezed. Nothing. I tried again focusing all my atten-
tion in the muscles in the palm of my hand. One of the
monkey's arms moved slowly downward, but there was
no sound.
Mom sounded delighted, though. "That's good, Carol.
Try to do it faster." She wrapped her hand around mine.
"Like this." She squeezed. Whump, whump.
"Again, Mommy," my eyes lit up. Squeeze. Tap, tap.
"Now you try again. You know how it feels."
Ssqueeezze. Whump.
"I did it, Mommy!" Squeeze. Whump. Squeeze. Tap, tap.
"I can do it!"
I think it was the first exercise I chose to do on my own.
I wonder if the family didn't eventually get sick of the
continual whump, whump . . . tap, tap, but I don't recall
anyone ever asking me to stop. Whump, whump . . . tap,
tap. Maybe it was music to their ears.
Some time later, Mom persuaded me to shift to using
my left hand. Things were quieter for a while. It took me
a long time to get it. Some days I'd give up and switch
back to my right. But by then doing it with my right hand
was too easy. I'd get bored.
So doing it with my left had become a challenge, and I
learned to give myself credit for getting the arm to move
at all. I'd squeeze the bulb with my right hand, watching
every muscle I could see, feeling how my wrist tightened,
how my fingers curled, how my thumb rolled toward the
fist.
Then I'd try to get the left hand to feel like that. Tighten,
curl, roll. A furry arm would descend halfway to the drum
and then bounce back. "Come on, Monkey, hit it," I'd say,

as if the little guy was resisting me on purpose.

Tighten, curl, roll. The other arm would move to the drum head, but not fast enough. "Aw, you almost had it."

Tighten, curl, roll. Whump! Tighten, curl, roll. Whump, whump. "I'm doing it, Mommy!" It was working! Whump, whump. "Come see!" Squeeze. Tap, tap.

"I can hear it, Honey. Is that your left hand?" She came to the side of the bed.

"Yeah! Look!" Whump, whump . . . tap, tap.

"That's wonderful! Do it again!" Whump, whump . . . tap, tap. "Oh, Carol, that's great!"

Of such small victories is recovery built. Sound the trumpet. Beat the drum.

Carol Barre

The Letter

To send a letter is a good way to go somewhere without moving anything but your heart.

Phyllis Theroux

I sat at my dining-room table, signing my name to the most difficult letter I'd ever penned. The letter was to my son Luke's birth mom. This was not the first time I had reached out to the woman whose name I didn't know. I'd sent several letters over the years with photos of Luke, which the adoption agency had agreed to forward, but had never received a single reply. I didn't know if Luke's birth mom had even read my letters.

Please read this letter, I prayed as I folded the paper and slipped it into its envelope. *Luke's life may depend on it.*

With four teenagers of our own, my husband Mark and I still felt we had more love to give. And so we adopted Luke, now six, and two years later Matthew.

When Luke was one year old the pediatrician ran a routine blood test: "Your son has sickle-cell disease," the doctor grimly informed us.

"People die from that!" I gasped.

A gene inherited from both of his birth parents had caused Luke to be born with defective red blood cells.

"As he grows older Luke will probably suffer anemia and extremely painful swelling in his joints," the doctor said. "But we can give Luke monthly transfusions of healthy blood to help keep up his strength."

I thanked God for every healthy day Luke enjoyed. But when Luke was three, he caught a cold and was having trouble breathing. We admitted Luke to the hospital immediately for IV antibiotics.

Luke had acute chest syndrome. Large clumps of sickle-shaped red blood cells were clogging the vessels in his lungs. The blockage was preventing Luke's blood from getting enough oxygen. This caused further sickling, which led to even more blockage in a vicious cycle that was spiraling dangerously out of control.

I held Luke's tiny hand while a heart-lung bypass machine struggled to raise his blood-oxygen levels.

Finally, Luke began to rally.

"Luke has been through quite an ordeal, but he is feeling much better now," I wrote to my son's birth mom, who, I had learned from the adoption agency, was a single mother of three with little money, struggling to finish her education.

After his crisis Luke's doctor increased his transfusions from monthly to every third week, but this only forestalled the inevitable. Soon Luke was back in the hospital, fighting once again for his life.

Luke recovered from the second crisis, but I knew it was only a matter of time before my son succumbed to his illness. "Isn't there anything more we can do?" I begged the doctors.

Then, Luke's hematologist related some exciting news. "There's a chance Luke's sickle-cell disease could be cured with a bone-marrow transplant," he told us. "The new marrow would produce healthy blood cells that wouldn't carry the sickle-cell disease."

My heart soared, but it landed with a thud when the doctor inquired, "Do you know if Luke has any siblings?" To perform a transplant, they would have to locate a matching donor. "A blood brother or sister would offer the best hope for a successful antigen match," the doctor explained.

I anguished over what to do. "Do I even have the right to ask Luke's birth mother for help?" I asked an adoption agency counselor.

"Luke is your child. You have a right to do whatever it takes to save his life," the counselor replied without hesitation.

And so I penned a letter describing the situation to Luke's birth mom. "Would you consider having your other children tested as possible marrow donors?" I wrote. I dropped the letter into the mailbox and then waited and prayed.

Two weeks later the hematologist called. "Luke's birth mom had her children tested, and I just got the results from her doctor," he said, excited. "One of them is a 100 percent match, and he can't wait to become his brother's marrow donor."

"She brought him into this world, and now he'll have a second chance to live a long and happy life," I told Mark.

The cutting-edge transplant was performed at the University of Michigan Medical Center in Ann Arbor. Luke received eight days of strong chemotherapy to kill off his diseased bone marrow. Meanwhile, many hundreds of miles away, one of Luke's older brothers visited a local hospital where doctors extracted a few ounces of his healthy bone marrow. The precious cargo was rushed to Michigan, where the doctor used a simple IV line to infuse the life-giving marrow cells into Luke's bloodstream.

Within weeks, tests revealed that Luke's new bone marrow was taking hold and already producing healthy red blood cells. Two weeks later Luke was ready to go home, his sickle-cell disease gone forever.

In a letter I shared the happy news with Luke's birth mom, who this time wrote back:

> *I've written many letters but never had the courage to mail them. Many times I've felt like I did the wrong thing, but now I know it was right. I never could have given Luke the medical attention he needed. Now I know he's right where God needed him to be. Luke has two families who love him. He's a very lucky little boy.*

I think I'm the lucky one. I get to watch Luke grow up healthy and strong.

Julane DeBoer
As told to Bill Holton

Just Do What You Can

It was a chilly fall day when the farmer spied the little sparrow lying on its back in the middle of his field. The farmer stopped his plowing, looked down at the frail, feathered creature and inquired, "Why are you lying upside down like that?"

"I heard the sky is going to fall today," replied the bird.

The old farmer chuckled. "And I suppose your spindly little legs can hold up the sky?"

"One does what one can," replied the plucky sparrow.

D'ette Corona

2

LIVING YOUR DREAM

The future belongs to those who believe in the beauty of their dreams.

Eleanor Roosevelt

New Directions

You may have a fresh start any moment you choose, for this thing we call "failure" is not the falling down, but the staying down.

Mary Pickford

In 1903 the late Mrs. Annie Johnson of Arkansas found herself with two toddling sons, very little money, and a slight ability to read and add simple numbers. To this picture add a disastrous marriage and the burdensome fact that Mrs. Johnson was a Negro.

When she told her husband, Mr. William Johnson, of her dissatisfaction with their marriage, he conceded that he too found it to be less than he expected, and had been secretly hoping to leave and study religion. He added that he thought God was calling him not only to preach but to do so in Enid, Oklahoma. He did not tell her that he knew a minister in Enid with whom he could study and who had a friendly, unmarried daughter. They parted amicably, Annie keeping the one-room house and William taking most of the cash to carry himself to Oklahoma.

Annie, over six feet tall, big boned, decided that she

would not go to work as a domestic and leave her "precious babes" to anyone else's care. There was no possibility of being hired at the town's cotton gin or lumber mill, but maybe there was a way to make the two factories work for her. In her words, "I looked up the road I was going and back the way I come, and since I wasn't satisfied, I decided to step off the road and cut me a new path." She told herself that she wasn't a fancy cook but that she could "mix groceries well enough to scare hunger away from starving a man."

She made her plans meticulously and in secret. One early evening, to see if she was ready, she placed stones in two five-gallon pails and carried them three miles to the cotton gin. She rested a little, and then, discarding some rocks, she walked in the darkness to the sawmill five miles farther along the dirt road. On her way back to her little house and her babies, she dumped the remaining rocks along the path.

That same night she worked into the early hours boiling chicken and frying ham. She made dough and filled the rolled-out pastry with meat. At last she went to sleep.

The next morning she left her house carrying the meat pies, lard, an iron brazier and coals for a fire. Just before lunch she appeared in an empty lot behind the cotton gin. As the noon dinner bell rang, she dropped the savories into boiling fat, and the aroma rose and floated over to the workers who spilled out of the gin, covered with white lint, looking like specters.

Most workers had brought their lunches of pinto beans and biscuits or crackers, onions and cans of sardines, but they were tempted by the hot meat pies that Annie ladled out of the fat. She wrapped them in newspapers, which soaked up the grease, and offered them for sale at a nickel each. Although business was slow, those first days Annie was determined. She balanced her appearances between the two hours of activity.

So, on Monday if she offered hot fresh pies at the cotton gin and sold the remaining cooled-down pies at the lumber mill for three cents, then on Tuesday she went first to the lumber mill presenting fresh, just-cooked pies as the lumbermen covered in sawdust emerged from the mill.

For the next few years, on balmy spring days, blistering summer noons, and cold, wet, and wintry middays, Annie never disappointed her customers, who could count on seeing the tall, brown-skinned woman bent over her brazier, carefully turning the meat pies. When she felt certain that the workers had become dependent on her, she built a stall between the two hives of industry and let the men run to her for their lunchtime provisions.

She had indeed stepped from the road which seemed to have been chosen for her and cut herself a brand-new path. In years that stall became a store where customers could buy cheese, meal, syrup, cookies, candy, writing tablets, pickles, canned goods, fresh fruit, soft drinks, coal, oil and leather soles for worn-out shoes.

Each of us has the right and the responsibility to assess the roads which lie ahead, and those over which we have traveled, and if the future road looms ominous or unpromising, and the roads back uninviting, then we need to gather our resolve and, carrying only the necessary baggage, step off that road into another direction. If the new choice is also unpalatable, without embarrassment, we must be ready to change that as well.

Maya Angelou
Submitted by Katy McNamara

Dare to Imagine

The doctors told me I would never walk again, but my mother told me I would, so I believed my mother.

Wilma Rudolph,
"The fastest woman on Earth,"
three-time gold medalist, 1960 Olympics

When people find out that I competed in the Olympics, they assume I've always been an accomplished athlete. But it isn't true. I was not the strongest, or the fastest, and I didn't learn the quickest. For me, becoming an Olympian was not developing a gift of natural athletic ability, but was, literally, an act of will.

At the 1972 Olympics in Munich, I was a member of the U.S. pentathlon team, but the tragedy of the Israeli athletes and an injury to my ankle combined to make the experience a deeply discouraging one. I didn't quit; instead I kept training, eventually qualifying to go with the U.S. team to Montreal for the 1976 Games. The experience was much more joyous, and I was thrilled to place thirteenth. But still, I felt I could do better.

I arranged to take a leave of absence from my college coaching job the year before the 1980 Olympics. I figured that twelve months of "twenty-four-hour-a-day training" would give me the edge I needed to bring home a medal this time. In the summer of 1979, I started intensively training for the Olympic trials to be held in June of 1980. I felt the exhilaration that comes with single-minded focus and steady progress towards a cherished goal.

But then in November, what appeared to be an insurmountable obstacle occurred. I was in a car accident and injured my lower back. The doctors weren't sure exactly what was wrong, but I had to stop training because I couldn't move without experiencing excruciating pain. It seemed all too obvious that I would have to give up my dream of going to the Olympics if I couldn't keep training. Everyone felt so sorry for me. Everyone but me.

It was strange, but I never believed this setback would stop me. I trusted that the doctors and physical therapists would get it handled soon, and I would get back to training. I held on to the affirmation: I'm getting better every day and I will place in the top three at the Olympic trials. It went through my head constantly.

But my progress was slow, and the doctors couldn't agree on a course of treatment. Time was passing, and I was still in pain, unable to move. With only a few months remaining, I had to do something or I knew I would never make it. So I started training the only way I could—in my head.

A pentathlon consists of five track and field events: the 100-meter hurdle, the shot put, the high jump, the long jump and the 200-meter sprint. I obtained films of the world-record holders in all five of my events. Sitting in a kitchen chair, I watched the films projected on my kitchen wall over and over. Sometimes, I watched them in slow motion or frame by frame. When I got bored, I watched them backwards, just for fun. I watched for hundreds of hours, studying and absorbing. Other times, I lay on the couch and visualized the experience of competing in minute detail. I know some people thought I was crazy, but I wasn't ready to give up yet. I trained as hard as I could—without ever moving a muscle.

Finally, the doctors diagnosed my problem as a bulging disc. Now I knew *why* I was in agony when I moved, but I still couldn't train. Later, when I could walk a little, I went to the track and had them set up all five of my events. Even though I couldn't practice, I would stand on the track and envision in my mind the complete physical training routine I *would* have gone through that day if I had been able. For months, I repeatedly imagined myself competing and qualifying at the trials.

But was visualizing enough? Was it truly possible that I could place in the top three at the Olympic trials? I believed it with all my heart.

By the time the trials actually rolled around, I had healed just enough to compete. Being very careful to keep my muscles and tendons warm, I moved through my five events as if in a dream. Afterwards, as I walked across the field, I heard a voice on the loudspeaker announcing my name.

It took my breath away, even though I had imagined it a thousand times in my mind. I felt a wave of pure joy wash over me as the announcer said, "Second place, 1980 Olympic Pentathlon: Marilyn King."

Marilyn King
As told to Carol Kline

The Little Girl Who Dared to Wish

As Amy Hagadorn rounded the corner across the hall from her classroom, she collided with a tall boy from the fifth grade running in the opposite direction. "Watch it, Squirt," the boy yelled, as he dodged around the little third-grader. Then, with a smirk on his face, the boy took hold of his right leg and mimicked the way Amy limped when she walked. Amy closed her eyes for a moment. *Ignore him,* she told herself as she headed for her classroom. But at the end of the day Amy was still thinking about the tall boy's teasing. And he wasn't the only one. Ever since Amy started the third grade, someone teased her every single day, about her speech or her limping. Sometimes, even in a classroom full of other students, the teasing made her feel all alone.

At the dinner table that evening, Amy was quiet. Knowing that things were not going well at school, Patti Hagadorn was happy to have some exciting news to share with her daughter. "There's a Christmas wish contest at the local radio station," she announced. "Write a letter to Santa and you might win a prize. I think someone with blond curly hair at this table should enter." Amy giggled and out came pencil and paper. "Dear Santa

Claus," she began. While Amy worked away at her best printing, the rest of the family tried to figure out what she might ask from Santa. Amy's sister, Jamie, and Amy's mom both thought a three-foot Barbie doll would top Amy's wish list. Amy's dad guessed a picture book. But Amy wouldn't reveal her secret Christmas wish.

At the radio station WJLT in Fort Wayne, Indiana, letters poured in for the Christmas Wish contest. The workers had fun reading about all the different presents the boys and girls from across the city wanted for Christmas. When Amy's letter arrived at the radio station, manager Lee Tobin read it carefully.

> *Dear Santa Claus,*
> *My name is Amy. I am nine years old. I have a problem at school. Can you help me, Santa? Kids laugh at me because of the way I walk and run and talk. I have cerebral palsy. I just want one day where no one laughs at me or makes fun of me.*
>
> *Love, Amy*

Lee's heart ached as he read the letter: He knew cerebral palsy was a muscle disorder that might confuse Amy's schoolmates. He thought it would be good for the people of Fort Wayne to hear about this special little girl and her unusual wish. Mr. Tobin called up the local newspaper.

The next day, a picture of Amy and her letter to Santa made the front page of *The News Sentinel*. The story spread quickly. Across the country, newspapers and radio and television stations reported the story of the little girl in Fort Wayne, Indiana, who asked for such a simple, yet remarkable Christmas gift—just one day without teasing.

Suddenly, the postman was a regular at the Hagadorn house. Envelopes of all sizes addressed to Amy arrived daily from children and adults all across the nation, filled with holiday greetings and words of encouragement. During that busy Christmas season, over two thousand people from all over the world sent Amy letters of friendship and support. Some of the writers had disabilities; some had been teased as children, but each writer had a special message for Amy. Through the cards and letters from strangers, Amy glimpsed a world full of people who truly cared about each other. She realized that no form or amount of teasing could ever make her feel lonely again.

Many people thanked Amy for being brave enough to speak up. Others encouraged her to ignore teasing and to carry her head high. Lynn, a sixth-grader from Texas, sent this message:

> I'd like to be your friend, and if you want to visit me, we could have fun. No one will make fun of us, because if they do, we will not even hear them.

Amy did get her wish of a special day without teasing at South Wayne Elementary School. Additionally, everyone at school got an added bonus. Teachers and students talked together about how teasing can make others feel. That year, the Fort Wayne mayor officially proclaimed December 21 as Amy Jo Hagadorn Day throughout the city. The mayor explained that by daring to make such a simple wish, Amy taught a universal lesson. "Everyone," said the mayor, "wants and deserves to be treated with respect, dignity and warmth."

Alan D. Shultz

Perseverance

When all the world is looming dark
And things seem not so clear,
When shadows seem to hover 'round
Lord, may I persevere.
When it seems everything's been tried
And there's no way to go,
Just let me keep remembering
Sometimes the journey's slow.
I may just need to stop and rest
Along the path I trod,
A time to try to understand
And have my talk with God.
As I gain new strength to carry on
Without a doubt or fear,
Somehow I know things will be right,
And so, I persevere.

Anne Stortz

Never Give Up

Opportunity . . . often it comes disguised in the form of misfortune or temporary defeat.

Napoleon Hill

"You have the MRI of someone in a wheelchair, Jason," said the doctor, in a voice his profession reserves for severe illness. "Eventually, you may lose your eyesight, coordination, even your bladder control."

The words hit my wife and I squarely. I was twenty-seven and had multiple sclerosis. I wanted to come to grips with this news, but right now all I could think of was ending this office visit. This doctor offered no hope—and he was scaring my wife and me in the process. I stole a glance at Tracy, who began to cry softly. I reached over to comfort her, my soul mate. We mumbled hurried good-byes and left.

I was in the construction business along with my dad, who owned the company. We raised buildings from the ground up and it was hard, demanding labor filled with long hours. But I loved it. I had walked the slender steel beams since the tender age of fourteen and probably felt more at home on a construction site than anywhere else. My dad taught me the ropes.

I couldn't bear the thought of letting him down now.

After I dropped Tracy off at home, I mentioned that I had to stop by the office for something. But actually, I wanted to pay a visit to a place that I had known for a very long time.

I sat in the church pew, feeling childhood memories wash over me. My eyes were squeezed shut as I anxiously prayed. "Dear Lord," I said. "I'm not afraid for myself, but I am afraid that I will let my wife and family down—they count on me for so much. Please, please help me beat this," I whispered.

I got up, left the church and hoped that my prayers would be answered. If ever there was a time to keep my faith up, it was now.

A few weeks later, the local paper featured an article in the sports section on a man named Pat. It was like a little miracle had come my way. Pat was a coach at the state college, and had conquered MS with the help of a strict diet.

At last I had found an ally, someone with the same symptoms, and likely the same doubts and fears. Pat and I met and talked for hours about food supplements, vitamins and working out. But these eight words echoed in my brain: "You can do it, Jason. Never give up."

I started a special diet and workout regime designed for MS patients, and stuck faithfully to it.

There were plenty of dark days, too. Days when I had to ask Tracy to help me finish dressing. Through all of this, she was spectacular, giving me the love and support I needed. I felt so blessed. Gradually, my recovery took shape. In time, the words of the doctor seemed far away.

Finally, I felt ready to set a goal for myself.

The challenge came in the form of natural bodybuilding. I had played football in high school and college, and I was certainly no stranger to the weight room. I began working out diligently with a trainer six days a week. He put me through different weight routines. My goal was to compete in a bodybuilding contest.

A few months later, all the hours of sweat and training brought me to a competition that included one three-minute routine. I found myself in front of an auditorium filled with people.

I completed my routine—flexing, stretching, showing off the body I had fought so hard to achieve—and walked off. As I waited for the judges to tally my score, I spotted my family and friends in the fourth row. When the judges announced that I had placed sixth, I felt a rush of pride and relief. As I took a bow, I stole a quick glance at my family, who were all standing up and clapping and cheering as hard as they could.

Before we left to celebrate at a nearby restaurant, my dad came over and put both his hands squarely on my shoulders. "Jason, I'm so proud of you. As far as I'm concerned, you are number one!" he said.

He looked me right in the eye. "We build foundations in our business, but let me tell you, the real foundations in life are family."

I hugged my dad tightly then, and as I did, I saw Tracy give me the thumbs-up sign and dazzle me with a smile as big as all outdoors.

Today, Tracy and I are the proud parents of two little girls. They are more precious than we could have ever imagined. And every day I remember my father's words: The *real* foundations in life are family.

Jason Morin

How to Be New and Different

If I could wish for my life to be perfect, it would be tempting, but I would have to decline, for life would no longer teach me anything.

Allyson Jones

The year 1993 wasn't shaping up to be the best year of my life. I was into my eighth year as a single parent, had three kids in college, my unmarried daughter had just given birth to my first grandchild and I was about to break up with a very nice man I'd dated for over two years. Faced with all this, I was spending lots of time feeling sorry for myself.

That April, I was asked to interview and write about a woman who lived in a small town in Minnesota. So during Easter vacation, Andrew, my thirteen-year-old, and I drove across two states to meet Jan Turner.

Andrew dozed most of the way during the long drive, but every once in a while I'd start a conversation.

"She's handicapped, you know."

"So what's wrong with her? Does she have a disease?"

"I don't think so. But for some reason, she had to have both arms and legs amputated."

"Wow. How does she get around?"

"I'm not sure. We'll see when we get there."

"Does she have any kids?"

"Two boys—Tyler and Cody—both adopted. She's a single parent, too. Only she's never been married."

"So what happened to her?"

"Four years ago Jan was just like me, a busy single mother. She was a full-time music teacher at a grade school and taught all sorts of musical instruments. She was also the music director at her church."

Andrew fell asleep again before I could finish telling him what little I did know about what had happened to Jan. As I drove across Minnesota, I began to wonder how the woman I was about to meet could cope with such devastating news that all four limbs had to be amputated. *How did she learn to survive? Did she have live-in help?*

When we arrived in Willmar, Minnesota, I called Jan from our hotel to tell her that I could come to her house and pick her and the boys up, so they could swim at our hotel while we talked.

"That's okay, Pat, I can drive. The boys and I will be there in ten minutes. Would you like to go out to eat first? There's a Ponderosa close to your hotel."

"Sure, that'll be fine," I said haltingly, wondering what it would be like to eat in a public restaurant with a woman who had no arms or legs. *And how on earth does she drive?* I wondered.

Ten minutes later, Jan pulled up in front of the hotel. She got out of the car, walked over to me with perfect posture on legs and feet that looked every bit as real as mine, and extended her right arm with its shiny hook on the end to shake my hand. "Hello, Pat, I'm sure glad to meet you. And this must be Andrew."

I grabbed her hook, pumped it a bit and smiled sheepishly. "Uh, yes, this is Andrew." I looked in the back seat of her car and smiled at the two boys who grinned back. Cody, the younger one, was practically effervescent at the thought of going swimming in the hotel pool after dinner.

Jan bubbled as she slid back behind the driver's seat, "So hop in. Cody, move over and make room for Andrew."

We arrived at the restaurant, went through the line, paid for our food, and ate and talked amidst the chattering of our three sons. The only thing I had to do for Jan Turner that entire evening was unscrew the top on the ketchup bottle.

Later that night, as our three sons splashed in the pool, Jan and I sat on the side and she told me about life before her illness.

"We were a typical single-parent family. You know, busy all the time. Life was so good, in fact, that I was seriously thinking about adopting a third child."

My conscience stung. I had to face it—the woman next to me was better at single parenting than I ever thought about being.

Jan continued. "One Sunday in November of 1989, I was playing my trumpet at the front of my church when I suddenly felt weak, dizzy and nauseous. I struggled down the aisle, motioned for the boys to follow me and drove home. I crawled into bed, but by evening I knew I had to get help."

Jan then explained that by the time she arrived at the hospital, she was comatose. Her blood pressure had dropped so much that her body was already shutting down. She had pneumococcal pneumonia, the same bacterial infection that took the life of Muppets creator Jim Henson. One of its disastrous side effects is an activation of the body's clotting system, which causes the blood vessels to plug up. Because there was suddenly no blood flow to her hands or feet, she quickly developed gangrene in all four extremities. Two weeks after being admitted to the hospital, Jan's arms had to be amputated at mid-forearm and her legs at mid-shin.

Just before the surgery, she said she cried out, "Oh God, no! How can I live without arms and legs, feet or hands? Never walk again? Never play the trumpet, guitar, piano or any of the instruments I teach? I'll never be able to hug my sons or take care of them. Oh God, don't let me depend on others for the rest of my life!"

Six weeks after the amputations as her dangling limbs healed, a doctor talked to Jan about prosthetics. She said Jan could learn to walk, drive a car, go back to school, even go back to teaching.

Jan found that hard to believe so she picked up her Bible. It fell open to Romans, chapter twelve, verse two: "Don't copy the behavior and customs of this world, but be a new and different person with a fresh newness in all you do and think. Then you will learn from your own experience how his ways will really satisfy you."

Jan thought about that—about being a new and different person—and she decided to give the prosthetics a try. With a walker strapped onto her forearms near the elbow and a therapist on either side, she could only wobble on her new legs for two to three minutes before she collapsed in exhaustion and pain.

Take it slowly, Jan said to herself. *Be a new person in all that you do and think, but take it one step at a time.*

The next day she tried on the prosthetic arms, a crude system of cables, rubber bands and hooks operated by a harness across the shoulders. By moving her shoulder muscles she was soon able to open and close the hooks to pick up and hold objects, and dress and feed herself.

Within a few months, Jan learned she could do almost everything she used to do—only in a new and different way.

"Still, when I finally got to go home after four months of physical and occupational therapy, I was *so* nervous about what life would be like with my boys and me alone in the house. But when I got there, I got out of the car, walked up the steps to our house, hugged my boys with all my might, and we haven't looked back since."

As Jan and I continued to talk, Cody, who'd climbed out of the hotel pool, stood close to his mom with his arm around her shoulders. As she told me about her newly improved cooking skills, Cody grinned. "Yup," he said, "She's a better mom now than before she got sick, because now she can even flip pancakes!" Jan laughed like a woman who is blessed with tremendous happiness, contentment and unswerving faith in God.

Since our visit, Jan has completed a second college degree, this one in communications, and she is now an announcer for the local radio station. She also studied theology and has been ordained as the children's pastor at her church, the Triumphant Life Church in Willmar. Simply put, Jan says, "I'm a new and different person, triumphant because of God's unending love and wisdom."

After meeting Jan, I was a new and different person as well. I learned to praise God for everything in my life that makes *me* new and different, whether it's struggling through one more part-time job to keep my kids in college, learning to be a grandmother for the first time or having the courage to end a relationship with a wonderful friend who just wasn't the right one for me.

Jan may not have real flesh-and-blood arms, legs, hands or feet, but that woman has more heart and soul than anyone I've ever met before or since. She taught me to grab on to every "new and different" thing that comes into my life with all the gusto I can muster . . . to live my life triumphantly.

Patricia Lorenz

I Was Thirty-Seven Years Old at the Time

Youth is a gift of nature,
Age is a work of art.

Helen M. Carrall

For years, you've watched everyone else do it.

The children who sat on the curb eating their lunches while waiting for their bus.

The husband you put through school who drank coffee standing up and slept with his hand on the alarm.

And you envied them and said, "Maybe next year I'll go back to school." And the years went by and this morning you looked into the mirror and said, "You blew it. You're too old to pick it up and start a new career."

This wisdom is for you.

Margaret Mitchell won the Pulitzer Prize for Fiction for *Gone with the Wind* in 1937. She was thirty-seven years old at the time.

Margaret Chase Smith was elected to the Senate for the first time in 1948 at the age of forty-nine.

Ruth Gordon picked up her first Oscar in 1968 for *Rosemary's Baby*. She was seventy-two years old.

Billie Jean King took the battle of women's worth to a tennis court in Houston's Astrodome to outplay Bobby Riggs. She was thirty-one years of age.

Grandma Moses began a painting career at the age of seventy-six.

Anne Morrow Lindbergh followed in the shadow of her husband until she began to question the meaning of existence for individual women. She published her thoughts in *Gift from the Sea* in 1955, at forty-nine.

Shirley Temple Black was ambassador to Ghana at the age of forty-seven.

Golda Meir in 1969 was elected prime minister of Israel. She had just turned seventy-one.

Barbara Jordan was given official duties as a speaker at the Democratic National Convention. She was forty years old.

You can tell yourself these people started out as exceptional. You can tell yourself they had influence before they started. You can tell yourself the conditions under which they achieved were different from yours. Or you can be like a woman I knew who sat at her kitchen window year after year and watched everyone else do it and then said to herself, "It's my turn."

I was thirty-seven years old at the time.

Erma Bombeck

The Secret Behind My Success

Be not afraid of going slowly. Be afraid of standing still.

Japanese Proverb

My career—TV, stage, movies, all of it—was founded on a strange event that was to be a deep mystery to me for years. Only after my life had changed drastically did I begin to solve the puzzle I was confronted with one long-ago June evening in California.

In those days I was one of a group of stage-struck drama-school students at UCLA, living on hopes and dreams and not much else. As school ended, one of our professors was leaving for a vacation in Europe. He had a house near San Diego, and a bon-voyage party was planned. It was suggested that some of us drama students might drive down and entertain his supper guests with scenes from musical comedies.

Nine of us agreed to go. One of the boys and I had rehearsed a scene from *Annie Get Your Gun*, and that was our part of the program. Everything went well. The guests seemed to enjoy our singing, and we enjoyed it, too.

After our performance, supper was announced. I was standing at the buffet when a man I had never seen before spoke to me pleasantly. He said he had admired our performance. Then he asked me what I intended to do with my life.

I told him that I hoped to go to New York some day and make a career for myself on the stage. When he asked what was stopping me, I told him truthfully that I barely had enough money to get back to Los Angeles, let alone New York. I might have added, but didn't, that at times my grandmother, my mother, my sister and I had been on welfare.

The man smiled and said he would be happy to lend me the money to go to New York. A thousand dollars, he added, should be enough to get me started. Well, in those days I was pretty innocent, but not that innocent. So I refused his offer politely. He went away, but in a few moments he was back with a pleasant-faced lady whom he introduced as his wife. Then he made his offer all over again. He was quite serious, he said. There were only three conditions. First, if I did meet with success, I was to repay the loan without interest in five years. Next, I was never to reveal his identity to anyone. Finally, if I accepted his offer, I was eventually to pass the kindness along, to help some other person in similar circumstances when I was able to do so.

He told me to think it over and telephone him when I got back to Los Angeles. He added that he was prepared to make a similar offer to my partner in the scene from *Annie Get Your Gun*, and he gave me his telephone number.

The next day, half convinced that I had dreamed the whole thing, I called the number. I was told that if I had decided to accept the conditions, I could drive down on Monday morning and pick up my check. Still unbelieving, I told my mother and grandmother. Their reaction, not surprisingly, was to urge me strongly not to have anything to do with this mysterious benefactor. But somehow I was convinced that the man was sincere, and I believed, furthermore, that God was giving me, Carol Burnett, a strong and unmistakable push. I was supposed to accept the offer. I was being guided. And if I didn't go, I would regret it for the rest of my life.

At sunup on Monday my partner and I were on the road. We drove for three hours. At nine o'clock, we were at the man's office. We had to wait perhaps half an hour—and believe me, that was the longest half hour of my life! But finally we were ushered in. Our friend was crisp, serious, businesslike. He reminded us of the conditions, especially the one about not revealing his identity. Then he had his secretary bring in the checks. I had never seen so many beautiful zeros in my life. We tried to thank him, but he just smiled and ushered us out. When we got to the car, still dazed, we realized we didn't have enough gasoline to get back to Los Angeles—and not enough cash to buy any. We had to go to a bank, present one of the checks, then wait while the astonished bank officials telephoned our friend's office to make sure that we weren't a pair of international forgers. But finally they did cash it for us.

Back in Los Angeles, I wasted no time. I spent a little of the money on a visit to the dentist, where I had two teeth filled and one extracted—I hadn't been able to afford a dentist for years. Then, with my family's anxious admonitions ringing in my ears, I headed for New York. In all of that vast city I knew just one soul, a girl named Eleanore Ebe. I called her up and found that she was staying at the Rehearsal Club, where in those days young theatrical hopefuls could find room and board for eighteen dollars a week. So I moved in with Ellie, and settled down to the long grind of finding work on the New York stage. It was the old story. No experience? Then no work. But how can you get experience if you can't get work? My funds got lower and lower. I went to work as a hat-check girl in a restaurant. Unfortunately, it catered mostly to ladies who had no desire or reason to check their hats. Still, I managed to make about thirty dollars a week from tips— enough to get by.

My grandmother wrote me sternly that if I hadn't found a job on the stage by Christmas, I had better come home. So I redoubled my visits to theatrical agencies. Finally one agent said wearily, "Why don't you put on your own show? Maybe then you'd stop bothering us!"

That sparked an idea. Back at the Rehearsal Club I talked to all my jobless friends. If we were really bursting with talent, as we were sure we were, why not hire a hall, send out invitations to all the agents and critics in town and put on our own revue?

Everyone agreed that it was a great idea. We started chipping in fifty cents apiece each night for a fund to hire the hall. Talented youngsters took on the task of creating scenery, writing music and lyrics, doing the choreography. When our first act was ready, we performed it for the board of directors of the club, who then gave us some additional help.

When the "Rehearsal Club Revue" finally opened and ran for three nights, it seemed to us that everyone in New York show business was in the audience. The day after it closed, three agents called me with offers of jobs. From that point on, the magic doors swung open, and I was on my way.

I reported all my progress to my benefactor back on the West Coast, but I heard very little from him. He continued to insist upon his anonymity. He showed no desire to share any spotlights, take any credit.

Five years to the day after I accepted his loan, I paid him back, and since then I've kept my pledge never to reveal his identity. He never told me his reasons for helping me in the manner he did, but as the years have gone by, I've been able to unravel the mystery of this man—at least to my own satisfaction—and in the process I've discovered a powerful spiritual principle to use in my own life.

I stumbled upon the key clue one day when I was glancing through a copy of the Living Bible. I had turned to the sixth chapter of Matthew, because I wanted to see how the Lord's Prayer had been translated. Suddenly, some verses seemed to leap out of the page: "When you give a gift to a beggar, don't shout about it as the hypocrites do. . . . When you do a kindness to someone, do it secretly . . . And your Father Who knows all secrets will reward you. . . ." (Matthew 6:2-4)

Do it secretly, the passage read, and at once I thought of my secretive friend. From that moment, what he had done and how he had done it began to make sense.

I began to see that when he made his offer to me, my benefactor had employed the spiritual principle of giving in secret without seeking credit. He had done it partly to be kind, of course, but also because he knew that great dividends flow back to anyone who is wise enough to practice this kind of giving.

So that's the story of how my career began. I shall always be grateful to my anonymous friend. With pride I repaid his loan, and with pride I have kept his name secret. As for his stipulation about passing the kindness along to others—well, that's my secret.

Carol Burnett

3

THE POWER
OF LOVE

There is a net of love by which you can catch souls.

Mother Teresa

No Greater Love

Whatever their planned target, the mortar rounds landed in an orphanage run by a missionary group in the small Vietnamese village. The missionaries and one or two children were killed outright, and several more children were wounded, including one young girl about eight years old.

People from the village requested medical help from a neighboring town that had radio contact with the American forces. Finally, an American navy doctor and nurse arrived in a jeep with only their medical kits. They established that the girl was the most critically injured. Without quick action, she would die of shock and loss of blood.

A transfusion was imperative, and a donor with a matching blood type was required. A quick test showed that neither American had the correct type, but several of the uninjured orphans did.

The doctor spoke some pidgin Vietnamese, and the nurse a smattering of high-school French. Using that combination, together with much impromptu sign language, they tried to explain to their young, frightened audience that unless they could replace some of the girl's lost blood, she would certainly die. Then they asked if anyone would be willing to give blood to help.

Their request was met with wide-eyed silence. After several long moments, a small hand slowly and waveringly went up, dropped back down and then went up again.

"Oh, thank you," the nurse said in French. "What is your name?"

"Heng," came the reply.

Heng was quickly laid on a pallet, his arm swabbed with alcohol, and a needle inserted in his vein. Through this ordeal Heng lay stiff and silent.

After a moment, he let out a shuddering sob, quickly covering his face with his free hand.

"Is it hurting, Heng?" the doctor asked. Heng shook his head, but after a few moments another sob escaped, and once more he tried to cover up his crying. Again the doctor asked him if the needle hurt, and again Heng shook his head.

But now his occasional sobs gave way to a steady, silent crying, his eyes screwed tightly shut, his fist in his mouth to stifle his sobs.

The medical team was concerned. Something was obviously very wrong. At this point, a Vietnamese nurse arrived to help. Seeing the little one's distress, she spoke to him rapidly in Vietnamese, listened to his reply and answered him in a soothing voice.

After a moment, the patient stopped crying and looked questioningly at the Vietnamese nurse. When she nodded, a look of great relief spread over his face.

Glancing up, the nurse said quietly to the Americans, "He thought he was dying. He misunderstood you. He thought you had asked him to give all his blood so the little girl could live."

"But why would he be willing to do that?" asked the navy nurse.

The Vietnamese nurse repeated the question to the little boy, who answered simply, "She's my friend."

Col. John W. Mansur
Excerpted from The Missileer

Dharma

Nearing the lake on that warm September morning, I heard a tiny mewing sound. My first inclination was to ignore the cries. *I've been through enough lately,* I thought; *I can hardly take care of myself.*

Three months earlier, at age thirty-seven, I had been diagnosed with breast cancer. Because the cancer was in more than one place, the doctor had recommended a radical mastectomy. It was scheduled for later that same month. I still remember the shock and denial I felt when I overheard my husband Gary, telling someone on the phone, "She's probably going to lose her breast." Those words seared through me like a knife. *No. No!* I silently cried to God, *I'm too young for that.*

A few weeks later, while I was recovering from the mastectomy, the surgeon called with more bad news: "The cancer has spread to your lymph nodes. Chemotherapy offers the best chance for survival." All I could do was sit there stunned, thinking, *Oh God, I'm going to die.*

I was terrified of dying. Many of my friends draw comfort from their beliefs about the afterlife or reincarnation. But I had trouble blindly believing in things I couldn't see or touch. I wanted proof. I prayed for God to show me the truth about death.

With the fear of dying in my heart, I decided to go on an aggressive clinical trial that included a combination of high-dose chemotherapy and a five-year follow-up with a hormone blocker.

The chemotherapy wiped me out completely. Even with the antinausea drugs, I was sick every time. Two months into the treatment, it was all I could do to get dressed and keep a little food down every day. In addition to working, my husband was doing his best to care for the house and me. Wonderful as he was, it was hard on both of us. I was irritable and lonely most of the time. This short walk to the lake was my first time outdoors in awhile.

Meow! Meow! The insistent pleas continued.

No, I really can't care for an animal right now, I thought as I passed by. Suddenly, ear-splitting shrieking and squawking filled the air. Four blue jays were dive-bombing the bush where the mewing sounds were coming from. Shooing the birds away, I ran and looked under the bush. Standing on wobbly legs was a tiny three-week-old orange tabby, with bright blue eyes, mewing his little head off. Gathering him up into my arms, I headed to the lake in hopes of finding his owner or else convincing someone to take him home.

The wind whipped all around us as the shaking kitten cuddled close, still scared to death. We sat together by the lake trying to find him a home. Asking a number of people and finding no takers, I decided to take him home temporarily until I could find him a home of his own. Still feeling exhausted from the chemo, I spent most of the day on the couch with the little kitty curled up on my chest purring. Later that evening, as my husband was leaving to go to a meeting, I asked him to take the kitten with him. "Try and find him a good home," I said, placing the kitten in a box. Little did I know, my heart had already been stolen.

An hour later, I beeped my husband. "Have you found him a home yet?" I asked.

"I was just giving him to someone," Gary replied.

"Don't," I said without hesitation. "Bring him home. I need him."

When Gary and the kitten returned home, the little orange tabby curled right back up on my chest like he'd never left.

For the next week, while I was bedridden, Dharma and I were constant companions. He just loved snuggling, sometimes trying to get right up under my chin. He didn't even notice my lack of hair or uneven chest. It felt good to love and be loved so unconditionally.

I chose the name Dharma because in India it means "fulfilling one's life purpose." Cancer-recovery research has shown that finding and following one's bliss or purpose supports the immune system and increases chances of survival. For me, I hoped this would include two deep-seated desires: writing and being of service to others. Dharma's name reminded me of that intention and so much more.

Arriving home from my biweekly doctor visits, I immediately picked him up like a baby and carried him around the house with me. I even carried him to the garage while I did laundry. We were inseparable. With Dharma around, I wasn't so needy and grouchy with Gary. And, boy, did Dharma purr loudly! It was so comforting hearing and feeling the love he expressed so freely.

As he grew, fighting, biting and clawing furniture became his favorite pastimes. We have a fenced-in backyard, so when he got too wild for me, I would let him play out back with other neighborhood cats.

Dharma also loved chasing butterflies. Last spring, I planted purple Porter's weed specifically to attract them.

The whole backyard, with its multitude of colorful butter-flies, was one big playpen for Dharma. I don't think he ever caught any, but I spent countless afternoons sitting on the back porch watching Dharma live his bliss. So free. No cares. My spirit soared as I watched him live his life so fully, and I decided it was time I do the same.

Late that December, I scheduled my final reconstructive surgery and let my office know I would be back to work in February.

Then, three days after my final surgery, the unthinkable happened. Escaping from the backyard, Dharma was hit by a car and killed instantly. My life, too, seemed to end at that moment. I was devastated and no one, not even Gary, could console me. I sat there on that same couch where Dharma and I had shared so much love and cried and cried for hours. *Why, God, why?* I asked in desperation. I wanted to turn back time and never let him outside. With all my might, I willed it not to be so. And still it was so.

Finally, Gary asked, "Do you want to see him?" Although I had never wanted to see a dead animal in the past, I answered, "Yes." Gary then placed Dharma in a towel in my arms, and I held him and wept. We decided to bury him in the backyard by the Porter's weed.

While Gary dug the hole, I held Dharma one last time, telling him all he meant to me and how much I loved him. I thought back on all the gifts he brought me in just the short time he was with me: unconditional love, laughter, a playful spirit, a reminder to live fully and a sense of my life's purpose.

My husband said, "You know, I believe Dharma was sent by God to help you through a very rough time. Now that you're through the worst of it, it's time for Dharma to move on and help someone else."

"Do you really think so?" I asked, wanting so badly to believe it was true.

"Look at the timing," Gary said. "You hadn't been to the lake in months and the one day you venture out, you find Dharma blocks from our house in dire need of help, and in rescuing him you get rescued as well. All of his gifts can't be a coincidence. There's definitely a reason he was put in your life when he was and also taken out when he was. He was your little angel."

"Thanks," I said, letting my husband's healing words wash over me.

Watching Dharma lying so peacefully in my arms, I got the much-needed answer to my prayer about death. I realized that he would go on in me forever, the same as I would in the lives of everyone I touched. I believe Dharma gave his life so that I might know peace. When Dharma died, I awakened spiritually. I am no longer afraid of death. Through Dharma, God showed me there is nothing to fear. There is only peace. And love.

We buried him at the foot of his butterfly bush and on his headstone I wrote, "Dharma—My Little Angel." Now, whenever I sit on the back steps, I see Dharma chasing butterflies for all eternity.

Deborah Tyler Blais

Dear Jesse

Be like the bird
That, pausing in her flight
Awhile on boughs too slight,
Feels them give way
Beneath her and yet sings,
Knowing that she hath wings.
Victor Hugo

Dear Jesse,

So, here it is—the moment we've both been waiting for. Graduation has already taken on the shades of a memory, and college is just a few weeks away. You, I know, are quite anxious to be moving on. You've passed the "Get on your mark!" "Get set" stages, and you are simply ready to "GO!"

Believe it or not, I remember that feeling well. The summer before I went away to school, I simply wanted to get on with it. I couldn't wait to be independent, to prove myself. It's just so weird being on the other side of the gate. I can yell "Go"—it's just making my heart let go that seems to be the hang-up.

I know you've been looking forward to this moment for a long time. I've watched you during this past year, as the countdown has become reality. You've worked hard and planned. That's one of the things I like best about you, your ability to run a good race. To set a goal, train and then go for it.

Funny, goal-setting. When you were little and I held your tiny body in my arms and rocked and sang and read to you, my goal was to give you two essentials—roots and wings. I think I've done that. So it seems I'm just seconds away from one of my own finish lines. The problem is, I seem to be enjoying the race a little too much. Somehow I've lost my stride and want to run the rest of this particular race in slow motion.

The other problem is I've also lost my concentration. Instead of focusing on the finish line, I keep rerunning the race. I think about the tears in your father's eyes the first time he saw you. I think about how I'd wake up to the sound of you and your sister talking, way back when you used to share a room and giggles and secrets. And I remember your gentleness six years later when you would sit next to your baby brother and read to him.

Not that the course has been particularly easy. When you were almost ten and I watched you place your favorite *Star Trek* book in your dad's coffin, I wasn't even certain the race was worth running. It was then that I learned that sometimes things are not fair. There really are no guarantees. Sometimes you can have a great pace going and get a cramp. All you can do is give it your best shot. Guess that's where I learned that if you keep going, somehow it's possible to get past the wall.

I suppose that when I got cancer and was almost

pulled out of the game, I realized exactly how precious this race was to me. I'm not certain you are aware of what an impact you had on getting me over that hurdle. I know it must have been difficult for you, but you were always there cheering me on by listening and talking me through. You filled in as my coach at that meet, and you instinctively knew a secret—great coaching involves shouting and listening. Thanks.

If life is a race—though I really don't like to think this experience is anything we should rush through—I think you're going to do well. You're in shape, you've trained hard and you have the tenacity to make it over the obstacles. I'm proud of you.

Enjoy the view. Remember you've got teammates who'll help when the course is rough. Take time to rest every once in a while, and whenever you need to . . . use your wings.

I love you,
Mom

Paula Bachleda Koskey

The Other Mother

"Hey, Mrs. Prins!" I shout while waving at her kitchen window. Standing on top of the monkey bars, I stretch across the school boundary fence toward her house, waving frantically, but she doesn't seem to notice. Her husband does though. He closes the kitchen curtains.

Mrs. Prins is my third-grade teacher, though sometimes I accidentally call her "Mom." I know she isn't my mother, but I can't stop hoping that she will adopt me if my mother dies from cancer. Mrs. Prins knows nothing of this hope, but she knows I like her enough to fight the kids after school who make fun of her curled-up mouth. Half her mouth is always smiling because she had a nerve operation, and kids sit at their desks curling up half their mouths, mocking Mrs. Prins behind her back.

As I hang off the monkey bars, I can't understand why Mr. Prins has closed the kitchen curtains on me. This makes about as much sense as the kids teasing Mrs. Prins. Maybe he didn't see me hanging off the bars, waving five feet from their window. Through their living-room curtains, I can see Mrs. Prins sitting on her couch reading the paper. I start waving and shouting hello again. Mr. Prins walks over and closes those drapes. Now I know he finds me a nuisance.

With all their drapes tightly closed, I remain on the monkey bars in the empty playground, dreading going home, wishing Mr. Prins didn't find me a pest. If he wasn't there, Mrs. Prins would invite me over. Just because school is done for the day, she can't suddenly find me a pest.

On the first day of school, Mrs. Prins had asked me, "Aren't you the girl that used to have that pretty long hair?" I didn't know her yet and was worried about why she had noticed me. Before school started, I had cut my hair off to make sure one more year wouldn't be spent with a cruel teacher yanking it every time I did something wrong. Now all my hair rests in a paper bag in Mom's dresser drawer, safe from cruel teachers. Standing on the monkey bars with short-hair, I imagine what it would be like to have Mrs. Prins brush my long hair while sitting next to her on the couch. But there is no more hair and the drapes are pulled.

As the sky darkens, Mrs. Prins walks into her yard and offers me a few peanut-butter cookies and a glass of milk. Instead of walking around the playground, I climb the fence, hoping to impress her with my strength, but she looks worried as I rip my shirt coming down on her side of the fence. For once there's no blood, just a torn shirt, not a bruised body.

"Don't you have to go home after school?" she asks.

"Of course, but not right away."

We sit on lawn chairs eating our cookies. Now that I'm finally in her yard, I don't know what to say.

"Did you just make these cookies?"

"After school."

"They're the best I ever had," I say, certain she made them especially for me.

When the cookies are finished, I know it's time to walk back home down the half-mile hill. I thank Mrs. Prins for the cookies, leaving her quiet home behind, slowly cutting through the alleys and looking over fences at dogs, wondering if my dad will be home for dinner or at a bar drinking. I feel guilty for having not gone home right away to fix dinner, making Mom have to cook knowing she's not feeling well. I wonder what Mrs. Prins is having for dinner and figure it won't be frozen fish sticks and a box of macaroni and cheese. That's what we'll be having.

At night, I write a story about Pepper, our dog. Mrs. Prins wants the class to write stories about people who are important to us, but it seems like all my important humans would make a sad story. Pepper's different. He's stuck at home, not dying or drinking, just waiting for someone to play with him.

A few days after I hand my story in, Mrs. Prins asks if she can talk with me after school. I agree and then spend the entire day worrying about what I did wrong. Three times I go into the bathroom and cry, certain I have hurt her feelings somehow. But after school, Mrs. Prins takes my story out of her desk drawer and asks, "May I keep this?"

"Why?"

"Because I want to save it in a special drawer at home with all my favorite stories." She looks like she is about to cry, and I want to ask for the story back, just to read what I had said that could make her feel this way; but I can't speak without crying. Then she hugs me and my eyes swell with tears.

Walking home I know that even if I never get to sleep in her house, my story does, and that is enough to make Mrs. Prins seem like my mother. This will be my mother with half a face smiling while the eyes are tearing. The mother I can watch by climbing the monkey bars. And most importantly, the mother who understands my stories.

Diane Payne

A Prayer for Children

We pray for children
Who give us sticky kisses,
Who hop on rocks and chase butterflies,
Who stomp in puddles and ruin their math workbooks,
Who can never find their shoes.

And we pray for those
Who stare at photographers from behind barbed wire,
Who've never squeaked across the floor in new sneakers,
Who've never "counted potatoes,"
Who are born in places we wouldn't be caught dead,
Who never go to the circus,
Who live in an X-rated world.

We pray for children
Who bring us fistfuls of dandelions and sing off key
Who have goldfish funerals, build card-table forts
Who slurp their cereal on purpose
Who put gum in their hair, put sugar in their milk
Who spit toothpaste all over the sink
Who hug us for no reason, who bless us each night.

And we pray for those
Who never get dessert,
Who watch their parents watch them die,
Who have no safe blanket to drag behind,
Who can't find any bread to steal,
Who don't have any rooms to clean up,
Whose pictures aren't on anybody's dresser,
Whose monsters are real.

We pray for those
Who spend all their allowance before Tuesday,
Who throw tantrums in the grocery store
And pick at their food,
Who like ghost stories,
Who shove dirty clothes under the bed
And never rinse out the tub,
Who get quarters from the tooth fairy
Who don't like to be kissed in front of the carpool,
Who squirm in church and scream on the phone,
Whose tears we sometimes laugh at
And whose smiles can make us cry.

And we pray for those
Whose nightmares come in the daytime,
Who will eat anything,
Who have never seen a dentist,
Who aren't spoiled by anybody,
Who go to bed hungry and cry themselves to sleep,
Who live and move, but have no being.

We pray for children
Who want to be carried,
And for those who must.
For those we never give up on,
And for those who don't have a chance.
For those we smother,
And for those who will grab the hand of anybody kind
  enough to offer.

Ina J. Hughs

Washing Teddy Bears

Should you shield the canyons from the wind-storms, you would never see the beauty of their carvings.

                                        Elisabeth Kübler-Ross

We are washing teddy bears—my eldest daughter and I. Old childhood toys. She has recently separated from her husband of seven years, and we are washing teddy bears.

Last week I helped her get settled in her new apartment. For the first time in her life, she is living alone and she is struggling to make a new life—just her and her bears.

She has just told me a story about two eighty-year-old women she met at the Laundromat yesterday. One of them was washing her teddy bears. The old woman gingerly explained to her the proper way to wash teddy bears.

"You put them into a pillowcase and pin the end of the case shut with a safety pin. Then you wash and dry them and they come out nice and clean and fluffy."

The old woman went on to explain that ever since her

husband passed away, whenever she gets lonely or anxious, she holds her teddy bear pressed close to her face for a long while and then she feels better. She says it always works.

They got to talking, and my daughter explained that she had always wanted to wash her bears but was afraid that they would be ruined in the process. She was delighted by the old woman and her tale and they continued to talk. My daughter explained that she was recently separated and that she was fixing up her new apartment and thanked the woman for the advice.

The old woman said that if she were her daughter, she would scoop her up and take her home with her. That she would not be living alone. I wanted to tell my daughter that the old woman's sentiments were also mine. I knew she had to find her own way. Although I wanted to rescue her, in my heart I knew that was not what was best for her.

Doing what is best for your child can be so difficult sometimes. Watching my daughter struggle—emotionally, financially and otherwise—is tugging at my heartstrings. I really do want to scoop her up and take her home and tuck her and her teddy bears into bed.

She was and is a beautiful child. Although she is a twenty-eight-year-old woman now, it is difficult for me sometimes to think of her as one.

We finish washing bears, and she is on her way home now. Her bears are clean, all present and accounted for. And I know that she will press them close to her face for a long time on many days and nights to come—and that they will help her feel better. They will listen as only teddy bears can. They will soak up her tears and hug her back when she needs it. And they will smile back at her when her own smile finally returns.

Watch over my little girl, Teddy Bears. Love her extra hard. The big wide world can be a pretty scary place. Hold her hand, tuck her in at night and remind her how very much her dad and I and her sisters love her. Help her to find that peaceful, teddy-bear place inside each one of us—that warm and fuzzy place that brings us to a "knowing" that everything will be all right, that tomorrow is another day, that all the answers we need are inside us. Remind her that time heals, that out of pain comes tremendous personal growth. And that there are no boogeymen under the bed.

Sweet dreams, my precious daughter. May the glory of your morning sun and the light of your magnificent moon dry all your tears and mend your heart and spirit. And may each new tomorrow bring you, my beloved child, deep and lasting joy, and teddy-bear peace.

Jean Bole

To Love Enough

My mother isn't speaking to my father. She hasn't spoken to him in five years, and for that, my father is truly grateful.

I was crying the last time she did speak to him. I saw the exchange though I could not hear the words. His whisperings, her whisperings.

The two of them silhouetted against the window light at the end of the long hall. My father leaning over my mother's gurney, pressed forehead to forehead. The word "Surgery" on the doors behind them forming a caption for the picture they made. Hands clasped together as if believing they held each other's hearts. As longingly as the first time they had reached for each other, as desperately as two lovers being forced apart.

Being forced to part on this day of life and death.

They had made the decision together, to do or die . . . to do and die. These two who had lived for and in each other's dreams these past forty years.

My mother with a disease that was cutting the blood flow to her brain. It was deteriorating her life and it would take it in three years. Her life could be prolonged if the surgery was done now. Twelve brave hearts had gone before her but only three of them had walked away.

I watched their process of decision making, both prayerful in the face of death. My mother wanting to live, wanting to try. The churning and turning until there was peace.

How brave we knew she was; we three sisters gathered around her hospital bed feeling time pushing us toward her fate the next day. We were quick to smile, slow to leave, hoping our "Good nights" were not our good-byes.

Our father was left to keep his prayerful, loving vigil. It was painful to leave him that night, too painful to think of him alone. But he reminded us that he would not be alone, at least for this night, he had his Love.

And morning came. We gathered and prayed. We kissed our mother, hugged our father and then followed her gurney until we were told that only one of us could go any farther.

My father continued to walk alongside her as he always had. Two people who had stood together against all odds. My mother orphaned at a young age and moved from place to place. My father the youngest of nine in a family hurting with poverty.

They who had found their home in each other.

We children were loved in their home. Given by these two what they had not been given in their own childhoods: safety, nurturing, moral guidance.

We knew that we were created from their love but that their love was an entity separate from us, a circle complete within itself.

I see the kiss, the parting. My mother wheeled through the door, alone. My father, his back to me, placing his hand on that door, praying love and strength and hope to the woman on the other side.

He turned and walked slowly toward me. The sunrise lit his face and I glimpsed the depth of this man's love.

This love of great self-sacrificing. A love so great that he was willing to bear the pain of being the one to walk alone.

And though surrounded by our love, my father walked alone for the two weeks we waited out her coma, the months of doubt and rehabilitation.

In the end, my mother had lost her speech but she had won her fight to live.

She has not spoken to my father for five years, and for that, he is truly grateful.

Cynthia M. Hamond

The Angel Who Fetched

Life is the little shadow which runs across the grass and loses itself in the sunset.

Crowfoot
Last Words, 1890

Two years ago, I paced away the longest day of my life in a windowless medical exam room, waiting for the results of a biopsy. My doctor finally gave me the news: I had metastasized squamous-cell carcinoma of the neck. I was told bluntly that I could expect little in terms of long-term survival.

I drove home in a stupor and vomited away the rest of the night. I prayed constantly and desperately those first few months for something—anything—that would help me get a hold on my life, but all that kept coming to mind was my old dog, Keesha.

Twenty years before, I had bought Keesha as a tiny puppy for five dollars. She was the offspring of a German shepherd and an Alaskan malamute—the runt of the litter. She had black-and-sand face markings and one ear that never quite stood all the way up.

Keesha grew into a sleek beauty with manners so

polished I could take her anywhere with pride. She snuggled beside me on camping trips and taught me how to play "throw-the-stick" so that she could fetch. When I cried, she licked my face.

She was my constant companion all through my late teens and early twenties. When I took a position as educator for a local Humane Society, we even became co-teachers. For four years, we visited classrooms and businesses, and taught the community how to avoid being bitten by nasty dogs. Keesha had a flair for theatrics and would peel her lips back and spit out hair-curling snarls on command. She put on hundreds of convincing performances as the world's most vicious animal. And children loved her—especially the sloppy kisses she delivered at the close of each performance.

One day everything changed: Keesha coughed up blood. I learned just hours later that she had cancer. But Keesha kept on teaching between visits to the vet for radiation treatments.

Keesha's cancer appeared as a rapidly growing ulcer in her mouth, which later advanced into her throat. She approached her discomfort during her meals with patience, though, and learned to take smaller, slower bites. Nevertheless, her enthusiasm for dinner never left. The minute her bowl came out of the cupboard, her eyes flashed and her tail rose like a banner. Each meal was welcomed as the best of all.

I remembered Keesha's attitude toward meals after my first cancer surgery left me with a shortened tongue. My tongue was so swollen, meals were impossible. So was speaking.

Thanksgiving was just ten days away. With Keesha as my inspiration, I practiced for the event with Cream-of-Wheat and mashed potatoes. Somehow I managed to swallow turkey and pie that holiday. They remain the best I've ever tasted.

I continued coping with my illness through positive, moment-to-moment living. This was no small task for me. Again I thought of Keesha. Deep into her disease, she was still chewing bones, savoring our marsh walks, barking at birds, splashing through rain puddles. Cancer had slowed her movements and shortened her breath, but her spirit remained light. She trotted along each trail with her ear-to-ear, good-dog grin, tail held high. Her life unfolded in front of her one paw at a time.

A year into my own cancer, I had another biopsy. Whoever said "Sticks and stones will break my bones, but words will never hurt me" never waited three days for lab results. I took one step at a time out of the doctor's office and into the pre-Christmas weekend, determined to value each moment as it came. I bought myself a sparkling dress for my office Christmas party, scheduled an ornament-making day with my dearest friend, and enjoyed the smell of Christmas-tree lots and popcorn in the malls. Monday afternoon finally arrived: The results were negative. Another crisis was behind me.

I've spent the past two years coming to grips with who I am today, as opposed to who I was before my surgeries. I've lost a few parts. My tongue has been shortened. Several large muscles were removed from my neck and shoulder, so I'm unable to turn my head easily or look up at the sky. Radiation treatments have caused some arthritis in my jaw. The worst, though, is that the radiation also destroyed my salivary glands, leaving me with perpetual "cotton mouth."

Here too, Keesha's approach to her failing body had been marvelously practical and inspirational—she adapted. When tumors in her shoulder made it impossible to race along her favorite paths, she seemed just as satisfied to limp along and smell the dirt at a slower pace. When she could no longer trudge up the hill in front of our house, she let herself be carried home. When swimming became too much for her, she'd lie in the water and snap at the ripples, barking loudly.

In my efforts to heal my life, I've learned that by confronting and accepting the truth of my own mortality, I am able to free up powerful healing energy that lies trapped under my fears of death. During this process, I am often drawn to the memory of Keesha's last day with me.

One day several years ago, I took her back to my office at the Humane Society where she had spent so many afternoons asleep under my desk. She walked beside me on unsteady legs, her breathing low and labored. No one can tell me an animal doesn't know what death is. Keesha reached her paw out to me, and my hands shook as I inserted the needle and emptied the syringe. She died quietly, resting against my shoulder, entering fearlessly into that greatest of all mysteries.

How can I ever express what it was like to lose her? There are no words. She was my friend and my teacher. She had faced her life with a dignity I can claim only on my best of days. I mourned her loss as deeply as I would later grieve the loss of a friend or family member. With prayers and tears, I scattered her ashes over the salt marsh where we had shared so many walks.

I have been free of cancer for two years now. For my condition, it's a miracle of sorts, and I'm celebrating wholeheartedly. My doctors now tell me that I might expect a full life if all continues to go well. I know it will.

I also know that when I do leave this world, Keesha will be the first to greet me—tail flying and voice sounding out joyously—on the other side. I will stoop and wrap my arms around her neck and feel the grace of her slobbering tongue on my face again.

And when I finally meet my creator, I will offer my heartfelt gratitude for answered prayers and angels that play fetch.

Susan McElroy

Ben

A baby is God's opinion that the world should go on.

Carl Sandberg

Ben was born on September 20, 1989. Not long after his birth, we learned of his blindness and deafness. By age three, we knew he would never walk either.

From the day Ben was two days old, our family traveled a road we had never envisioned. Hundreds and hundreds of miles to the best doctors and the best hospitals. Hundreds of needles and X-rays, CT scans and MRIs. After that came the contact lenses, braces, hearing aids, wheelchairs, walkers and crawlers—along with all the therapists to show us how to use all of these things. The operations never stop.

Ben's life today consists of his regular teacher, a teacher of the visually impaired, a teacher of the hearing impaired, an inclusion specialist, an occupational therapist, a physical therapist, a speech and language pathologist, a pediatrician, a neurologist, orthopedic doctors, a pediatric ophthalmologist, an ear-nose-throat doctor, an audiologist, a dentist, an oral surgeon and an orthodontist—and he is only eight years old.

Yet every morning my little man wakes up with the biggest smile on his face as if to say, "I am here for another day everybody, and I am so glad."

Our daughter was born three years before Ben. I remember her dad and I staring at her for lengths of time when she was a toddler waiting for the next sound or word to spill out. Every time one did, it was a marked moment in history—a topic of proud conversation with whomever had the patience to listen. We truly had a brilliant and remarkable child. We still do.

After Ben was born, our love for him changed our views on what was truly important about our children. It no longer was important how many words were spoken at what age, or what phenomenal development took place sooner than any of the baby books predicted. Our children became individuals, each having wonderful qualities, not to be compared. Their lives were not to be measured by lack of ability or exceptional ability, but by the strength to persevere.

By the time Ben was four, he was quite expertly maneuvering his wheelchair, but he had never spoken a word— only open vowel sounds. So our family started putting a tape recorder at the table during dinner to record the sounds Ben was making because he clearly wanted to be a part of the dinner conversations. We thought maybe if he heard his recorded voice and ours, it would stimulate something in him.

One day in September 1993, the tape was rolling while I was feeding Ben and making some sounds, trying to stimulate an interest in him. Suddenly, time froze. I'll never forget the look in Ben's eyes, the concentration on his face, the formation of his mouth, how he was looking up at me from his wheelchair when he spoke his first three words: "I love you." I turned to my husband, and he tearfully looked at me and said, "Terry, I heard him!"

Ben said those words for me, and I have it on tape to play back whenever I need to. I'm grateful, too, because he has not said another word since.

But, you know, I don't play the tape that often; I don't need to. I will always recognize the look in his eyes—even though they are blind—as he reaches for my face to give me a kiss. That is all I need.

Terry Boisot

Heaven's Very Special Child

We were on our way to visit an institution in 1954 with our three daughters: Mary, twelve, Joan, nine, and Ruth, eighteen months old. Because of little Ruth, handicapped since birth, we were making this sad and silent trip. We had been advised to place her in a special home. "It will be less of a burden," "Ruth will be better off with children like herself," "Your other children will have a home free of the care of a disabled person."

To break the silence, I flipped on the car radio and heard the voice of a former classmate. I remembered him as a boy without legs. He was now president of an organization employing persons who are disabled.

He told of his childhood and of a conversation with his mother. "When it was time for another handicapped child to be born," his mother explained, "the Lord and his counselors held a meeting to decide where he should be sent . . . where there would be a family to love him. Well, our family was chosen."

At this, my wife Edna leaned over and turned off the radio, her eyes shining with unshed tears. "Let's go home," she said.

I touched Ruth's tiny face. She looked like a beautiful symbol of innocence. I knew at that moment Ruth was given to us for a purpose. How miraculous it was that the voice of a friend, with whom I'd had no contact for twenty years, should that day speak to me. Mere coincidence? Or was it God's unseen hand helping us hold on to a little girl who would enrich our lives immeasurably in the years that followed?

That night, Edna awoke at three o'clock in the morning with thoughts that demanded to be written. A pad was on the night table, and in the morning we pieced her notes together into the poem, "Heaven's Very Special Child":

A meeting was held quite far from Earth;
"It's time again for another birth."
Said the angels to the Lord above,
"This special child will need much love.
Her progress may seem very slow.
Accomplishments she may not show,
And she'll require extra care
From the folks she meets way down there.
She may not run or laugh or play,
Her thoughts may seem quite far away.
In many ways she won't adapt,
And she'll be known as handicapped.
So let's be careful where she's sent,
We want her life to be content.
Please, Lord, find the parents who
Will do a special job for you.
They will not realize right away
The leading role they're asked to play,
But with this child sent from above
Come stronger faith and richer love.
And soon they'll know the privilege given
In caring for this gift from heaven.
Their precious charge, so meek and mild,
Is heaven's very special child."

John and Edna Massimilla

Lavender Roses

My education about autism began in the 1940s. As the youngest child in my family, by the age of four I knew Scott was our secret, an embarrassment we sent to a back bedroom when company came. His pain and the pain of him were too private to share with others. My sisters and I left as soon as we could, marrying young or attending college across the country. Years later, I heard a psychologist classify our behavior as "sibling flight." It was flight all right, but Scott hadn't chased us away. Fear, shame and confusion had made our home unbearable.

Early on, I thought Scott's disability was the worst curse a family could suffer. I'd seen my parents break under the burden and knew I couldn't follow. Could it happen again? Was it possible that I might father a "child who never grows up"?

This fear plagued me in my twenties, but after five years of marriage, I knew I had to start a family or lose the woman I loved. I traded my nightmares for hopes, and we conceived our first child.

At Ted's birth, I nagged the doctor for reassurance. Was there a chance—even a small chance—that this perfectly formed infant had a flaw? Ted passed every screening. In spite of a cesarean delivery, he earned a nine out of ten on the newborn scale—a champion in the delivery room!

Like many men, I didn't know much about babies, but I knew no other baby could compare with my firstborn. Each move, every step and word, seemed precocious and brilliant!

By Ted's second birthday, we noticed little "quirks," eccentricities that suggested he was different (but surely better!) than other children. His language was odd (maybe he didn't need to ask questions). He didn't play with other children (perhaps he preferred adults). His scores on developmental charts started to slip (maybe the charts were wrong).

By his third birthday, we suffered through a series of diagnoses that seemed more like professional guesses: "brain-damaged," "neurologically impaired," and finally, "autistic." We searched for help, ways to "fix" Ted. But the more we learned, the less we hoped. It looked like my worst nightmare had come true—my second family seemed as doomed as my first.

On the positive side, my wife and I had resources my parents had never known: steady employment, better education and access to a university-based training center. Furthermore, society had begun to recognize the rights and needs of people with disabilities. Unlike Scott who'd been born in the 1920s, my child of the seventies wouldn't have to stay home. The law guaranteed him an "appropriate" education. Medical understanding had progressed, too. Doctors no longer blamed parents for the disability.

The stigma was lifting like a cloud. We decided we'd never hide this child. We weren't ashamed of him.

Reviewing the past, I realized my childhood family had it all wrong: Scott hadn't been "our problem"—we were his! Confronting that truth hurt, but the pain brought a rush of adrenaline and determination. It hit me like a bolt of lightning: *whether something's a curse or a blessing depends on our interpretation.*

As my wife and I struggled to understand Ted, we were determined not to neglect our second child, born three years later. Having been Scott's brother, I could identify with my younger son's concerns and needs, though he never spoke them. He craved a "normal" brother and worried through his adolescent quest for identity.

Raising two sons with such different needs tested us to the fullest. We stumbled through their childhoods, waiting for graduation like a light promised at the end of the tunnel.

Ted's twenty-second birthday found us well-prepared for his passage into the adult world. He'd graduate at the end of the year. Between part-time jobs and some government help, he'd have a reasonable income. His supervisors knew him well and had trained him during student internships. We even fixed up a basement apartment for him.

We thought everything was planned for graduation, but Ted didn't agree. That spring, in his senior year, he caught us off-guard with his announcement: "I'm going to the prom."

He had thought about it for years. At eighteen, he'd seen kids his own age plan their prom night. Now Ted saw his chance. All he needed was a date.

But he simply couldn't get a date on his own. Some of the girls called him "cute" and tolerated his attention at assemblies, but none would actually date him. However, a family friend had a daughter named Jennifer. A striking blonde, Jennifer had met Ted and liked him. And she understood what prom night meant to him.

As the big evening approached, we helped Ted prepare. We dusted off the family tuxedo; it fit Ted better than me.

He agreed to let me chauffeur him in the family car. He even planned their dinner before the dance. Only one detail remained: *the corsage.*

I could have ordered that corsage in two minutes flat, but I wanted Ted to have the experience. I poignantly wondered if he would ever have occasion to present a woman with flowers again.

Before the trip to the florist, Ted "role-played." Practicing the words at home makes it easier to say them in another setting. Ted gave me the florist's role, so I invited him into my imaginary shop. We rehearsed until Ted seemed letter perfect. Then we strolled to our neighborhood florist.

Hearing the door, the florist stopped filing and turned her attention toward us. I waited for Ted to speak, looking at him expectantly. It grew very quiet in the shop. His entire body had grown rigid. Then he drew his face into a grimace and blurted out, "I'm Ted. I'm here to rent the purple flowers."

The clerk looked startled. She glanced at me as I calmly prompted, "Let's try that again, Ted." He drew a couple of deep breaths and furrowed his brows.

I encouraged him to stay calm and speak slowly. Finally he was able to explain.

He needed a corsage for Saturday. His date wanted to wear it on her wrist. He preferred lavender roses. He'd pay when he picked it up Saturday afternoon.

I hadn't expected the clerk's reaction. "You have a lot of patience," she told me. "I could never be so patient."

"No!" I'd wanted to shout. This isn't patience, this is understanding. Our nervous systems work. They transmit signals instantaneously from memory banks to nerve centers to vocal cords and back. Ted has to labor these pathways, struggling upstream toward a life the rest of us take for granted. The florist was admiring the wrong person! Unknown to her, Ted had climbed mountain-high barriers and swum oceans of confusion to reach this point. Saturday night wouldn't find him working a jigsaw puzzle, as his Uncle Scott had done so often. Ted was going to the prom!

On prom night, I dropped Ted and Jennifer at the dance. At home, I called one of my sisters. We talked about our brother's stunted life and the amazing progress Ted had already made. We cried.

I keep a photo from the dance on my desk. Jennifer stands beside Ted. On her wrist, she wears a corsage of lavender roses.

Charles A. Hart
Submitted by Edna Smith

4

THE POWER
OF SUPPORT

When spider webs unite, they can tie up a lion.

Ethiopian Proverb

The Ludenschide Connection

One day, the people of the world will want peace so much that the governments are going to have to get out of their way and let them have it.

Dwight D. Eisenhower

Bill Porter, an American prisoner of war in Germany, braced himself against the icy winds—and German guards with guns. A shadow of his former high school football physique, the twenty-year-old infantryman knew he was in real trouble not only from starvation, chronic dysentery and a festering leg wound, but from an increasing, familiar pain—the agony of corneal ulcers, which had threatened to blind him each time he caught a cold or got run down during his childhood years. Now, without medication, Bill was losing his sight, and the morning came when he collapsed in the line-up of prisoners being forced to rebuild a bombed-out railroad track. He was trucked to a hospital in Ludenschide.

The temporary hospital for care of German war casualties had been set up in the town's three-story elementary school. Although Bill was a prisoner, his leg was treated and he was placed in the eye-injury ward on the third floor. There he shared a space with the only other American prisoner, a pilot whose eyes had been burned when he bailed out over Germany, robbing him of sight. Since Bill could see out of one eye, he quickly became the blind pilot's companion and guide. He fed him—the pilot's hands and wrists had been burned as well—and took him for walks up and down the halls of the building. But empty hours haunted both young men.

"If only we had something to read, a newspaper, magazine, anything," Bill said to his friend one day. "I could read to you . . . just as long as it's in English."

"I have a book," the pilot responded in the warm, midwestern drawl Bill had come to know so well. "Take a look in my jacket pocket." He paused for a moment. "It's . . . it's my Bible."

From that moment on, day in and day out, through his unbandaged seeing eye, Bill read the Old Testament aloud. Then he read the New Testament and favorite passages until the entire Bible had been read and reread many times. They didn't realize it then, but through the words of the Bible, a bond was growing between them as they found comfort and the strength they needed to survive.

One morning as they walked down the hall, they heard the unmistakable drone of approaching American bombers. It wasn't until they stopped for a moment to talk with a nurse that Bill detected the whine of misdirected bombs overhead. With no time to search for shelter, he grabbed his friend, threw him to the floor and shoved him under a baby-grand piano. The hospital received a direct hit . . . an explosion that burst Bill's eardrums.

Bill has no idea how long it was before he regained

consciousness or felt the pain from multiple head injuries and an eight-inch shaft of steel through his face. At first, he couldn't hear the shouts of German soldiers outside the ruptured building, or the cries of victims. As a matter of fact, he couldn't hear anything except his own heart hammering in his chest. But he smelled smoke and knew he had to get out. With his one free arm he struggled to extricate himself from confining plaster, planks and debris. Then, with a final upward push, he broke through the fallen roof—and caught "a glimpse of hell."

The dead lay everywhere: the nurse he had been talking to only moments before, doctors, the wounded, the sick. Everyone was dead—except himself. *And his friend? Where was he?* Could the old piano have withstood the crushing weight of roofing beams, falling bricks and cement?

That's when the thought struck him. If his friend had survived, he would not only be blind; he'd be buried alive. Bill's ears screamed. His head hurt. What was his friend's name anyway? He couldn't remember. Was he losing his mind? What difference did it make? He had to crawl back down and find him. Now! *Please God,* he prayed, *let him be alive.*

The searing pain from the steel in his face dimmed amid thoughts of what he might find. He reached under the piano. He felt a leg move. "Are you okay, buddy?" he asked.

"I think so," the voice replied.

Somehow during the next ten minutes, Bill maneuvered them both down two flights of shattered stairwells. Outside, the street was milling with a confusion of police, medics, ambulances and fire engines. He found an empty bench, and the two huddled together for warmth in the bitter cold. All the while Bill dodged the Germans spitting at the Americans who had lived while their own had perished. Still others grabbed the glinting steel protruding from his face and tried to pull it out. Perhaps they were only trying to help? What did it matter? Unable to fight them off any longer, he put his head between his knees and covered himself with his arms.

"Bill," the pilot's teeth chattered, "do you think you can get back inside and get us a blanket—and my Bible?"

"Sure," he said. "I'll try. Just don't go anywhere," he added jokingly. "I'll be back. I promise."

The climb back up the stairs took longer than Bill thought it would, but his friend's treasured Bible and dog tags were on the bed where he'd left them. He grabbed a blanket, and, with everything clutched in his arms, hurried back down the broken stairs and out to the bench. His buddy was gone.

Where was he? His voice a plea, he shouted at passersby. "Has anyone seen a guy with bandages over his eyes?" He held up two fingers and pointed to his own patch. No one responded. No one spoke English. *God! Keep him safe,* he prayed. *The guy can't see!*

Alone now, and in excruciating pain, Bill crouched behind the bench and covered his head with the blanket. Hours of sirens, shouts and running footsteps passed before a young Ludenschide doctor peered under at the blanketed figure. He took Bill to his office in a nearby building. There, after giving him a shot of Schnapps, the doctor sliced into his cheek and jaw to relieve the pressure and removed the steel and other pieces of metal embedded in his head. Finally, he rebandaged the eye. Still a prisoner of war, Bill was packed into a boxcar and later forced to walk to Fallingbastel, fifty miles away, where he was interred in another prison camp until the war ended.

When he returned to the United States, Bill wrote to the War Department and asked them to search for his friend.

He placed the letter in a box along with the pilot's dog tags—and the well-read Bible. Then he printed his return address: 7 Sigma Nu Fraternity, Lehigh University, Bethlehem, Pennsylvania.

Nightmares, panic at sudden sounds and mood swings would plague Bill for the rest of his life, as they do most victims of post-traumatic stress disorder. But even as a young father and a grandfather, he would always find joy in reminiscing about the good things in life—before the war and after.

He never talks about his time as a prisoner. He prefers instead to tell stories about his years as a rancher, one hundred miles from town, where he felt closer to God and his family. He especially likes to tell his children and grandchildren stories about when he was in college fifty-three years ago—especially the day an unfamiliar car pulled up in front of Sigma Nu.

From the second-floor landing of the fraternity, he remembers glancing out the window at the blue Chevy pulling up to the curb. It was lunch time. He knew he should hurry on down to the living room where the rest of the brothers were waiting for the lunch gong, but there was something about the stranger walking up the sidewalk to the front door that stopped him. The bell chimed. His roommate, Jack Venner, got up to answer. "Hello! Can I help you?" he said.

From where he stood, Bill felt sudden moisture dampen his forehead. He had to grip the banister to remain steady.

"Yes," said a voice with a warm, midwestern twang. "I'm looking for an old friend of mine named Bill Porter. I want to thank him . . . for lots of things." He smiled, looking anxious as he stood in the crowded living room. "And this might sound sort of crazy," he added, "but I wouldn't

know him even if I saw him. I . . . I've never seen him
before."

Penny Porter

POSTSCRIPT: *The two ex-POWs talked all night. They promised
to keep in touch. But life has its demands. It takes curious twists
and turns, and they lost each other. Today, Bill is seventy-four. He
can't remember the pilot's name, but the bond born in Ludenschide
remains. He hopes someone that does remember will read this story
—so he can give the pilot a call.*

The Day I Finally Cried

I didn't cry when I learned I was the parent of a men-tally handicapped child. I just sat still and didn't say any-thing while my husband and I were informed that two-year-old Kristi was—as we suspected—retarded.

"Go ahead and cry," the doctor advised kindly. "Helps prevent serious emotional difficulties."

Serious difficulties notwithstanding, I couldn't cry then nor during the months that followed.

When Kristi was old enough to attend school, we enrolled her in our neighborhood school's kindergarten at age seven.

It would have been comforting to cry the day I left her in that room full of self-assured, eager, alert five-year-olds. Kristi had spent hour upon hour playing by herself, but this moment, when she was the "different" child among twenty, was probably the loneliest she had ever known.

However, positive things began to happen to Kristi in her school, and to her schoolmates, too. When boasting of their own accomplishments, Kristi's classmates always took pains to praise her as well: "Kristi got all her spelling words right today." No one bothered to add that her spelling list was easier than anyone else's.

During Kristi's second year in school, she faced a very traumatic experience. The big public event of the term was a competition based on a culmination of the year's music and physical education activities. Kristi was way behind in both music and motor coordination. My husband and I dreaded the day as well.

On the day of the program, Kristi pretended to be sick. Desperately I wanted to keep her home. Why let Kristi fail in a gymnasium filled with parents, students and teachers? What a simple solution it would be just to let my child stay home. Surely missing one program couldn't matter. But my conscience wouldn't let me off that easily. So I practically shoved a pale, reluctant Kristi onto the school bus and proceeded to be sick myself.

Just as I had forced my daughter to go to school, now I forced myself to go to the program. It seemed that it would never be time for Kristi's group to perform. When at last they did, I knew why Kristi had been worried. Her class was divided into relay teams. With her limp and slow, clumsy reactions, she would surely hold up her team.

The performance went surprisingly well, though, until it was time for the gunnysack race. Now each child had to climb into a sack from a standing position, hop to a goal line, return and climb out of the sack.

I watched Kristi standing near the end of her line of players, looking frantic.

But as Kristi's turn to participate neared, a change took place in her team. The tallest boy in the line stepped behind Kristi and placed his hands on her waist. Two other boys stood a little ahead of her. The moment the player in front of Kristi stepped from the sack, those two boys grabbed the sack and held it open while the tall boy lifted Kristi and dropped her neatly into it. A girl in front of Kristi took her hand and supported her briefly until Kristi gained her balance. Then off she hopped, smiling and proud.

Amid the cheers of teachers, schoolmates and parents, I crept off by myself to thank God for the warm, understanding people in life who make it possible for my disabled daughter to be like her fellow human beings.

Then I finally cried.

Meg Hill

The Sound of One Hand Clapping

There's a wonderful story about Jimmy Durante, one of the great entertainers of a few generations ago. He was asked to be a part of a show for World War II veterans. He told them his schedule was very busy and he could afford only a few minutes, but if they wouldn't mind his doing one short monologue and immediately leaving for his next appointment, he would come. Of course, the show's director agreed happily.

But when Jimmy got on stage, something interesting happened. He went through the short monologue and then stayed. The applause grew louder and louder and he kept staying. Pretty soon, he had been on fifteen, twenty, then thirty minutes. Finally, he took a last bow and left the stage. Backstage someone stopped him and said, "I thought you had to go after a few minutes. What happened?"

Jimmy answered, "I did have to go, but I can show you the reason I stayed. You can see for yourself if you'll look at the front row."

In the front row were two men, each of whom had lost an arm in the war. One had lost his right arm and the other had lost his left. Together, they were able to clap, and that's exactly what they were doing, loudly and cheerfully.

Tim Hansel

The Joy of Usefulness

*Some of us are like wheelbarrows—only useful
when pushed, and very easily upset.*

Jack Herbert

I became a pastor because I wanted to help people.
Why the yearning to help others led to the pastoral ministry and not, say, to a career in medicine is a mystery I've
yet to decipher. It's all the better if you can follow your
joy and drive a nice car, too. Still, I'm not complaining. I
like being a pastor, especially on those rare occasions
when I've helped someone along life's way.

I call them rare occasions because the people in my
Quaker meeting haven't asked me for much help lately.
They're an amazingly self-sufficient group who bear life's
burdens with silent equanimity. In addition to their stoic
nature, they are incredibly robust. Thus, I am seldom
called to help them.

Two of my best friends, Stan and Jim, are also pastors.
They spend their days traveling from hospital to hospital,
comforting one troubled soul after another. At night they
collapse in their beds, content with the memory of a

useful day. I linger near the phone, praying for a call to take me away from my warm home to the bedside of a wretched parishioner. The call seldom comes.

Is it too much for me to expect my people to have problems? If they've asked me to be their pastor, am I wrong to expect them to have an occasional challenge that might occupy my time and help me feel needed?

I don't think this is too much to expect. My friend's congregation was decimated by a pernicious virus. I'm not asking for that. I don't want to be so busy that I'd miss watching *The Andy Griffith Show* every lunch hour. But if a few persons could see their way clear to contracting a mild disease, that would be considerate. It wouldn't have to be anything exotic. Once a lady in my meeting was afflicted with Bell's palsy. It caused her mouth to droop, and she lost all the feeling on one side of her face. Then, after I spent two glorious days by her bedside, her condition grew better and she was completely healed. It was a wonderful illness! She received much-needed bed rest, and I knew the exquisite joy of helpful ministry.

I know I'm not alone in my desire to feel useful. If a woman spends twelve years learning to be a surgeon, I bet she's anxious to perform her first operation. If a man goes away to technical school and studies car repair, he probably can't wait to crawl underneath a chassis. Doesn't a free country owe its citizens the right to ply their chosen trades? Isn't that what America is all about?

Back when I was growing up, our town had a volunteer fire department. They screeched the fire alarm once a week, and all the firefighters practiced rushing to the station. After a while, they grew discouraged, because real fires were few and far between. One of our more thoughtful citizens, on a beautiful autumn weekend afternoon, set his field ablaze, thereby earning the gratitude of many of our townspeople. Our policeman got to block the nearby roads. Our firefighters got to fight a real fire. Our news-paper reporter got to write a story. Our insurance agent got to process a claim for damaged crops. And the minister at the Baptist church got to visit the considerate citizen that very evening and profess thanksgiving that no one was hurt. By day's end, everyone felt the pleasant exhaustion of usefulness and went to bed happy. It was one of our town's finer days.

Keith Miller once said, "Jesus never went out of his way to help anybody." The first time I heard that, it angered me. That's an awful thing to say about Jesus. Then I thought about it for a while and understood what Miller was saying. Jesus never went out of his way to help any-body because helping people was never "out of his way." It was the very reason for his existence.

I've told my wife that when I die I want that chiseled on my gravestone: "Here lies Philip Gulley. He never went out of his way to help anybody." Though, knowing my luck, they'll run out of room and just put: "Here lies Philip Gulley. He never helped anybody."

Which might be closer to the truth, unless my church starts cooperating.

Philip Gulley

The Writer

I can live for two months on a compliment.

Mark Twain

Nineteenth-century life had dealt the ten-year-old London lad a bad hand. While his father languished in debtors' jail, painful pangs of hunger gnawed at his stomach. To feed himself, the boy took a job pasting labels on blacking bottles in a grim, rat-infested warehouse. He slept in a dismal attic room with two other street urchins, while secretly dreaming of becoming a writer. With only four years of schooling, he had little confidence in his ability. To avoid the jeering laughter he expected, he sneaked out in the dead of night to mail his first manuscript.

Story after story was refused, until finally one was accepted. He wasn't paid for it, but still, one editor had praised his work.

The recognition he received through the printing of that one story changed his life. If it hadn't been for the encouragement of that one editor, he might have spent his entire working life in a rat-infested factory.

You may have heard of this boy, whose books brought about so many reforms in the treatment of children and the poor: his name was Charles Dickens, author of *A Christmas Carol.*

Willy McNamara

Tzippie

One hot summer day, a young couple and their four-year-old daughter, Tzippie, were on their way to the mountains for a few weeks' vacation. Suddenly, a huge truck in the oncoming lane collided head-on with the family's small car. The couple was injured seriously, and little Tzippie sustained many fractures. They were immediately taken to the nearest hospital, where Tzippie was brought to the children's ward and her parents were taken to the intensive care unit. As can well be imagined, Tzippie was not only in great pain, but she was also very frightened because her parents were not nearby to give her comfort.

Martha, the nurse who was assigned to Tzippie, was a single, older woman. She understood Tzippie's fear and insecurity and became very devoted to her. When Martha finished her shift, instead of going home, she would volunteer to stay with Tzippie at night. Of course, Tzippie grew very fond of her and depended on her for her every need. Martha brought her cookies, picture books and toys; she sang songs to her and told her countless stories.

When Tzippie was able to be moved, Martha put her in a wheelchair and took her to visit her parents every day.

After many months of hospitalization, the family was discharged. Before they left the hospital, the parents blessed Martha for her devoted and loving care and invited her to visit them. Tzippie would not let go of Martha, and insisted that she come to live with them. Martha also did not want to be parted from her little Tzippie, but her life was in the children's ward of the hospital, and she could not think of leaving. There was a tearful parting as Tzippie and the loving nurse said good-bye to each other. For a few months the family kept up a close relationship with Martha—through phone calls only, since they lived quite a distance from her. When they moved abroad, however, they lost contact with each other.

Over thirty years passed. One winter Martha, who was now in her seventies, became seriously ill with pneumonia and was hospitalized in the geriatric ward of a hospital near her home. There was a certain nurse on duty who noticed that Martha had very few visitors. She tried her best to give the elderly lady special care, and she saw that she was a sensitive, clever person.

One night when the nurse was sitting near her elderly patient and they were chatting quietly, she confided in her as to what had prompted her to become a nurse. When she was four years old, she explained, and her parents had been injured in an automobile accident, there had been a wonderful nurse who had brought her back to health with her loving, caring devotion. As she grew older, she determined that one day she, too, would become a nurse and help others—from the young to the old—just as that nurse had done for her.

After she graduated from nursing school overseas, she had met a young man from America, and when they married, they moved to the States. A few months earlier they had moved to this city, where her husband had been offered a very good job, and she was happy to get a position as a nurse in this hospital. As the nurse's story unfolded, tears flowed from the elderly patient's eyes, as she realized that this must surely be her little Tzippie, whom she had cared for after the accident.

When the nurse had finished her story, Martha said softly, "Tzippie, we are together again, but this time you are nursing me!" Tzippie's eyes opened wide as she stared at Martha, suddenly recognizing her. "Is it really you?" she cried out. "How many times I have thought about you and prayed that someday we would meet again!"

When Martha recovered from her illness, Tzippie—this time—did not beg her to come and live with her family. Instead, she just packed up Martha's belongings and took her home with her. She lives with Tzippie to this day, and Tzippie's husband and children have welcomed her like a most special grandmother.

Ruchoma Shain

Sharing Beauty

Circumstances are like a mattress: When we are on top, we rest in comfort; when we are underneath, we are smothered.

Anonymous

I think it was 1982. I know it was October. A friend had business dealings in the city of Reno, Nevada, and I was asked to accompany her on an overnight trip. While she conducted her business, I was aimlessly wandering down Virginia Street, headed into a most gloriously beautiful sunset. I had an urge to speak to someone on the street to share that beauty, but I couldn't make eye contact with anyone. It seemed everyone was shuffling along looking at their feet.

I took the next-best action. Quickly I ducked into a department store and asked the lady behind the counter if she could come outside for just a minute. She looked at me as though I were from some other planet and said, "Well ... "

I said, "It will only take a moment." Seemingly against her better judgment, she moved toward the door.

When she got outside I said to her, "Just look at that

sunset! Nobody out here was looking at it and I just had to share it with someone."

For a few seconds we just looked. Then I said, "God's in his heaven and all's right with the world." I thanked her for coming out to see it; she went back inside and I left. It felt good to share the beauty.

I forgot about the episode.

Four years later my situation had altered considerably. I had come to the end of a twenty-year marriage. I was alone and on my own for the first time in my life and in drastically reduced circumstances. I lived in a trailer park which, at the time, I considered a real come-down, and I had to do my wash in the communal laundry room.

One day, while my clothes were going around, I picked up a *Unity Magazine* and read an article about a woman who had been in similar circumstances. She had come to the end of a marriage, moved to a strange community, and the only job she could find was one she disliked: cosmetic sales in a department store. We had a lot in common. She was as bummed out as I was.

Then something happened to her that changed everything. She said a woman came into her department store and asked her to step outside to look at a sunset. The stranger had said, "God's in his heaven and all's right with the world," and she had realized the truth in that statement and that she simply had not been seeing it. From that moment on, she turned her life around.

Sherry Maddox

[EDITORS' NOTE: *Sherry returned to the laundry room but the magazine was gone. She wrote* Unity Magazine, *but they were moving when they received her letter and couldn't help. She wants the woman in Reno to know that she has done the same thing for her. The gift has come full circle.*]

Mama's Visit

Do what you can, with what you have, where you are.

Theodore Roosevelt

In the early morning, I lay snuggled under the quilt my grandmother had made for me. I was small for my seven years, but Granny always told me I was "full of spunk." As I sat up, rubbing sleep from my eyes, I suddenly realized what day it was! Excitement coursed through my entire body. I struggled with the quilt to free my legs. Once free, I bounded out of bed.

"Granny! Granny!" I cried as I ran through the house. My hand reached out to grab the doorjamb that led into the kitchen. I tried to stop but my body swung around the corner with such force that my feet went one way, my arms another and I went sprawling across the kitchen floor.

My grandmother looked up in time to see me fall. A robust woman with salt and pepper hair, Granny had a very stern face, which almost never smiled. From the floor, I saw that she had one hand in the mixing bowl and the other floured hand rested on her hip. One of her eyebrows began to rise while the other one stayed perfectly still. I knew when that eyebrow came up, I was about to be in trouble. But I was too excited to care.

"Granny, guess what?" I said. "Know what day this is? Do ya? Do ya know?"

The eyebrow slowly went down and I saw a hint of a smile.

"I reckon I know what day it is," Granny said with amusement in her voice. As she spoke, I scrambled to get up, grabbing hold of Granny's dress to get an extra lift.

Granny shook her head, "Lord child, you will be the death of me." She turned her attention back to the bowl where she continued to knead the dough for biscuits. "Now go on, wash up for breakfast." I knew better than to argue and did what I was told.

When breakfast was on the table, I started eating the biscuits and gravy as fast as I could stuff them into my mouth.

"Victoria," Granny said in a commanding voice. I stopped chewing and looked up at my grandmother, my cheeks stuffed with food.

"Slow down. We do not eat like pigs here!"

I managed to answer, "Yes, Ma'am." When my mouth was finally clear, I said, "But I've gotta get ready, Granny. Mama's coming today!"

Granny looked into my wide blue eyes with an expression I couldn't read and said, "So she said, child. So she said."

I went on, "Can I wear my best dress today? Can I? Oh please Granny." My words tumbled out so fast Granny couldn't get a word in.

When she did reply, her voice sounded old and very tired, "I suppose so."

Granny had told me my mother was planning to come,

but she'd warned me that she might not make it. What I didn't know then was how many times my mother had called to say, "I'm coming to see Victoria" only never to arrive. Granny had soon decided not to tell me so I wouldn't be disappointed. But this time, my mother had sounded so earnest that Granny had said something. Now she hoped she hadn't made a mistake.

I ran to my closet and reached for my favorite dress. It was navy blue gingham with a white pinafore. As soon as I was dressed, with my hair pulled back in a ponytail and a white bow, I ran out the front door, down the steps and through the yard. I had already picked out the place where I would wait for my mother.

There was an old telephone pedestal that sat by the edge of the road just wide enough for me to sit on. From there, I could see the entire road from all directions.

The sun was bright and I had to hold my hand over my eyes to see. Nothing in sight except for our neighbor, old Mr. Bearden, who was plowing his fields.

Then I saw something coming down the road. It was black, but too far away for me to see what it was. I waited, my feet swinging back and forth hitting the pedestal with satisfying thumps. The black thing moved closer—it was too small and slow to be a car. I smiled when I saw it was an old mama dog running down the road with two puppies nipping at her heels.

I loved puppies, though Granny wouldn't let me have one. I jumped off the pedestal and walked towards the dog. I could play with the puppies for a while, I thought, but I thought better of it when I looked down at my best dress. With a sigh, I turned back.

The sun moved through the sky. Three hours passed, then five hours and still no sign of my mother. Granny made me a sandwich for lunch, but I fed it to the ants to watch them scurry around, snatching every last crumb.

Beads of sweat gathered on my forehead as the afternoon sun grew hotter but I never moved too far from the pedestal. I counted five cars come . . . and go. Each time my heart would race faster when they approached . . . then sink as they sped past me.

I kept busy watching the ant piles. I watched the cows eating grass at Mr. Bearden's farm but even that wasn't fun anymore.

The sun sank lower, casting shadows across the yard. As darkness fell, Granny came out on the front porch. She watched me pace back and forth straining to see if just one more car would come. But the car never came.

Finally Granny called to me, "Come in, Victoria, it's getting dark now."

I ignored my grandmother's words as tears welled in my eyes. My hands clenched into fists at my side, I whispered to myself, "No! I won't go in! My mama will come! She will!"

I stood there a few minutes, tears making little rivers that ran down my dust-covered face. Then I caught a movement out of the corner of my eye. I strained harder to see and then I heard a whimper. It was a puppy, limping down the road, one leg held up off the ground. He looked just like the puppies who'd passed by with their mama so many hours ago.

He was covered in dust and was so tired he could barely walk. I knelt down to get a better look and he hobbled toward me. I picked the puppy up, holding him tight against my white pinafore. He licked my tear-stained face, and I held him closer.

"I guess you're looking for your mama, too."

Granny had come up behind me and heard my words. The old woman picked me and the dusty puppy up and headed for the rocking chair on the porch.

She rocked us back and forth. No words were spoken; no words would do.

Granny looked down at that little puppy and stroked his matted fur. He licked her hand. Finally Granny spoke, her voice gentle, "Victoria, I guess the angels sent you someone to love."

Comforted, I held the puppy tight as I snuggled against Granny.

The night was still. The only sound was my grandmother's soft singing, "Hush little baby, don't you cry, Granny's gonna sing you a lullaby . . ."

Victoria Robinson

Margaret of New Orleans

If you ever go to the beautiful city of New Orleans, somebody will be sure to take you down into the old business part of the city, where there are banks and shops and hotels, and show you a statue erected in 1884 that stands in a little square there. It is the statue of a woman, sitting in a low chair, with her arms around a child who leans against her. The woman is not at all pretty. She wears thick, common shoes, a plain dress with a little shawl and a sunbonnet. She is stout and short, and her face is a square-chinned Irish face. But her eyes look at you like your mother's.

Now there is something very surprising about this statue. It was one of the first that was ever made in this country in honor of a woman. Even in old Europe there are not many monuments to women, and most of the few are to great queens or princesses, very beautiful and very richly dressed. You see, this statue in New Orleans is not quite like anything else.

It is the statue of a woman named Margaret. Her whole name was Margaret Haughery, but no one in New Orleans remembers her by it, any more than you think of your dearest sister by her full name. She is just Margaret.

This is her story, and it tells why people made a monument honoring her.

When Margaret was a tiny baby, her father and mother died, and she was adopted by two young people as poor and kind as her own parents. She lived with them until she grew up. Then she married and had a little baby of her own. But very soon her husband died, and then the baby died, too, and Margaret was all alone in the world. She was poor, but she was strong and knew how to work. All day, from morning until evening, she ironed clothes in a laundry. And every day, as she worked by the window, she saw the little motherless children from the orphanage nearby working and playing about. After a while, a great sickness came upon the city, and so many mothers and fathers died that there were more orphans than the orphanage could possibly take care of. They needed a good friend now. You would hardly think, would you, that a poor woman who worked in a laundry could be much of a friend to them? But Margaret was. She went straight to the kind Sisters who ran the orphanage and told them she was going to give them part of her wages and was going to work for them besides. Pretty soon she had worked so hard that she had some money saved from her wages. With this, she bought two cows and a little delivery cart. Then she carried her milk to her customers in the little cart every morning, and as she went, she begged the leftover food from the hotels and rich houses, and brought it back in the cart to the hungry children in the orphanage. In the very hardest times that was often all the food the children had.

A part of the money Margaret earned went every week to the orphanage, and after a few years it was made very much larger and better. And Margaret was so careful and so good at business that, in spite of her giving, she earned more money and bought more cows. With this, she built a home for orphan babies; she called it her baby house.

After a time, Margaret had a chance to get a bakery, and then she became a bread-woman instead of a milk-woman.

She carried the bread just as she had carried the milk, in her cart. And still she kept giving money to the orphanage.

Then the great war came, the Civil War. In all the trouble and sickness and fear of that time, Margaret drove her cart of bread, and somehow she always had enough to give to the starving soldiers, and for her babies, besides what she sold. And despite all this, she earned enough so that when the war was over, she built a big steam factory to bake her bread. By this time everybody in the city knew her. The children all over the city loved her. The businessmen were proud of her. The poor people all came to her for advice. She used to sit at the open door of her office in a calico gown and a little shawl, and give a good word to everybody, rich or poor.

Then, by and by, one day Margaret died. And when it was time to read her will, the people found that, with all her giving, she had still saved a great deal of money— thirty thousand dollars—and that she had left every cent of it to the different orphanages of the city—each one of them was given something. Whether they were for white children or black, or Jews, Catholics or Protestants, it made no difference; for Margaret always said, "They are all orphans alike." And just think, that splendid, wise will was signed with a cross instead of a name, for Margaret had never learned to read or write!

When the people of New Orleans knew that Margaret was dead, they said, "She was a mother to the motherless. She was a friend to those who had no friends. She had wisdom greater than schools can teach. We will not let her memory go from us." So they made a statue of her, just as she used to look, sitting in her own office or driving in her own little cart. And there it stands today, in memory of the great love and the great power of plain Margaret Haughery, of New Orleans.

Sara Cone Bryant
Submitted by Rochelle Pennington

Bridge Builder

An old man going down a lone highway
Came in the evening cold and gray
To a chasm vast and deep and wide
Through which was flowing a sullen tide.

The old man crossing in the twilight dim;
That swollen stream held no fears for him;
But he turned when safe on the other side
And built a bridge to span the tide.

"Old man," said a fellow pilgrim near,
"You are wasting your strength with building here;
Your journey will end with the ending day;
You never again must pass this way;
You have crossed the chasm deep and wide—
Why build you this bridge at the eventide?"

The builder lifted his old gray head.
"Good friend, in the path I have come," he said,
"There followeth after me today.
A youth whose feet must pass this way.
This swollen stream which was naught to me
To that fair-haired youth may a pitfall be;
He, too, must cross in the twilight dim;
Good friend, I am building the bridge for him."

Will Allen Dromgoole

The Yellow Ribbon

It was a hot, muggy day during the summer between second and third grade. My hair was in a French braid with my favorite yellow ribbon—the one my Great Aunt Lilly had given me before she died. "Flaunt it, Honey," she'd told me, whatever that meant.

Like every summer day, I was in my front yard playing with Wilma Wynonna Willett, my imaginary friend. Since I wasn't allowed to leave my yard and no one my age lived nearby, "Triple W," as I called her, was my best friend.

Suddenly out of nowhere came a big yellow moving truck. I heard an annoying beep and realized our new neighbors were moving in. I was excited, though I prayed there wouldn't be any boys, because boys, of course, had "cooties." But then, I saw an unusual object being removed from the truck—a wheelchair. It looked cold and heavy. What kind of people were moving in? They were obviously not like the neighbors I had grown to expect in my sheltered life.

Soon I learned these neighbors had a daughter my age named Laura. She could not walk or talk, however, and she was confined to the wheelchair. I didn't know how to respond. Should I go over, shake hands and introduce myself as my parents had taught, or should I hide under my bed so I would never have to meet her?

The problem was solved when my mom announced that the new neighbors were coming for dinner Friday night. When the doorbell rang, I answered and introduced myself. Laura's parents quickly explained that Laura had been born with cerebral palsy, an incurable condition that limited her mobility, controlled her muscles and destroyed her speech. Pretty sobering news for an eight-year-old whose previous hurts were healed with a kiss and a bandage.

Timidly, I said "Hello." Then I heard it, stammering from the bottom of her stomach and exploding from her lips: the loudest, strongest and most peculiar laugh I had ever heard. My mom told me that Victor Borge once said, "Laughter is the shortest distance between two people," and this couldn't have been more accurate. Even though Laura could not speak, her laugh did not need any explanations. Instantly I knew this was the beginning of a very special friendship.

I could not understand why the other kids could not perceive Laura as I did. Instead they made fun of her, threatened her and even tipped her wheelchair. I, too, was teased because I was friends with "Cripple." No matter how hard I tried, I couldn't make the other children stop.

What did I learn from my friendship with Laura? I learned bad things happen to nice people. Life was unfair! I learned lessons no other situation could have taught: I learned patience as I watched Laura painstakingly perform simple tasks that took forever because she was not physically able to do them any faster. I learned compassion when I heard the teasing and saw the hurt in Laura's eyes. I learned about courage as I watched Laura face the battles she had each day with her body and speech.

Each morning, Laura awakens to powerful, painful muscle cramps; eating is a chore because she is fed every meal; talking is only something she and her parents dream of. Laura cannot stand, but if she could, she would be five feet six inches tall. She has big brown eyes, soft curly hair and, of course, that great big laugh. Laura is able to understand when spoken to; she simply cannot respond with speech. Instead, she communicates by pointing to the communication board on the tray of her wheelchair.

This past summer, I had the honor and privilege of being Laura's able-bodied person in the Special Olympics. My job consisted of helping Laura do anything she would have done if she were not handicapped. I wrapped her clenched hand around the ball before we threw it. Our hands swung that bat together, and I cheered the loudest when she won the wheelchair race. We were a team and our bodies worked together to pursue the "gold."

Watching each Special Olympian compete in his or her event made my heart cheer and cry at the same time. Most of all, it made me appreciate the many blessings of life I had taken for granted. Helping Laura win the gold in two of her events was a gift we gave each other. I took the yellow ribbon that was in my hair that day and tied it around Laura's long, curly ponytail.

"Flaunt it, Honey," I whispered, finally understanding what Great Aunt Lilly had meant.

Nikki Willett

And, And, And

Peeking out from the corner of my desk blotter is a note, slowly yellowing and bent from time.

It is a card from my mother, containing only four sentences, but with enough impact to change my life forever.

In it, she praises my abilities as a writer without qualification. Each sentence is filled with love, offering specific examples of what my pursuit has meant to her and my father.

The word "but" never appears on the card. However the word "and" is there almost a half dozen times.

Every time I read it—which is almost every day—I am reminded to ask myself if I am doing the same thing for my daughters. I've asked myself how many times I've "but-ted" them, and me, out of happiness.

I hate to say that it's more often than I'd like to admit.

Although our eldest daughter usually got all As on her report card, there was never a semester when at least one teacher would not suggest that she talked too much in class. I always forgot to ask them if she was making improvement in controlling her behavior, if her comments contributed to the discussion in progress or encouraged a quieter child to talk. Instead, I would come home and greet her with, "Congratulations! Your dad and I are very proud of your accomplishment, but could you try to tone it down in class?"

The same was true of our younger daughter. Like her sister, she is a lovely, bright, articulate and friendly child. She also treats the floor of her room and the bathroom as a closet, which has provoked me to say on more than one occasion, "Yes, that project is great, but clean up your room!"

I've noticed that other parents do the same thing. "Our whole family was together for Christmas, but Kyle skipped out early to play his new computer game." "The hockey team won, but Mike should have made that last goal." "Amy's the homecoming queen, but now she wants two hundred dollars to buy a new dress and shoes."

But, but, but.

Instead, what I learned from my mother is that if you really want love to flow to your children, start thinking "and, and, and . . ." instead.

For example: "Our whole family was together for Christmas dinner, and Kyle mastered his new computer game before the night was through." "The hockey team won, and Mike did his best the whole game."

"Amy's the homecoming queen, and she's going to look gorgeous!"

The fact is that "but" feels bad—"and" feels good. And when it comes to our children, feeling good is definitely the way to go. When they feel good about themselves and what they're doing, they do more of it, building their self-confidence, their judgment and their harmonious connections to others. When everything they say, think or do is qualified or put down in some way, their joy sours and their anger soars.

This is not to say that children don't need or won't respond to their parents' expectations. They do and they will, regardless of whether those expectations are good or bad. When those expectations are consistently bright and positive and then are taught, modeled and expressed, amazing things happen. "I see you made a mistake. And I know you are intelligent enough to figure out what you did wrong and make a better decision next time." Or, "You've been spending hours on that project, and I'd love to have you explain it to me." Or, "We work hard for our money, and I know you can help figure out a way to pay for what you want."

It's not enough just to say we love our children. In a time when frustration has grown fierce, we can no longer afford to limit love's expression. If we want to tone down the sound of violence in our society, we're going to have to turn up the volume on noticing, praising, guiding and participating in what is right with our children.

"No more buts!" is a clarion call for joy. It's also a challenge, the opportunity fresh before us every day to put our attention on what is good and promising about our children, and to believe with all our hearts that they will eventually be able to see the same in us and the people with whom they will ultimately live, work and serve.

And if I ever forget, I have my mother's note to remind me.

Robin L. Silverman

5

INSIGHTS AND LESSONS

Experience is a hard teacher, because she gives the test first, the lesson afterwards.

Vernon Saunders' Law

The Day at the Beach

Put your troubles in a pocket with a hole in it.

Old Postcard

Not long ago, I came to one of those bleak periods that many of us encounter from time to time, a sudden drastic dip in the graph of living when everything goes stale and flat, energy wanes, enthusiasm dies. The effect on my work was frightening. Every morning I clenched my teeth and muttered: "Today life will take on some of its old meaning. You've got to break through this thing. You've got to."

But the barren days dragged on, and the paralysis grew worse. The time came when I knew I needed help.

The man I turned to was a doctor. Not a psychiatrist, just a doctor. He was older than I, and under his surface gruffness lay great wisdom and experience. "I don't know what's wrong," I told him miserably, "but I just seem to have come to a dead end. Can you help me?"

"I don't know," he said slowly. He made a tent of his fingers, and gazed at me thoughtfully for a long while. Then, abruptly, he asked, "Where were you happiest as a child?"

"As a child?" I echoed. "Why, at the beach, I suppose. We had a summer cottage there. We all loved it."

He looked out the window and watched the October leaves sifting down. "Are you capable of following instructions for a single day?"

"I think so," I said, ready to try anything.

"All right. Here's what I want you to do."

He told me to drive to the beach alone the following morning, arriving not later than nine o'clock. I could take some lunch, but I was not to read, write, listen to the radio or talk to anyone. "In addition," he said, "I'll give you a prescription to be taken every three hours."

He tore off four prescription blanks, wrote a few words on each, folded them, numbered them and handed them to me. "Take these at nine, twelve, three and six."

"Are you serious?" I asked.

He gave me a short honk of laughter. "You won't think I'm joking when you get my bill!"

The next morning, with little faith, I drove to the beach. It was lonely, all right. A northeaster was blowing; the sea looked gray and angry. I sat in the car, the whole day stretching emptily before me. Then I took out the first of the folded slips of paper. On it was written: *Listen carefully.*

I stared at the two words. *Why,* I thought, *the man must be mad.* He had ruled out music and newscasts and human conversation. What else was there?

I raised my head and listened. There were no sounds but the steady roar of the sea, the croaking cry of a gull, the drone of some aircraft overhead. All these sounds were familiar.

I got out of the car. A gust of wind slammed the door with a sudden clap of sound. *Was I supposed,* I asked myself, *to listen carefully to things like that?*

I climbed a dune and looked out over the deserted beach. Here the sea bellowed so loudly that all other sounds were lost. And yet, I thought suddenly, there must be sounds beneath sounds—the soft rasp of drifting sand, the tiny wind-whisperings in the dune grasses—if the listener got close enough to hear them.

Impulsively, I ducked down and, feeling fairly ridiculous, thrust my head into a clump of seaweed. Here I made a discovery: If you listen intently, there is a fractional moment in which everything pauses, waiting. In that instant of stillness, the racing thoughts halt. The mind rests.

I went back to the car and slid behind the wheel. *Listen carefully.* As I listened again to the deep growl of the sea, I found myself thinking about the white-fanged fury of its storms. Then I realized I was thinking of things bigger than myself—and there was relief in that.

Even so, the morning passed slowly. The habit of hurling myself at a problem was so strong that I felt lost without it.

By noon the wind had swept the clouds out of the sky, and the sea had a hard, polished and merry sparkle. I unfolded the second "prescription." And again I sat there, half-amused and half-exasperated. Three words this time: *Try reaching back.*

Back to what? To the past, obviously. But why, when all my worries concerned the present or the future?

I left the car and started tramping reflectively along the dunes. The doctor had sent me to the beach because it was a place of happy memories. Maybe that was what I was supposed to reach for—the wealth of happiness that lay half-forgotten behind me.

I decided to work on these vague impressions as a painter would, retouching the colors, strengthening the outlines. I would choose specific incidents and recapture as many details as possible. I would visualize people complete with dress and gestures. I would listen (carefully) for the exact sound of their voices, the echo of their laughter.

The tide was going out now, but there was still thunder in the surf. So I chose to go back twenty years to the last fishing trip I made with my younger brother. He had died during World War II, but I found that if I closed my eyes and really tried, I could see him with amazing vividness, even the humor and eagerness in his eyes.

In fact, I saw it all: the ivory scimitar of beach where we fished, the eastern sky smeared with sunrise, the great rollers creaming in, stately and slow. I felt the backwash swirl warm around my knees, saw the sudden arc of my brother's rod as he struck a fish, heard his exultant yell. Piece by piece I rebuilt it, clear and unchanged under the transparent varnish of time. Then it was gone.

I sat up slowly. *Try reaching back.* Happy people were usually assured, confident people. If, then, you deliberately reached back and touched happiness, might there not be released little flashes of power, tiny sources of strength?

This second period of the day went more quickly. As the sun began its long slant down the sky, my mind ranged eagerly through the past, reliving some episodes, uncovering others that had been completely forgotten. Across all the years, I remembered events, and knew from the sudden glow of warmth that no kindness is ever wasted, or ever completely lost.

By three o'clock the tide was out and the sound of the waves was only a rhythmic whisper, like a giant breathing. I stayed in my sandy nest, feeling relaxed and content—and a little complacent. The doctor's prescriptions, I thought, were easy to take.

But I was not prepared for the next one. This time the three words were not a gentle suggestion. They sounded more like a command. *Reexamine your motives.*

My first reaction was purely defensive. *There's nothing wrong with my motives,* I said to myself. *I want to be successful—who doesn't? I want to have a certain amount of recognition, but so does everybody. I want more security than I've got—and why not?*

Maybe, said a small voice somewhere inside my head, those motives aren't good enough. Maybe that's the reason the wheels have stopped going around.

I picked up a handful of sand and let it stream between my fingers. In the past, whenever my work went well, there had always been something spontaneous about it, something uncontrived, something free. Lately it had been calculated, competent—and dead. Why? Because I had been looking past the job itself to the rewards I hoped it would bring. The work had ceased to be an end in itself; it had become a means to make money, pay bills. The sense of giving something, of helping people, of making a contribution, had been lost in a frantic clutch of security.

In a flash of certainty, I saw that if one's motives are wrong, nothing can be right. It makes no difference whether you are a mailman, a hairdresser, an insurance salesman, a stay-at-home mom or dad—whatever. As long as you feel you are serving others, you do the job well. When you are concerned only with helping yourself, you do it less well. This is a law as inexorable as gravity.

For a long time, I sat there. Far out on the bar I heard the murmur of the surf change to a hollow roar as the tide turned. Behind me the spears of light were almost horizontal. My time at the beach had almost run out, and I felt a grudging admiration for the doctor and the "prescriptions" he had so casually and cunningly devised. I saw, now, that in them was a therapeutic progression that might well be valuable to anyone facing any difficulty.

Listen carefully: To calm a frantic mind, slow it down, shift the focus from inner problems to outer things.

Try reaching back: Since the human mind can hold but one idea at a time, you blot out present worry when you touch the happiness of the past.

Reexamine your motives: This was the hard core of the "treatment." This challenge was to reappraise, to bring one's motives into alignment with one's capabilities and conscience. But the mind must be clear and receptive to do this—hence the six hours of quiet that went before.

The western sky was a blaze of crimson as I took out the last slip of paper. Six words this time. I walked slowly out on the beach. A few yards below the high-water mark I stopped and read the words again: *Write your troubles on the sand.*

I let the paper blow away, reached down and picked up a fragment of shell. Kneeling there under the vault of the sky, I wrote several words on the sand, one above the other. Then I walked away, and I did not look back. I had written my troubles on the sand. And the tide was coming in.

Arthur Gordon
Submitted by Wayne W. Hinckley

A Lesson in Cloud Recognition

It had been another long week of conducting training sessions throughout the country. I generally like to relax on the flight home, do some easy reading, maybe even close my eyes for a few minutes. I try to be open to whatever does happen, though. I usually say a little prayer: *Whoever is supposed to sit next to me, let it be so, and help me be open to that.*

On this particular day, I boarded the plane and noticed a young boy, around eight years old, sitting in the window seat next to mine. I love kids. However, I was tired. My first instinct was, *Oh boy, I'm not sure about this.* Trying my best to be friendly, I said "Hello" and introduced myself. He told me his name was Bradley. We struck up a conversation and, within minutes, he took me into his confidence, saying, "This is the first time I have ever been on a plane. I'm a little bit nervous."

He told me that he and his family had driven to see his cousins, and that he got to stay longer after his family had returned home. Now he was flying home, all by himself.

"Flying is a piece of cake," I tried to reassure him. "It is one of the easiest things you'll ever do." I paused, thinking for a moment, and then asked him, "Have you ever been on a roller coaster?"

"I love roller coasters!"

"Do you ride them without hands?"

"Oh, yeah, I love to." He giggled. I acted as if I were horrified.

"Do you ever ride in the front?" I asked with a pretense of fear on my face.

"Yeah, I try to get in the front seat every time!"

"And you're not afraid of that?"

He shook his head no, clearly sensing that he was now one up on me.

"Well, this flight will be nothing compared to that. I won't even ride roller coasters, and I'm not the least bit afraid to fly."

A smile edged its way onto his face, "Is that right?" I could see that he was starting to think that maybe he was brave after all.

The plane began to taxi down the runway. As we ascended, he looked out the window and began describing with great excitement everything he was experiencing. He commented on the cloud formations, and the pictures they seemed to paint in the sky. "This cloud looks like a butterfly, and that one looks like a horse!"

Suddenly, I saw this flight through the eyes of an eight-year-old boy. It was as if it were the first time that I had ever flown. Later Bradley asked me what I did for a living. I told him about the training that I conduct and mentioned that I also do radio and television commercials.

His eyes lit up. "My sister and I did a television commercial once."

"You did? What was that like for you?"

He said that it was very exciting for them. Then he told me that he needed to go to the bathroom.

I stood up to let him out into the aisle. It was then that I noticed the braces on his legs. Bradley slowly made his way down to the bathroom and back. When he sat back down, he explained, "I have muscular dystrophy. My sister has it too—she's in a wheelchair now. That's why we did that commercial. We were poster children for muscular dystrophy."

As we began our descent, he looked over, smiled, and spoke in a hushed, almost embarrassed voice, "You know, I was really worried about who would sit next to me on the plane. I was afraid it would be someone crabby who didn't want to talk with me. I'm so glad I sat next to you."

Thinking about the whole experience later that night, I was reminded of the value of being open to the moment. A week that began with me being the trainer ended with me being the student. Now when times get rough—and they inevitably do—I look out the window and try to see what images the clouds are painting in the sky. And I remember Bradley, the beautiful child who taught me that lesson.

Joyce A. Harvey

A Story to Live By

You've got to dance like nobody's watching, and love like it's never going to hurt.

Source Unknown

My brother-in-law opened the bottom drawer of my sister's bureau and lifted out a tissue-wrapped package.

"This," he said, "is not a slip. This is lingerie."

He discarded the tissue and handed me the slip. It was exquisite: silk, handmade and trimmed with a cobweb of lace. The price tag with an astronomical figure on it was still attached.

"Jan bought this the first time we went to New York, at least eight or nine years ago. She never wore it. She was saving it for a special occasion. Well, I guess this is the occasion."

He took the slip from me, and put it on the bed with the other clothes we were taking to the mortician. His hands lingered on the soft material for a moment, then he slammed the drawer shut and turned to me.

"Don't ever save anything for a special occasion. Every day you're alive is a special occasion."

I remembered those words through the funeral and the days that followed, when I helped him and my niece attend to all the sad chores that result from an unexpected death. I thought about them on the plane returning to California from the midwestern town where my sister's family lives. I thought about all the things that she hadn't seen or heard or done. I thought about the things that she had done without realizing that they were special.

I'm still thinking about his words, and they've changed my life. I'm reading more and dusting less. I'm sitting on the deck and admiring the view without fussing about the weeds in the garden. I'm spending more time with my family and friends and less time in committee meetings. Whenever possible, life should be a pattern of experiences to savor, not endure. I'm trying to recognize these moments now and cherish them.

I'm not "saving" anything: We use our good china and crystal for every special event—such as losing a pound, getting the sink unstopped, the first camellia blossom.

I wear my good blazer to the market if I feel like it. My theory is if I look prosperous, I can shell out $28.49 for one small bag of groceries without wincing. I'm not saving my good perfume for special parties: Clerks in hardware stores and tellers in banks have noses that function as well as my party-going friends.

"Someday" and "one of these days" are losing their grip on my vocabulary. If it's worth seeing or hearing or doing, I want to see and hear and do it now. I'm not sure what my sister would have done had she known that she wouldn't be here for the tomorrow we all take for granted. I think she would have called family members and a few close friends. She might have called a few former friends to apologize and mend fences for past squabbles. I like to think she would have gone out for a Chinese dinner. I'm guessing; I'll never know.

It's those little things left undone that would make me angry if I knew that my hours were limited. Angry because I put off seeing good friends whom I was going to get in touch with—someday. Angry because I hadn't written certain letters that I intended to write—one of these days. Angry and sorry that I didn't tell my husband and daughter often enough how much I truly love them. I'm trying very hard not to put off, hold back or save anything that would add laughter and luster to our lives.

And every morning when I open my eyes, I tell myself that it is special. Every day, every minute, every breath truly is . . . a gift from God.

Anne Wells

Sensory Deprivation

[EDITORS' NOTE: *The following piece was sent to us by a female prisoner. We don't know what the crime was.*]

I want to go dancing and wear a dress that swirls and floats around me, and laugh.

I want to feel the shimmer of silk as it glides over my arms and down my body, the joy of fingering its whispery softness.

I want to sleep in my own bed and luxuriate in the cool crispness of clean sheets, and rest my head on my own soft pillow. And go to sleep when I want to, with all the lights out, and wake up when I'm ready.

I want to stretch out on my couch under my blue-plaid afghan and listen as my favorite music seeps from the speakers and into my being, watering the parched land-scape of my soul.

I want to sit on my porch and sip hot coffee from my stoneware mug, and read the newspaper, and hear the dog bark at blowing leaves and trespassing squirrels.

I want to answer the phone and call my friends and family and talk until we catch up on all the words we've saved for each other, and laugh.

I want to hear the train hoot through Loveland, the gravel crunch in the driveway, and car doors slam as friends come to visit. And the tinkle and clink of silverware on china, the hiss and gurgle of the coffee maker.

I want to feel my bare feet on the cool whiteness of my kitchen floor, and the soft blueness of my bedroom carpet.

I want to see the colors, all of them, every color ever spun into existence. And white, true white, pristine and unblemished. And acres of green trees, and miles of yellow-ribbon highways, and yards of Christmas lights. And the moon.

I want to smell bacon sizzling, a steak broiling, Thanksgiving dinner and my father's tomato vines. And fresh laundry, hot tar on a parking lot. And the ocean.

But more than all of this, I want to stand in the doorway of my son's room and watch him sleep. And hear him get up in the morning and see him come home at night. And touch his face and comb my fingers through his hair, and ride in his truck and eat his grilled-cheese sandwiches.

And watch him grow and laugh and play and eat and drive and *live*. Mostly, mostly, live. And put my arms around him and hold him until he laughs and says, "Mom, that's enough!"

And then be free to do it again.

Deborah E. Hill

The Birthday Present

I have a dream my four little children will one day live in a nation where they will not be judged by the color of their skin but by the content of their character. . . .

Martin Luther King Jr.

[EDITORS' NOTE: *This story was penned in 1969.*]

A week after my son started first grade, he came home with the news that Roger, the only African-American in the class, was his playground partner. I swallowed and said, "That's nice. How long before someone else gets him for a partner?"

"Oh, I've got him for good," replied Bill.

In another week, I had the news that Bill had asked if Roger could be his desk partner.

Unless you were born and reared in the deep South, as I was, you cannot know what this means. I went for an appointment with the teacher.

She met me with tired, cynical eyes. "Well, I suppose you want a new desk partner for your child, too," she said.

"Can you wait a few minutes? I have another mother coming in right now."

I looked up to see a woman my age. My heart raced as I realized she must be Roger's mother. She had a quiet dignity and much poise, but neither trait could cover the anxiety I heard in her questions: "How's Roger doing? I hope he is keeping up with the other children? If he isn't, just let me know."

She hesitated as she made herself ask, "Is he giving you any trouble of any kind? I mean, what with his having to change desks so much?"

I felt the terrible tension in her, for she knew the answer. But I was proud of that first-grade teacher for her gentle reply: "No, Roger is not giving me any trouble. I try to move all the children around the first few weeks until each has just the right partner."

I introduced myself and said that my son was to be Roger's new partner and I hoped they would like each other. Even then I knew it was only a surface wish, not a deep-felt one. But it helped her, I could see.

Twice Roger invited Bill to come home with him, but I found excuses. Then came the heartache that I will always suffer.

On my birthday, Bill came home from school with a grimy piece of paper folded into a very small square. Unfolding it, I found three flowers and "Happy Birthday" crayoned on the paper—and a nickel.

"That's from Roger," said Bill. "It's his milk money. When I said today was your birthday, he made me bring it to you. He said you are his friend, 'cause you're the only mother who didn't make him get another desk partner."

Mavis Burton Ferguson

Mrs. George

Go confidently in the direction of your dreams.
Live the life you have imagined.

Henry David Thoreau

I first met Mrs. George, the teacher for Dr. J. P. Lord's new high school, in a small room designed for one teacher and one student.

The room had been converted into a classroom for four teenage boys. Three of us were in wheelchairs and one walked with a cane. Those of us in the class had a variety of medical problems. The student with the cane was legally blind. As for the three in wheelchairs, one was the victim of a gunshot wound in the head, one had muscular dystrophy, and one had cerebral palsy.

I was the one with cerebral palsy. When I tried to vocalize, Mrs. George kidded me by saying that it sounded like the mating call of a bull moose.

Each of us had different academic and emotional needs, ranging from preparing for college to preparing for death. Mrs. George did everything she could to help the first class of Dr. J. P. Lord High.

Mrs. George, in her fifties, was about five feet tall, had graying black hair (which turned a lot more gray by the end of the school year), olive skin and a high-pitched voice. She had a habit of talking too fast, and she ended her explanations with, "Do you see that?"

She greeted us the first day of school with a cheery, "Good morning, you guys. This room was thrown together at the last minute, but I think we'll do okay. This high school is the first of this kind in Nebraska, so we are pioneers. Pioneers have to put up with a few troubles. I understand all of you know one another except Bill and David. David, this is Bill. He has cerebral palsy. He left school about the time you came, because this school didn't offer high school then. Bill, David is a Hawaiian transplant, and he has muscular dystrophy. He'll be nineteen on May 6. We'll have a birthday party with dancing girls."

I wondered if she knew what muscular dystrophy was. I knew that David wouldn't last until his birthday. He already had more birthdays than most suffering from this disability. Already his lungs were affected, which meant his breathing would require effort all year.

"Now I'll get you started on what I want you to do. I have expectations for all of you, do you see that?" the new, idealistic teacher stated.

When she came to me, I was classifying rocks to fulfill a requirement in earth science. Sitting down beside me, she said, "I hear you have been taking correspondence courses from the University of Nebraska at Lincoln and haven't gotten very far for the past three years. I know these courses are bear-cats and take a lot of time. But I will help you with them, and we will shoot for graduation next spring. Also, I'll feed you lunch if that's okay with you. I know you would rather have one of those young chicks that are just out of college, but you're stuck with the old hen. Do you have any questions?"

"I don't think David will make it to his birthday. His lungs are too weak, and these winters are hard on anybody," I spelled out slowly on my letter board with a stylus attached to my head, commonly referred to as a headstick.

"You and I know that, but he doesn't know that. Just as you want that diploma, David wants his nineteenth birthday cake."

Mrs. George was true to her word. I completed courses and started new ones at amazing speed. However, David worsened during the holiday season. He was afraid to go to sleep at night for fear that he wouldn't wake up. So Mrs. George let him sleep in class saying, "We have hospitals across the street, and if we have to visit them, we can be there in five minutes. So, David, you are safer here than anywhere else."

Once when David was having trouble breathing, she had to massage his chest all afternoon. While she was doing it, she said to the physical-therapist aide standing by with oxygen, "David is helping me build up my tennis arm, so if you see a five-foot woman with bulging biceps on the tennis court, it will be me. This is fantastic exercise! Do you see that?"

One day we were discussing some dull subject for my world-history course when she said, "When I'm working with the other two guys, I can't keep an eye on David's breathing so I'll leave it up to you, Bill, okay? If he slumps over, make one of your bull-moose noises to get my attention. He doesn't look good, does he? But we'll keep him in school as long as possible. At least his mother doesn't have to watch over him when he is here. Now we should be able to finish this damn history course in March, if we are lucky. This is a dry course, and I'm sure you're fed up with it, because I am!"

Frequently, when he was gasping for air, David would

look at me and say, "I'm all right, Bill. I'm all right. Thanks for watching over me."

Fortunately, my bull-moose yell was never needed. The vigil, however, matured me greatly. I watched David, and in doing so, I became aware of his desire to live. Seeing him fight for every breath he took, I suddenly knew the value of living. So when I had to do some boring research, I didn't mind, because at least I could do it without worrying about breathing. I think this was the lesson that Mrs. George was teaching me by having me keep an eye on David.

April 10 was David's last day of school. That night he took a turn for the worse. He was rushed to the hospital, where life-support machines could maintain his breathing.

On April 15, 1975, I had planned to visit him after school. But that morning I found a handwritten note beside my typewriter saying, "Don't go to the hospital tonight; David died in his sleep. I didn't want to tell the other guys, because today the school is going to the circus, and there's no reason to spoil that. We will mourn him together. J. George."

Although Mrs. George couldn't make David's dream of a nineteenth birthday come true (God knows she tried!), she made my dream of a high-school graduation come true.

As I sat on the stage on a warm May evening in 1976, listening to the commencement song, "The Impossible Dream," the words seemed to fit the lady dressed in yellow, proudly watching me receive my diploma, because she "dreamed the impossible dream" and made it come true.

William L. Rush

A Bowl of Humility

Honk, honk, slice, splash, stop, start. Thick traffic. Teeming rain. My seven-year-old Volkswagen jerked along the freeway like a bug on sticky tape. Problems droned angrily around in my head. For weeks I'd been pouring all my hopes and energy into preparing an interior design presentation for a fat-cat client, and I'd just learned that I'd lost the job to a competitor. *But your biggest mistake, Linda,* I scolded myself, *was counting on the money. When will you learn not to assume?*

Traffic ground to a stop, and I fished my checkbook out of my purse and opened it. Balance, less than forty dollars. I was nearly broke—again. I couldn't begin to stretch that to cover what my fifteen-year-old son Tim, and I were going to need until my next check.

Since my divorce the problems had come pouring down like the rain dimming my view through the windshield. Not only scarce money, but long hours at a stressful job, guilty feelings for once again not making it to the school basketball game, the always-present feeling of "being in this all alone," the self-imposed pressure of expecting peak-level, super-human performance from myself at all times and in all kinds of different situations.

The car ahead of me inched forward and I turned off on my exit ramp. I had planned to stop by the grocery store, but with my make-up streaked from crying and my checkbook balance what it was, I decided to drive past and make dinner with what we had at home.

This afternoon Tim wasn't scheduled to work at his weekend and after-school job at the local Tastee-Freez. I knew he'd be home before me, and he might have started cooking dinner. He enjoyed the kitchen and managed to cook for us quite often. Right now his specialty was chili, so there was a good chance that we'd be having it tonight. *I hope so,* I thought. *Chili would taste good on a cold, rainy night like this.*

I started to make plans for the evening. *I deserve to pamper myself,* I decided—so no bookwork tonight. Dinner, a hot bath, maybe a little television. I'd done a load of laundry before leaving that morning and had told Tim to put it in the dryer for me. I would fold that and then I'd be done.

I pulled into our gravel drive, parked and hurried inside. Coming through the kitchen door, I was greeted by the tangy aroma of simmering chili. *Oh good!* I thought. *Tim has set the table with the dill pickles we had canned last summer, crackers, tall glasses of milk—and he has even baked chocolate chip cookies!*

"Hi, Tim," I called as I scurried downstairs to fold the laundry.

I opened the door of our antique clothes dryer and saw—a big black hole. An empty black hole. Tim had forgotten to put the laundry in the dryer. My just-beginning-to-rise spirits went clunk. "All I do is work and worry." Slowly, I walked back up the stairs. Tim was watching television.

"I would like to talk to you, Tim." One look at my face and the warm smile left his.

"Things haven't been exactly easy around here," I began. "I am trying to maintain this house and a way of life for us both. I get no assistance from your father, so it's up to me. I don't ask you to do much, but when I do, I expect it done—like putting clothes in the dryer.

"I need some help every now and then, Tim. I have to depend on you. We have to depend on each other. Do you know what would happen to us if I forgot to do what was expected of me today?"

Tim looked as if I'd slapped him, but he sat quietly and waited for me to finish. Then he got up from the sofa, came over and took my hand. I will never forget that moment. His expression was that of a man, not a young boy. "Okay Mom, I'm sorry if I let you down. But I want to ask you something. Next time you get together with your friends and someone says their sister is dying or their oldest son is on drugs or their mother is in a nursing home, are you going to say, 'That's nothing. Tim forgot to put the clothes in the dryer'?"

He was not being flippant. He was earnest. In that instant, with those words, we had changed roles. He was the parent and I was the child.

That was many rainy afternoons ago. But Tim's clear perspective continues to help me see past the obstruction when problems seem to jam up my life.

Everyone has problems: single parents like me, young folks, old folks, married people, unmarried people. It isn't the problems themselves that are harmful. It's letting them block you from feeling the powerful force that God had given you to compensate for them.

Linda LaRocque

Wind Beneath My Wings

"Mom, can I go see Luke now?" Arlyn asked, jangling her car keys in her hand.

Hmmm, I thought. *Since when had Arlyn asked for permission to go anywhere?* She was eighteen; she had graduated from high school two months before.

"Of course," I replied. Maybe Arlyn wasn't eager to leave home, after all. I worried about whether she would be strong enough to survive the rough, scary world outside our safe nest in rural Georgia. Sometimes she accused me of being over-protective. In two weeks, however, Arlyn would leave for college, whether she was ready or not.

But I was wrong. Very wrong. She did not wait two weeks to leave; she left that very afternoon.

Arlyn said good-bye and drove out into the country. She turned down a long, deserted dirt road and parked her car near a stream. She got out, took an old hunting rifle out of the trunk, placed its barrel into her mouth and pulled the trigger.

Around 3:30, I answered a knock on my door. A man identified himself as a deputy and walked in. He strode across the room to a large photograph hanging on the wall. "Is this your daughter?" he asked, as he glanced from the picture to me.

"Yes," I replied proudly, too surprised to realize that this was not a social call. "That's Arlyn."

He stared at the picture for a moment, then sat down in a chair near the door. He described Arlyn's car, and I confirmed it was hers. Then he said, "Your daughter is dead." Just like that.

I wrote and gave the eulogy for my daughter's funeral. For a week, I had no time to think, no time to feel, just time to exist. I functioned as a wooden puppet whose jerky movements are the result of strings pulled by an invisible hand. Others quietly kept order in my surroundings.

Then my family and friends left, and I could feel the silence. I called my child's name aloud, over and over. The telephone rang; I picked it up and waited to hear her voice on the other end, but it was never her. I checked her bedroom a thousand times, hoping to see her, but all I saw was her worn stuffed bunny lying on her pillow. Her clothes hung in her closet and her acceptance letter to the university lay on the floor. When I heard the back door open, I would smile. I expected Arlyn, with her guitar slung over her shoulder, to dance in and give me a hug. When someone else appeared, my smile faded and my heart went numb.

I held on to the fantasy that Arlyn would return. I sat in her car, breathing in her lingering scent. I listened to her music, and I wore some of her clothes.

One night, I drank tea at her favorite coffee shop. A tall, slender brunette with long hair walked in; I leaned forward to get a better look. I stood up, ready to dash across the room and throw my arms around her; but when she moved, I saw that she was not Arlyn. At night, I lay in bed stiffly, corpse-like. I stared blankly at the ceiling hour upon hour, until the morning light slipped through the blinds. Then I would get up; or I wouldn't.

Every minute of the day, I struggled desperately to understand what had happened. Arlyn would never have killed herself. My daughter found joy in living; she laughed, learned and loved. Arlyn was in tune with nature and peace. How could she have taken her own life?

I ransacked her bedroom, searching for clues. In her closet, in dresser drawers, under her bed and on shelves, I found several journals and dozens of pages of her writing. I collected them all into one mountainous pile. Then I sat down to read.

"I keep asking myself why. For my entire life, all I have ever wanted was to be dead, to not be. Why?" she had written.

"I don't know why I didn't kill myself in fifth grade when I had the chance," she had also written. I shook my head, confused. The handwriting was Arlyn's, but these words could not be hers.

I thought back to when Arlyn was in sixth grade, ten years old. One day, the school held a talent contest. Arlyn signed up to sing. She picked out a long, green Victorian-style dress to wear, and I tied a matching bow in her hair.

When Arlyn stepped up in front of the crowd and took the microphone in her hand, she scanned the audience until she spotted me. Then she smiled. The students talked and laughed with each other, ignoring the shy little girl standing in front of them. I wanted to shout at them to pay attention, but I couldn't.

The music started, and Arlyn began to sing. Her song was "Wind Beneath My Wings," one popularized by Bette Midler.

After a moment, the students stopped chatting and noticed Arlyn. Her strong voice caressed them gently, and they focused completely on her.

That afternoon as we drove home, I glanced at the

small trophy in her lap. "When you sing," I asked, "do you think about the words?" Arlyn replied, "When I sing 'Wind Beneath My Wings,' I always think of you."

But now, Arlyn was dead, and I was in her bedroom, reading that she had wanted to kill herself in fifth grade. I could not comprehend. My husband and I turned her writings over to a psychiatrist. He said he would do a "psychological autopsy" (an evaluation of someone based on information from writings or other sources). A few weeks later, he called us in.

He told us that Arlyn was manic-depressive. He said she knew "something" was not right, so she had been tormented by confusion and shame and fear. He explained that the chemicals in her mind were imbalanced and that they had altered her perception of reality. This chemical imbalance had also produced her thoughts of suicide.

The psychiatrist also told us that her brilliant mind made it possible for Arlyn to hide this part of herself from others. He insisted she did not want to die.

I went home and devoured materials on manic depression (also called bipolar disorder) and on suicide. I began to understand that Arlyn may have viewed death as an escape from emotional pain. It was as though her heart was carrying a heavy weight, and it became unbearable.

So Arlyn, my sensitive, fragile child, carried this burden inside her for years; but one day, she simply could not carry it any more. She knew that if she just stopped walking, that if she closed her eyes and let go, the weight would go away forever. So, she killed herself.

A common theme in science fiction is projecting ourselves into the future. Some of us visit psychics, in hopes of learning what tomorrow will bring. Of course, we only want to hear about the "good" things. We know bad things happen, but we generally don't expect them to happen to us.

If we really knew the future, we would alter our behavior profoundly. Since we don't, however, we simply plod along, oblivious to the fact that disaster may happen at any moment. If I had known Arlyn's last day alive would have been August 7, 1996, I would have focused on her exclusively. I would have quit my job to spend more time with her. I would have unplugged the telephone and television, so I could listen to her more carefully. I would not have let her out of my sight for even a nanosecond, so I could have savored her presence. Nothing else would have mattered. But I did not know.

One of the most profound lessons Arlyn's death has taught me is that the only guaranteed moment is this one; therefore, if we live our lives expecting a future that may not exist, we may regret our choices forever.

This knowledge should inspire us to change the way we interact with others. We may choose to treat those we care about with extra attention and sensitivity every moment of every day, or we may plod on about our lives, oblivious to the reality that each moment could be our last—or theirs.

It only takes a little more effort to listen carefully, to give an extra hug, to say kind words. A moment given now may prevent a lifetime of regret.

In closing, I'd like to offer you words from the author Harriet Beecher Stowe. She wrote, "The bitterest tears shed over graves are for words left unsaid and deeds left undone."

Karyl Chastain Beal

Sorrow

In this sad world of ours, sorrow comes to all,
and it often comes with bitter agony.
Perfect relief is not possible,
except with time.
You cannot now believe that you will ever feel better.
But this is not true.
You are sure to be happy again.
Knowing this,
truly believing it,
will make you less miserable now.
I have had enough experience to make this statement.

Abraham Lincoln

How I Came to Terms

The richness of the human experience would lose something of rewarding joy if there were no limitations to overcome.

Helen Keller

I didn't want to believe my own eyes. *There must be some other explanation for what I saw,* I kept telling myself, struggling to hide my concerns. I was sitting with my wife, Diane, after the birth of our second child, Sandra. Diane was radiant as she lay in her hospital bed talking to her folks on the phone. But Diane hadn't seen our new baby yet. She'd been spared the look of alarm in the nurse's eyes just seconds before she whisked our baby out of sight. There had been no tests. No advance warning.

I lost all hope when the doctor came in and took a chair. He waited patiently for Diane to finish her conversation and hung up the phone, and then he delivered the devastating news: "I'm sorry. Your baby has Down's syndrome."

Diane took the news in stride. She'd had nine months to bond with her baby. Even before they brought Sandra in for her to hold, my wife already loved our new daughter with all her heart. But not me. I had to excuse myself and flee from the room.

I walked the hospital corridors for hours, slamming my fists into walls and crying hot, stinging tears. "Why did you have to do this to my child?" I railed at a God I suddenly despised. "Why her? Why me?"

Why couldn't Sandra be perfect—like my three-year-old son, Aaron? Aaron was the apple of my eye. I loved taking long walks with him in the rain and pointing out the nightcrawlers and snails wriggling across the sidewalk. We always had fun together Friday nights when Diane worked late and stayed with her parents so she wouldn't have to make the hour-and-a-half drive home and then back again Saturday morning. We played with plastic trucks and dinosaurs. I read him stories at bedtime.

When Aaron asked me not to leave, I gathered pillows and blankets and sacked out on the floor beside his bed. By morning, he was always curled up on the floor beside me. He'd open his sleepy eyes and ask, "Daddy, can we watch cartoons?"

"You bet, Son," I'd reply.

With Sandra things couldn't have been more different. After we brought her home, I hurried to the library and read everything I could find about Down's syndrome. I desperately searched for some tiny shred of hope. But the more I read, the more discouraged I became. There was no magic cure for what I called "Sandra's condition." Back then I couldn't even bring myself to utter the words, "Down's syndrome."

Diane and I enrolled in a support group, but after a few weeks I couldn't go back. Listening to the parents of older Down's syndrome children describing the many health problems they faced made me utterly heartsick. *Is this our future?* I couldn't help but wonder.

Indeed, when Sandra was six months old she needed heart surgery. "Dear God, please don't take Sandra from me," Diane prayed, but it was a prayer I couldn't share. *Maybe it would be for the best,* I secretly thought, and didn't allow myself to contemplate—best, for whom?

As weeks flowed into months, I dutifully carried Sandra back and forth to doctors and therapists. I massaged her legs and tried to build up her muscle tone. I tried to teach her how to walk and talk, and I grew more frustrated and depressed with each developmental milestone she missed.

I devoted myself to making Sandra better. I was determined to "fix" her, but that was all I was doing—trying to make repairs. I wasn't loving my daughter. I only took her from her crib to change her diaper or to do one of her therapies. I never picked her up just to hold her in my arms and luxuriate in that powdery baby smell. I never smiled at her or played peek-a-boo.

"You don't love Sandra the same way you love Aaron," Diane observed mildly one afternoon, and I had to admit that she was right.

"I just need more time," I protested lamely.

I was ashamed of my feelings, and may God forgive me, I was ashamed of my little girl. I felt embarrassed to be seen with her. "Oh, she's so cute," people would coo, and I always felt like snatching them by the collar and shouting back: "You don't really think that! You think my daughter is ugly! You probably think she belongs in an institution!"

My anger soured into sadness, and my sadness faded into apathy and distance. Even taking walks or playing games with Aaron lost its thrill because it always reminded me of all the things Sandra could never do.

I went through the motions of caring for Sandra, but I grew increasingly hopeless and detached. "This is the way it's always going to be," I sighed one day about a year ago as I settled my two-year-old daughter into her high chair for lunch. I spooned baby food into a dish and wiped away tears of despair. I felt utterly empty inside.

But as I approached Sandra's high chair, she tilted her head and studied me with her large blue eyes. And then she reached out both tiny arms and hugged me with all the force she could muster, as if to say, "Daddy, I'll hug your sadness away."

I returned Sandra's hug and cried all the harder. Only now I wasn't crying from sadness. I was crying because my little girl had shown me what it felt like to be loved unconditionally. For a brief moment our roles had been reversed. Sandra had given me the love I had been so long unable to give to her.

I had grieved because my daughter wasn't perfect, but who was I to expect perfection when I had such a long way to go myself? Who was I to cry for what might have been, instead of accepting and cherishing my daughter for the very special being she is and will always be?

Sandra taught me how to open my heart and give my love willingly and without expectations. I'd spent so much time and energy taking care of Sandra's needs, I'd all but forgotten to take the time to simply enjoy being with her. I don't make that mistake anymore.

These days I read to both of my children at bedtime, and Saturday mornings you'll find all three of us curled up on the couch watching cartoons together. And whenever I'm making Sandra laugh with funny faces, or playing ball with her or hugging one of her dolls, it never fails to occur to me: Now that I've finally opened my heart to Sandra, every day she fills it to the brim with joy and love.

Mike Cottrill
As told to Bill Holton

Like Me

I went to my dad, and I said to him,
There's a new kid who's come to my school.
He's different from me and he isn't too cool.
No, he's nothing at all like me, like me,
No, he's nothing at all like me.

He runs in a funnyish jerkyish way,
And he never comes first in a race.
Sometimes he forgets which way is first base,
And he's nothing at all like me, like me,
No, he's nothing at all like me.

He studies all day in a separate class,
And they say that it's called Special Ed.
And sometimes I don't understand what he's said,
And he's nothing at all like me, like me,
No, he's nothing at all like me.

His face looks kind of different from mine,
And his talking is sometimes slow.
And it makes me feel funny and there's one thing I know;
He is not at all like me, like me,
No, he's nothing at all like me!

And my father said, "Son, I want you to think
When you meet someone different and new
That he may seem a little bit strange, it's true,
But he's not very different from you, from you,
No, he's not very different from you."

Well I guess, I admitted, I've looked at his face;
When he's left out of games, he feels bad.
And when other kids tease him, I can see he's so sad.
I guess *that's* not so different from me, from me,
No, that's not very different from me.

And when we're in Music, he sure loves to sing.
And he sings just like me, right out loud.
When he gets his report card, I can tell he feels proud.
And that's not very different from me, from me,
No, that's not very different from me.

And I know in the lunchroom he has lots of fun;
He loves hot dogs and ice cream and fries.
And he hates to eat spinach and that's not a surprise,
'Cause that's not very different from me, from me,
No, that's not very different from me.

And he's always so friendly, he always says hi,
And he waves and he calls out my name.
And he'd like to be friends and get into a game,
Which is not very different from me, from me,
No, I guess that's not different from me.

And his folks really love him, I saw them at school,
I remember on Open School Night—
They were smiling and proud and they hugged him real
   tight,
And that's not very different from me, from me,
No, that's not very different from me.

So I said to my dad, "Hey, you know that new kid?"
Well, I've really been thinking a lot.
Some things are different . . . and some things are not . . .
But *mostly* he's really like me, like me,
Yes, my new friend's . . . a lot . . . like me.

Emily Perl Kingsley

6

ON COURAGE
AND
DETERMINATION

You can't be afraid of stepping on toes if you want to go dancing.

Lewis Freedman

The Best Advice I Ever Had

Courage is resistance to fear, mastery of fear—not absence of fear.

Mark Twain

Life was just about perfect, I told myself, feeling immensely thankful that fate had been so good to me. Truly I was sitting on top of the world. I had been the star of a hit musical revue on the Paris stage for a year. I'd been signed to make four movies at an important studio. Best of all, I had scores of good friends whom I saw often.

That was in 1922. I did not know then how soon all my good luck was to end.

Looking back later on what happened at *Les Bougges Parisiens* that evening, I realized there had been warning signs. For months I had been working too hard, sleeping too little, and exhaustion occasionally caught up with me—a terrible heaviness of spirit, a draining of morale. I had ignored it, however. "Momentary fatigue," I would say, and move out before the footlights, forcing the gaiety that the audience awaited.

This night, however, was to be different. At a long

lunch with friends, I'd foolishly indulged in too much rich food and too many wines. I had taken a nap, expecting to be myself again before curtain time. But at the theater my brain still seemed to be on fire. I had never felt this strange dizziness before, and I tried to dismiss it as I waited for my opening cue. When the cue came, though, the words seemed to reach me from far away. I responded with my customary lines—or so I thought. But something obviously had gone wrong. I could see it in my fellow actor's eyes.

When I answered his second speech, I saw surprise turn to alarm, and I realized with horror that I had replied to both his cues with lines not from the *first* act but the *third!* Desperately I tried to get back on the track, but my mind was now suddenly a jumble. I was hopelessly lost.

The actor with whom I played the scene covered up for me beautifully, whispering the opening words of each of my lines, as did others in subsequent scenes. Somehow the evening came to an end with only those backstage the wiser.

The rest of the cast laughed off the episode as a temporary upset. I wanted to believe them, but I was badly shaken. What if tonight was only the beginning? An actor who couldn't remember his lines—this could mean the end of a career which had brought me from rundown Montmartre cafés where I had sung for food to the finest theaters in Paris and a salary of thousands of dollars a week.

The next day I went over and over my lines, rehearsing speeches and songs I had known perfectly for a year. But that night the panic returned, and with it a nightmare existence I was destined to suffer for months. Onstage I found myself unable to concentrate on the lines I must say at the moment; instead, my mind would race to those which lay far ahead, trying to ready itself in advance. I hesitated, stammered; the debonair ease that had been my trademark as an entertainer was gone. And then came attacks of vertigo, when the floor would whirl up to meet me in a dizzying spin. I was afraid I might actually fall in the middle of a scene.

I visited one specialist after another. Nervous exhaustion, they said, and tried injections, electric massages, special diets. Nothing worked. People began to gossip openly that my performances were slipping. I tried to avoid my friends, certain that they must be aware that something was wrong.

With pressure building up inside me, a nervous breakdown seemed inevitable. It came. And with it came a conviction that I was really through.

The doctor ordered me to a rest home in Saujon, a tiny village in southwest France. The world of Maurice Chevalier had crumbled, I told myself, and nowhere would the pieces ever be put together again. But I reckoned without the wisdom and gentle patience of the graying, intelligent doctor who was awaiting me in Saujon. With my dossier before him, Dr. Robert Dubois outlined a simple treatment of rest and relaxation.

"It will do no good," I said wearily. "I'm beaten."

But in the weeks that followed I took the long, solitary walks on country roads that Doctor Dubois suggested, and I found a certain peace in the beauty of nature, which has never left me. There came finally a day when Doctor Dubois assured me that the damage to my nervous system had been repaired. I wanted to believe him, but I could not. The inner turmoil did seem to be gone, but I still had no confidence in myself.

Then one afternoon the doctor asked me to entertain a small group at a holiday celebration in the village. At the thought of facing an audience—any audience—I felt the blood drain from my head. I refused abruptly.

"I know you can do it, Maurice," he said, "but you must

prove it to yourself. This is a good place to start."

I was terrified. What guarantee would there be that my mind would not go blank again?

"There are no guarantees," Doctor Dubois said slowly. And then he went on with words that I can hear as clearly today as thirty-seven years ago: *"Don't be afraid to be afraid."*

I was not sure what he meant until he explained.

"You are afraid to step onto a stage again, so you tell yourself you're finished. But fear is never a reason for quitting; it's only an excuse. When a brave man encounters fear, he admits it—and goes on despite it."

He paused, waiting for my reply. There was a long moment before it came. I would try.

I returned to my room trembling at what lay ahead. I spent hours of torture during the next few days going over the words of the songs I would sing. Then came the final trial: when I stood in the wings of the tiny auditorium, waiting to go on.

For an instant, as panic mounted in me, I was tempted to turn and run. But the doctor's words echoed in my ear: *Don't be afraid to be afraid.* And then suddenly the amateur orchestra was playing my cue, and I moved onstage and began to sing.

Each word I sang and spoke that evening was anguish. But not once did my memory play me tricks. When I walked offstage to the sound of enthusiastic applause, I felt a triumphant joy welling up inside. Tonight I had not conquered fear; I had simply admitted it and gone on despite it. And the scheme had worked.

There was a road back after all. Probably I would never quite regain my old assurance, I told myself, for what had happened once could always happen again. But I could live with it now, and I was determined to prove it.

The path to Paris was not easy. I chose to begin it in Melun, only a few miles from the French capital. I selected a small movie theater, located the startled manager and offered to sing for a sum so low he thought I was joking. When I convinced him that he was helping me toward my comeback, he agreed, and I began a pattern that was to take me to city after city for many weeks. Each performance was an agonizing strain.

"So you are afraid," I would whisper to myself every time. "So what?"

I said that same thing when, at last, I waited for my cue in a magnificent new theater in Paris, willing finally to face the challenge of a Parisian appearance. The curtain fell that night on the beginning of a new world for me. Applause shook the theater. I answered calls for encores until I could physically do no more. Success, which I had once had and lost, was mine again.

Since that night, for almost four decades, I have gone on doing the work I love, playing for audiences everywhere. There have been many moments of fear, for the gentle doctor of Saujon was right: There are no guarantees. But being frightened has never again made me want to quit.

How often has fear been the barricade at which we have all halted in our tracks! We can see what we want beyond, but rather than admit we are afraid and go ahead nonetheless, we so frequently invent excuses and turn back in defeat.

But my own experience has taught me this: If we wait for that perfect moment when all is safe and assured, it may never arrive. Mountains may not be climbed, races won or lasting happiness achieved.

Maurice Chevalier

"Fear of getting caught is understandable, but your fear of water is an obstacle you'll have to overcome."

The Victim's Voice

A frightened woman speaks haltingly to Julie Alban, a thirty-one-year-old deputy prosecutor. Julie nods sympathetically as Lisa describes the night her boyfriend punched her in the eye. It was one blow too many in their turbulent relationship: For the first time, Lisa called the police. Now she must decide whether to speak out against the father of her baby—a man she says she still loves—or go home and forgive him once again.

Julie's advice is firm. "You don't want to stay with your boyfriend unless he gets counseling," she says, leaning forward in her wheelchair. "I'm very familiar with domestic violence. I'm in this chair because my ex-boyfriend tried to kill me."

Jarred out of her own dilemma, Lisa asks, "Oh my God, what happened?"

"I was breaking up with him," Julie answers, "and he shot me in the back."

That bullet shattered Julie's spine, paralyzing her below the waist. But she did not let it shatter her spirit. Instead, she used her anger, pain and frustration as fuel to launch a legal career and a personal crusade against domestic violence. Since joining the Long Beach district attorney's office in 1993, she has prosecuted thousands of domestic violence cases, handling as many as twenty-five a day—mostly on behalf of women battered by their husbands and boyfriends. (Only fifteen of these cases have gone to trial. Most defendants plead no contest, then undergo counseling.) Amazingly, although Julie is a tough advocate, she is not a wild-eyed avenger.

Julie once enjoyed a gilded life among the California elite as the daughter of a wealthy orthopedic surgeon and a former teacher. In the fall of 1987, during her senior year at university, Julie began dating a childhood playmate named Brad. Brad was then twenty-three, a one-time national junior tennis champion who was literally the boy next door.

At first, Julie felt she had found a soul mate. "Brad was so sensitive," she says. "He would cut roses from his parents' garden and bring them to my mother. He adored my father and even asked if he could call him Dad."

But Brad's feelings intensified too quickly for Julie. He began clinging to her oppressively and pressing her for marriage. However, neither she nor her family recognized Brad's behavior as a real obsession. Everyone assumed his feelings would pass.

Just before midnight on June 7, 1988, in the family room of the Albans' hacienda-style home, Julie broke off the affair. "I'll always love you. I'll always be your friend," she told him, "and you'll always be welcomed by my family."

Brad's apartment was forty-five minutes away, so Julie invited him to sleep in the guest room.

At seven o'clock the next morning, she heard her bedroom door open. "I pretended to be asleep. Then I heard this tremendously loud blast, and I was thrown to the floor."

A moment later, Brad pointed the gun at his own chest

and fired. Julie watched in horror and shock, not really aware that she had been wounded. She screamed for her parents, asleep at the other end of the house. When they didn't respond, she dragged herself to the next room, where she called 911.

Finally waking to Julie's screams, her father raced down the hall and gave CPR to the bleeding young man until paramedics arrived. Only then did he realize that Julie, still lying on the floor, was also in danger.

"Dad, I can't move my legs," Julie whimpered. When her father rolled her over, her spinal fluid was seeping out.

Compounding his distress, Julie's father realized his daughter had been shot with his own pistol. He belonged to the county sheriff's reserve, and he had invited Brad to the firing range the day before, afterwards leaving the gun in his unlocked car.

Julie and Brad were rushed to the hospital, where they lay in the emergency room separated by a thin curtain. Julie overheard doctors say Brad would survive. She told her mother through angry sobs, "He's going to walk out of here, and I'm never going to walk again."

Discharged from the hospital two weeks later, Brad was arraigned for attempted murder. His wealthy parents, members of the same Long Beach elite, posted the five-hundred-thousand-dollar bail, and he went home without serving any jail time.

Julie, meanwhile, began physical therapy. "I'd been an active young woman, ready to take on the world," she says. "And here I was, having to learn what to do if I fell in the shower."

After a month, Julie, too, went home. One day, as she lay anguished and immobile, she heard a familiar, repetitive "whup" through her bedroom window.

It was the sound of Brad swatting tennis balls on his private court next door.

At his trial in December 1988, Brad claimed that he had been despondent over gambling debts and had shot Julie accidentally after overdosing on Valium.

Unmoved, the jury convicted him. (Ultimately he served half of a fourteen-year prison term before his release on parole. He has since married.)

Julie last saw Brad in prison eight years ago, behind a glass partition. "I wanted to hear him say 'I'm sorry,'" she says. Instead, Brad told the woman he had paralyzed for life, "The worst part of this is, I know your father hates me."

With Brad behind bars, Julie got on with her life—a very different life than before. She could no longer participate in the usual social activities of her circle of girlfriends—friendships that had been based mostly, as she recalls, on playing tennis and shopping for cocktail dresses. Instead, Julie learned to operate a specially equipped car, although spasms of pain prevented her from driving it. And in 1990, she entered law school, a lifelong dream.

Despite chronic pain—eventually eased by surgery to remove bullet and bone fragments from her spinal canal—Julie fulfilled her ambition. She even took one final exam while recuperating on a gurney, graduating on time in 1993.

After passing the bar exam, Julie applied for a job with the district attorney's office. "I told my future boss that I would be the most determined prosecutor he ever hired," she says, "because I had a personal commitment to victims he wasn't going to find in other people."

About that, even her legal adversaries agree. "The biggest problem the prosecution has in these cases is that most victims recant," says Bill Hoffman, a public defender who has battled Julie in domestic-violence cases.

"But Julie Alban helps these women find a voice."

Lisa appears to be one of them. After speaking with Julie, she agreed to confront her boyfriend in court. He pleaded no contest to misdemeanor domestic violence and was ordered to undergo counseling and perform community service.

"He can't just smack me whenever he doesn't like what I say," Lisa declares, with new firmness and self-respect. "I can't let what happened to Julie happen to me."

Richard Jerome

Barriers or Hurdles?

Children were enthusiastically rehearsing and decorating the rural school for their approaching concert. As I glanced up from my teacher's desk, Patty stood waiting to lodge her urgent request.

"Every year I g-g-g-get to do quiet stuff. The other kids are always in a p-p-p-p-play or something. Talking. This year, I w-w-want to do a p-p-p-p-poem, myself!"

As I looked into those eager eyes, all possible excuses fizzled. Patty's yearning drew from me a promise that in a day or two she would have a special part—a "reciting" part. That promise proved to be very difficult to keep.

None of my resource books had any usable selection. In desperation, I stayed up most of the night writing a poem, carefully avoiding those letters that trip the tongue. It was not great literature, but it was custom tailored to cope with Patty's speech problem.

After only a few brief readings, Patty had memorized all the verses and was prepared to dash through them. Somehow we had to control that rush without shattering her enthusiasm. Day after day, Patty and I plodded through recitals. She meticulously matched her timing to my silent mouthing. She accepted the drudgery, eagerly anticipating her first speaking part.

Concert night found the children in a frenzy of excitement.

In a dither the master of ceremonies came to me, waving his printed program. "There has been a mistake! You have listed Patty for a recitation. That girl can't even say her own name without stuttering." Because there was not time enough for explanations, I brushed his objection aside with, "We know what we are doing."

The entertainment was moving well. As item after item was presented, parents and friends responded with encouraging applause.

When it was time for the questionable recitation, the MC again challenged me, insisting that Patty would embarrass everyone. Losing patience, I snapped, "Patty will do her part. You do yours. Just introduce her number."

I flitted past the curtains and sat on the floor at the foot of the audience. The emcee appeared flustered as he announced, "The next recitation will be by ... um ... Patty Connors." An initial gasp from the audience was followed by strained silence.

The curtain parted to show Patty, radiant, confident.

Those hours of rehearsing took possession of the moment. In perfect control, the little charmer synchronized her words to my silent mouthing below the footlights. She articulated each syllable with controlled clarity, and without a splutter or stammer. With eyes sparkling she made her triumphant bow.

The curtain closed. A hushed silence held the audience. Gradually the stillness gave way to suppressed chuckles, and then to enthusiastic applause.

Utterly thrilled, I floated backstage. My little heroine threw her arms around me and, bubbling with joy, blurted out, "We d-d-d-d-did it!"

Irvine Johnston

A Tribute to Courage

It was the middle of May and spring was in the air. The sun was warm against my face and the smell of wildflowers and cut grass was everywhere. I took a deep breath, which seemed to ease the pain growing in my abdomen. Heavy with child I called for my husband, "Honey, I think it's time to go. Honey . . . Now!" He came out of the garage at a steady pace, calculating each step to keep his balance. I could see worry and excitement fighting for dominance on his face. "Okay, Sweetheart, I'm coming! Just don't move!" Amusement crossed my face for a brief moment only to be replaced with pain as another contraction came. I carefully gained my balance as I rose from the chair, and he ushered me to the car and grabbed our daughter who was playing nearby. As he fumbled with the keys I placed my hand on his; he smiled, took a deep breath and started the car.

He paced up and down the hospital corridors with his daughter, small for the age of three, matching his strides, holding tightly to his strong hand. Glancing at the hospital walls—white and gleaming—the smell of antiseptic assaulted his nose. Nurses in starched white uniforms scurried up and down the halls with an assortment of needles, bandages and bags loaded in their arms.

He hated hospitals and all they represented; antiseptic and impersonal. His daughter looked up at him in quiet anticipation, hoping for a brother. "It won't be long now, Princess," he said understanding her dilemma. "Mommy will be fine," he added as he noticed fear creeping into her eyes.

As they sat in the waiting room he cradled his daughter protectively as his mind drifted back to when he was a small boy, in a place like this . . . for a very different reason. Yet the walls were not antiseptic and white, they were dirty and the rooms smelled of urine and disease. Death ran rampant through the halls taking one child and rejecting another.

It was the years when polio was ravishing children, claiming so many little victims. The nurses began to shut off their emotions just to deal with all they had seen, and the children in some hospitals were on their own, alone and scared. In one of those rooms lay a small frail boy, his eyes clouded by pain and confusion. He didn't understand why he was here and why his legs wouldn't move. He had heard the doctors and nurses talking about this thing called "polio." In all his nine years he had never heard the word before. Somehow it made everyone sad and it hurt children, he knew that much! All the questions that never seemed to be answered, like why his right arm worked and his left one didn't. He wished someone would tell him how long it would be before his left arm would work again; after all, he had baseball practice in the spring.

He heard the nurse outside the door. *Maybe if I shrink myself really small she won't find me!* He knew why she was coming: The daily dipping of the not-so-perfect-hand into a vat of hot wax . . . into the wax . . . let it seep through all the fingers . . . then harden and back in again. She never seemed to notice the tears rolling down his cheeks because the wax was so hot, or the pain in his eyes when they stuck another needle into his bruised flesh. He lay very quiet but to no avail, the nurse turned the covers back, "Okay, let's have the hand." He looked up at her with tears welling in his eyes as she lifted his hand from the bed.

Hours turned into days and days into months. The innocent little boy who first came to the hospital was replaced by a strong-willed fighter with determination and courage to survive. To occupy his time he played a game with the fingers on his good hand . . . up the stomach . . . down the stomach . . . inch by inch so his right hand would be strong. He waited daily for a visit from his parents, but they rarely came. They had other children to care for, and he thought because he wasn't perfect they had discarded him.

"Mr. Robinson, Mr. Robinson," he stirred, fighting to climb out of the darkness that enveloped him. He looked up as his mind cleared, his face drenched in sweat; his body trembled and he clutched his daughter tightly. "Mr. Robinson," the nurse smiled softly as she spoke. "You have a son." He didn't believe it at first. As his daughter giggled and jumped around his feet, he asked the nurse with great reluctance, "Does he have all his fingers and toes?" It was a question he also asked when his daughter was born. He had been told all his life that imperfect people produce imperfect children. The nurse smiled with understanding and replied, "He is healthy, all fingers and toes present and screaming bloody murder!"

He rose slowly and walked to the room where I lay sleeping. Touching my hair with tenderness he whispered, "I love you and I'm so grateful you believed in us. His thoughts drifted to his son, who would be able to play baseball, football and all the things he wasn't able to do.

He thought about his daughter who loved him as he was; to her he was her knight in shining armor.

As the years passed and the children grew, he taught them not to judge a person by the outward appearance, but by what is on the inside. The children knew this too well, from years of growing up around people too quick to judge their father.

It's been fourteen years since he paced the halls of the hospital, awaiting the arrival of his son.

It's Thursday night and we sit in the football stadium with our daughter. The band plays and the cheerleaders scream in unison. We wait for the announcer to call our son's name, "Robinson #10, quarterback." He runs across the field, strong and lithe, looks up in the stands, finds his father and smiles, holds his arm high, thumb in the air and mouths, "For you, Dad."

Victoria Robinson

Riley

We should consider every day lost in which we have not danced at least once.

Friedrich Nietzsche

In March 1995, my wife Teri and twin three-year-old daughters, Riley and Taylor, were living in Los Angeles with my wife's parents. I was working 250 miles away in El Centro, California, driving in on weekends to be with them. My wife was six months pregnant with our son Max. One day Riley complained of a headache and showed flu-like symptoms. Our family pediatrician examined her and told Teri that Riley probably had some childhood virus.

Twenty-four hours later, Riley was in the emergency room at Tarzana Medical Center. X-rays and MRIs revealed a mass at the base of her brain. My wife and I were told Riley's mass was in the brain stem; it had bled and was probably still bleeding. We prepared to say good-bye to our daughter. Then the doctor told us that she needed to be transported to UCLA Medical Center where pediatric neurosurgeons could try to help her. It was her only chance.

When Riley arrived at UCLA, we were met by Dr. Jorge Lazareff. He confirmed the seriousness of Riley's condition, but told us not to give up hope. The fact that Riley was still alive after such massive bleeding meant that she was a fighter.

The first of many surgeries followed, lasting fourteen hours. It involved removing a piece of Riley's skull, separating the two halves of the brain, manipulating the brain stem and then removing the mass. The veins within the mass can rupture at any time, causing a stroke. It is crucial to remove all of the mass to ensure that no additional strokes happen in the future.

Riley had five such surgeries. The staff at UCLA said it was a miracle that she was still with us.

During that first surgery, the doctors manipulated the brain stem, disconnecting it from the rest of the brain. This causes the brain to lose its ability to talk to the body. Riley lost all motor skills; for a while she needed a respirator just to breathe. Most of the doctors told us that we should not expect much from Riley and to be thankful she was even alive. However, Doctor Lazareff said that Riley might prove the medical establishment wrong again.

When we finally took Riley home, she could not eat, walk, talk or do even the basic movements expected of a newborn. My wife, Teri, worked daily with Riley, while I returned to work. Each weekend, when I returned to L.A., I witnessed a new miracle. With the love only a mother could give, Riley learned how to eat, talk and move her limbs again. During this period, after seeing a dance recital on television, Riley announced that she wanted to be a ballerina when she grew up. Riley's spirit was dreaming of dancing even before she had relearned to walk.

Then we received news that a recent MRI had shown more of the mass. In August, Riley once again went to UCLA. The single operation that would remove the remaining mass turned into seven more surgeries and five weeks in the hospital.

Once again, Riley beat the odds and survived the surgeries. Once again, her motor skills were sacrificed to reach the mass by manipulating the brain stem during the operation. Once again, she woke up only able to communicate her pain with her eyes. But once again, Riley did not give up.

By now I had relocated my job back to L.A., and I saw firsthand her daily struggle to do the simple things we all take for granted.

As I write this, Riley is a beautiful six-year-old girl. For the past three years, she has fought many battles and has gotten the upper hand on a war that most adults would have lost long ago. As with all wars, there are emotional and psychological wounds besides the physical damage. Yet Riley's laughter rings throughout our home every day. Physically she still battles some facial paralysis and has some vision problems, both of which are expected to improve with therapy. Yet, in June of this year, Riley's dream came true—she performed in her first ballet recital.

Jeffrey Weinstein

[EDITORS' NOTE: *Riley's amazing progress has inspired a new research foundation at UCLA headed by Dr. Lazareff called "Kidz 'n Motion." This foundation studies the brain's plasticity and searches for medical ways to improve disabilities caused by traumas to the brain.*]

You Can Beat the Odds and Be a Winner, Too

Bury him in the snows of Valley Forge, and you have a George Washington.

Raise him in abject poverty and you have an Abraham Lincoln.

Subject him to bitter religious prejudice, and you have a Disraeli.

Spit on him and crucify him, and you have Jesus Christ.

Label him "too stupid to learn," and you have a Thomas Edison.

Tell her she's too old to start painting at eighty, and you have a Grandma Moses.

Have him or her born black in a society filled with racial discrimination, and you have a Booker T. Washington, Harriet Tubman, Marian Anderson, George Washington Carver or Martin Luther King Jr.

Make him the first child to survive in a poor Italian family of eighteen children, and you have an Enrico Caruso.

Afflict him with periods of depression so severe that he cut off his own ear, and you have a Vincent van Gogh.

Tell her in the late 1800s and early 1900s that only men can be scientists, and you have a Madame Curie, who eventually won two Nobel Prizes—one for physics and the other for chemistry.

Tell a young boy who loved to sketch and draw that he has no talent, and you have a Walt Disney.

Take a crippled child whose only home he ever knew was an orphanage, and you have a James E. West, who became the first chief executive of the Boy Scouts of America.

Make him a second fiddle in an obscure South American orchestra, and you have a Toscanini.

Abigail Van Buren

Superman Learns How to Ride

It was the summer of 1967, and the moment was nearing when I would unlatch my training wheels and learn to ride a bike.

My family owned a humble roadside motel called the Bonaire in the tranquil, picturesque town of Flat Rock, North Carolina. We lived in the basement below the motel's lobby, where I shared a room with my older sister. My parents prayed for those nights when our neon Vacancy sign would no longer cast its orange glow across the empty country highway.

For an adventurous little boy unconcerned with matters like occupancy rates, it was a time to put my overactive imagination to good use. I shuffled along as the bookish Clark Kent, with an old straw hat, pipe-cleaner glasses and ragged gray overcoat. Then, at the first hint of something amiss, I disappeared into the motel phone booth and emerged moments later with a red towel hanging from the collar of my dirty blue T-shirt and an ironed-on S boldly emblazoned across my boy-sized chest.

"This is a job for Superman!" I would cry out as I flew to meet imaginary dangers that threatened the world.

"Hey, Superman, when are you going to learn to ride a bike?" the neighborhood kids would taunt as they rolled past. "The Man of Steel still uses training wheels!" they teased.

As I watched them ride away, I realized I was being left behind. To claim my place among their ranks, I needed to cast off my training wheels and learn to ride with the big kids. I enlisted my father's help.

"Okay, I'm going to let go, and you just remember to balance," Dad counseled as he rolled me across the lawn. We were on take number ten—I had already made nine falls onto the grassy field behind the motel. After each mishap, my father would take hold of my bicycle seat and we'd begin again. He was the engine, and I was the pilot. He'd propel me across the grassy runway and then let go. I would fly solo—careening through the meadow, holding my breath in nervous anticipation as the grass rolled beneath my wheels.

Suddenly I was riding! This time I had it! I dared to grin as my father's shouts of encouragement faded into the background. My smile widened. Victory was mine.

You are going to fall. The thought was at first a whisper and then grew louder and more convincing until I believed it must be true. After all, I had always fallen before. Why should this time be any different? My elation whooshed out of me like air out of a pricked balloon. Dread gripped me, and my confidence faltered. Sure enough, I tumbled to the grass.

"You almost had it," Dad said, catching his breath. "You listened to fear and you fell."

"I quit," I snapped, trying to stave off the tears of frustration. "I don't wanna learn to ride."

So I went back to my world of Clark Kent and Superman, but somehow it didn't feel the same. The intrepid reporter had left a story unfinished. The Caped Crusader had given up. And each time I swooped through the backyard en route to foil another bank robbery, I saw my bicycle leaning against the garage door, reminding me that there was work left undone.

Then one afternoon, I glanced over at my bike and a peculiar notion came to mind: I could do it. I was going to ride my bike this very day.

When I boldly grasped the handlebars, fear came again—closing its fingers around my insides. I quickly let go. Maybe tomorrow. But then, all of a sudden, I heard the shouts and laughter of the other children as they rode their bikes through the neighborhood. If they could do it, so could I!

I gripped the handlebars with renewed determination and pushed off, wobbling as I struggled for balance. Then I took a deep breath and began to pedal. I gathered momentum as I started up the driveway and, with my Superman cape flapping in the breeze, I rounded the front of the motel at full speed just as my father stepped out of the lobby door.

"Look, Dad! I'm riding!" I exclaimed.

He smiled and waved as I took a turn up the dirt road to join my friends at play.

The next morning I found my training wheels in the garbage can where my father had tossed them the previous afternoon. Superman had beaten an enemy called "fear," and once again the world was a safer, happier place.

Robert Tate Miller

A Father's Advice

Once I found a pink moth. Perhaps someone will tell me there is no such thing as a pink moth. There may be no such thing as a flying horse, or a golden calf, but I say once I found a pink moth.

The front door of the large, three-story house where I grew up was protected on the outside by four panels of windowpanes, nearly like a greenhouse. Before we entered the house, we had to turn into this small enclosure of glass, wipe our feet, turn the doorknob and step into the front hallway.

I found my pink moth in this enclosure. It is here that birds often took a wrong turn and flapped their wings in a rush of feathers and noise against the glass, trying to break through the invisible barrier. Here, also, spiderwebs collected, and bees buzzed angrily against the glass as they, too, were caught in the trap.

One morning—perhaps I was eight or ten—I stepped out through the front door. I noticed another moth was desperately trying to find its way out of the enclosure.

Each time I found a bee, a bird or a moth trapped in the porch vestibule, I caught it and let it go. But I noticed this insect was a color I had never seen before on a moth:

pink—completely pink. I caught the moth, held it in my cupped hands.

What does a boy do with a pink moth? I stepped back into the house, found a shoebox, filled it with grass and a soda cap of water and placed my moth in the box.

It died, of course. Things cannot be held too long. They need to be set free. I threw the shoebox, the soda cap and the grass into the garbage can. I buried the moth in the garden. I feel as though I am always being pulled between wanting to hold on to things and wanting to let them go.

I remember the afternoon Karen learned how to ride her bicycle alone for the first time. We began in the early fall, Karen and I. I took her training wheels off, but she insisted that I grasp the handlebars and the seat as we walked around the court.

"I'll just let go for a second, Karen."

"No!" she insisted.

Perhaps Karen will be a lawyer someday, or a singer. Perhaps she will invent something, make a discovery, give birth to her own daughter. I thought about these things as we wiggled and rattled our way around the block. It didn't take her long to understand how to turn the pedals with her feet. As I held on to the bicycle, Karen's head and dark hair were just to the right of my cheek. She always looked down toward the front of the bicycle, calling out suggestions or laughing a bit.

After a few weeks, Karen was comfortable enough with my letting the handlebars go, but I still had to clasp the rear of the seat.

"Don't let go, Daddy."

Halloween. Thanksgiving. The leaves disappeared. We spent less and less time practicing. Wind. Cold. Winter. I hung Karen's bicycle on a nail in the rear of the garage.

Christmas. One of Karen's favorite gifts that year was

five pieces of soap in the shape of little shells that her mother had bought.

New Year's Eve. Snow. High fuel bills. And then a sudden warm spell.

"Roe?" I said as we woke up. "Do you hear that bird? It's a cardinal. It's been singing for the past ten minutes. Listen." Roe listened. I listened. The children were downstairs watching television.

After I showered, dressed and ate breakfast, I found Karen in the garage trying to unhook her bicycle. In this last week of January, when it is usually too cold for the children to be outside on their bicycles, it was nearly sixty degrees. I walked into the garage and lifted the bicycle off the nail.

"I love my bicycle, Daddy."

She hopped on as I pushed her across the crushed stones of our driveway to the street. I gave her a slight shove. "Let go, Daddy!" And Karen simply wobbled, shook, laughed and pedaled off as I stood alone watching her spin those wheels against the blacktop.

Einstein spoke about time, about the speed of light and objects moving beside one another. I wanted to run to Karen, hold the seat of her bicycle, hold on to her handlebars, have her dark hair brush against my cheeks. Instead I kept shouting, "Keep pedaling, Karen! Keep pedaling!" And then I applauded.

There is no use holding on to a pink moth—or your daughter. They will do just fine on their own. Just set them free.

Christopher de Vinck

Highsights

There are some things you learn best in calm, and some in storm.

Willa Cather

Cessna planes flew me and my climbing team, along with overstuffed packs and sleds, across the Alaska range and onto the Kahiltna Glacier, the base camp of Mt. McKinley.

That day, we worked to carve a camp out of the harsh snow and ice of the glacier. Even in McKinley's extreme cold, the intense heat of the sun reflecting off the ice burned my eyes through my goggles.

When the snow walls were built and tents were set up, we sat around our gas stove feeling the temperature drop fifty degrees as the sun sank behind the mountains. Sam, my climbing partner, took my finger and began pointing it at prominent parts of the West Buttress Trail. Then I tried to point on my own towards the summit, but Sam only laughed and said, "Higher!" So I pointed higher and higher until I imagined I was pointing at the sun. "There," he said, "there's the summit of McKinley." For the first time I was afraid of what we'd undertaken.

Afterwards, we sat listening to the nightly weather report given by Base Camp Annie and other local stations. On one, we heard the voices of two Spanish climbers croaking their location to a rescue party. That morning, they had pushed for the summit but had been turned back by high winds and whiteout conditions. Now, ten hours later, they lay in their tent, suffering from high-altitude edema. The next morning, we learned that one of the climbers had died. I worried that this tragedy, on our first night, might be a bad omen.

Sam and I asked ourselves whether we were putting our lives at unnecessary risk by attempting this climb. I thought back to when I had begun training more than a year ago, by running trails with my guide dog in the desert. One day I had tripped over a cactus, landing on my hand. I needed a couple of stitches. The next day, I showed my fifth-grade class my bandaged hand and told them what happened. One very brave little girl stood up and asked, "Mr. Weihenmayer, if you fell down in the desert, how do you expect to climb that big mountain?" I didn't yet have an answer, but I knew within a year, I would have to!

For the next year, we trained by running up stairs in the tallest building in Phoenix with sixty-pound packs on our backs, going on many training climbs as a team to Mt. Rainier, Long's Peak and Mt. Humphrey, and reading several Braille books on McKinley.

Now I said, "Sam, we've come a long way in a year. We've made mistakes, but we've learned from them. We've taken risks, but they've been calculated ones. We've solved problems and compensated for all the things that could go wrong on the mountain. We've worked well as a team. We've prepared all we can."

Trying to fall asleep that night, I remembered hard lessons learned. For example, on our team's second training climb, we had worked our way up a steep ridge. It was getting dark and cold. I was assigned to set up the tents. But I found that, with my thick layers of gloves on, I couldn't feel the intricate sleeves and loops of the tent. Each time I took the gloves off to orient myself, tiny splinters of ice pricked my hands and they went instantly numb. Finally, I had to have a teammate set up the tent for me.

Frustrated and embarrassed, I made a promise to myself. The things I couldn't do—and there were many— I would let go, but the things that I could do—and there were also many—I would learn to do well.

Later, back in Phoenix in hundred-degree weather, I went often to a field near my school. With my thick gloves on, I worked on setting up the tent and breaking it down again. I wanted to contribute to the team, carry my share. I wanted the team to be able to put their lives in my hands, as I would put mine in theirs.

When I decided to attempt McKinley, I knew the risks. Risk is like the next hold on a rock face: you reach for it expecting that it's there, hoping that it's there, but ready to find the next hold if it's not!

The greatest risk I ever took was deciding, at sixteen, to rock climb. I went as part of a recreational program for the blind. The idea was that blind people, given the opportunity to challenge themselves, would become more independent and successful adults.

I had enough faith in myself to give it a try. Through trial and error, I found that I could hang from a hold with one hand while my other hand scanned for the next hold, then hang from that while scanning for the next. The technique was tedious, but I managed to work my way up my first rock face.

When I sat on top, my feet dangling over the edge, the heat of the rocks beneath my hands and the sound of space all around me, I knew that I would never catch a pop-fly in the seventh game of the World Series, and I would never drive a car in the Indy 500, but I could get to the top of almost anything I set my mind to—although I might have to get there a little differently.

Like risk taking, I've also learned how to create systems and strategies to compensate for my blindness. Before the McKinley climb, I worked on organizing and reorganizing my pack, memorizing where each piece of gear was stowed. On the mountain, losing a sock or glove could mean losing a toe or finger, and losing an ice axe or shovel could mean losing the life of a teammate. I also had to figure out how to follow the team, even in high winds when I couldn't hear their footsteps. I found that two ski poles were the answer. With my poles, I could scan the trail and stay almost exactly in Chris's, my leader's, footsteps.

One day, on the steepest part of the mountain, I couldn't seem to catch my breath. At 16,000 feet, a climber has only half of the oxygen of a person at sea level—a condition called pressure breath. Chris said, "You've got to breathe," but I couldn't seem to find my rhythm. My pack and sled seemed heavier than on other days; the hip straps cut sharply into my sides and kept slipping, putting more weight on my shoulders. I found myself wondering how far I could push myself before I collapsed in the snow. I feared that I had made a huge mistake in attempting this mountain, and I seriously doubted that I had the strength within me to reach the top. Somehow, though, I silenced the fear, concentrating on my breathing and the placement of each step.

That day I found the meaning of the climb: to show me that, with enough preparation, we are all capable of pushing ourselves far beyond our perceptions of our own limitations—even farther beyond those that others set for us!

On day fifteen, we reached our summit camp and hiked

out to a ledge that overlooked our starting point, the Kahiltna base camp, ten thousand feet below. It was hard to imagine how far we had come.

That evening began a five-day storm that blew wind above us at more than one hundred miles per hour. By the fifth day, we were running out of food and fuel, forced to contemplate the grim possibility that we might never reach the summit. Chris reminded us, "We don't decide when to climb a mountain. The mountain decides!"

The next morning, the sky was clearer. We decided to climb just to the saddle between the north and south summits, where we could reevaluate the weather. We left at 6:00 A.M., wading through a field of thigh-deep snow. I was sheltered from the minus-twenty-degree temperature by so many layers of polypropylene, fleece, down and Gortex. The howling wind and the frigid temperatures rendered my senses of hearing and smell useless, so that my only contact with the earth was the metal bite of my crampons in the deep snow.

When we reached the saddle, the weather seemed to be holding, so we went on to Pig Hill, the last "grunt" before the summit. Halfway up, Chris said, "I think we might make it." When we crested Pig Hill, the summit seemed very close. I didn't realize the hardest part of the entire climb was yet to come—the summit ridge. The ridge is two feet wide, with a one-thousand-foot drop on one side and a nine-thousand-foot drop on the other. The good news was that it didn't really matter which side one fell off of.

Chris said, "Boys, if you fall here, you'll drag us all off the side of the mountain."

I was nervous, taking each step slowly and carefully, knowing that the mountain would not tolerate any carelessness. I was concentrating so hard that I was taken by surprise when someone yelled over the wind, "Congratulations! You're standing on the top of North America."

All of us put our arms around each other and stood as a team on the 20,300-foot summit of Mt. McKinley. As we unfurled the American Foundation for the Blind flag, I thought about this magnificent adventure that had begun as a dream more than a year ago. Now it was real.

An hour before we summitted, we radioed out to Base Camp Annie who radioed in turn to a small air strip where my family waited. Now, as I stood on the summit, my dad, two brothers and girlfriend, Ellen, circled above me in a Cessna, sharing our joy.

We waved our ski poles and cheered at the plane as they flew overhead. I asked Sam if he thought my family would know which one was me, since we all wore identical jackets and hats.

"I think they will," he laughed. "You're the only one waving your ski pole in the wrong direction."

Erik Weihenmayer

Ode to the Champions

Who are these people—
These doers of deeds,
These dreamers of dreams
Who make us believe?

Who are these people
Who still win the day—
When the odds are against them
And strength fades away?

These people are champions,
For they never give in.
A heart beats within them
That is destined to win.

They follow their dreams
Though the journey seems far,
From the top of a mountain
They reach out to a star.

And when they have touched it—
When their journey is done—

They give to us hope
From the victories they won.

So here's to the champions—
To all their great deeds.
They follow their hearts
And become winners indeed.

Tom Krause

Ask Creatively

The chief buyer for a thriving company was particularly inaccessible to salespeople. You didn't call *him*. He called *you*. On several occasions when salespeople managed to get into his office, they were summarily tossed out.

One saleswoman finally broke through his defenses. She sent him a homing pigeon with her card attached to one leg. On the card she had written, "If you want to know more about our product, just throw our representative out the window."

The Best of Bits & Pieces

Dilbert, reprinted by permission of United Feature Syndicate, Inc.

Never Say Quit

The highest reward for a man's toil is not what he gets for it, but what he becomes by it.

John Ruskin

I was fresh out of college and had just started my teaching and coaching career at St. Bernard's, the same high school I had attended. Compared to the schools that surrounded us, we were rather small, with two to three thousand students. My first year I served as an assistant coach with our football and basketball teams; during the spring, I was in charge of the track program.

We had a phenomenal year. Our football team won ten games, finishing the season undefeated. Our basketball team won twenty-one games, losing only five. We emerged as conference champions in both sports.

Being young and naïve, I didn't recognize what extraordinary athletes we had that year. By the next fall, fourteen of our former students would be playing college football—four with major scholarships. Two others would be running track for Division I universities. In twenty-five years of coaching after that, I never encountered a more gifted group.

Yet the student who made the greatest impression on all of us wasn't one of these promising young men. Physically he was as different from them as a donkey from a thoroughbred. His name was Bobby Colson, and his impact will last the rest of my life.

Bobby was the freshman brother of our star two-mile runner, Mark Colson. Early in the season, Bobby stopped me in the school hallway. At five-three and 175 pounds, he looked like the model for the Pillsbury Dough Boy. He told me that he'd been doing some serious thinking about joining our track team and believed he could make an important contribution. He added that he didn't know in what events he could help us, but felt confident that he had something to offer. I was impressed by his presentation and self-confidence.

Given his physique, the logical role for Bobby was that of a "weight man"—an athlete who specializes in shot-put and discus throwing. We quickly encountered a setback, however: Even though Bobby's 175 pounds was a lot of weight for a freshman, he didn't have an ounce of visible muscle. Not only was he unable to put (throw) the shot, he could barely pick it up.

Undaunted, Bobby proceeded with me to the discus area. A discus is considerably lighter than a shot, so immediately we were off to a good start. I coached him in the proper grip, delivery and release. Things seemed to be going fairly well. On command, Bobby would assume a wide stance, bend his knees, spread his fingers, bring his arm back and fourth three times, and let fly.

That is, *most* of the time he'd let fly. Every few tries, though, he'd forget to let go, or he'd start to run right out of the circle, holding the discus in front of him in his pudgy little mitt. Whenever he actually released the discus, he would quickly spread out the measuring tape to see if his throw challenged the freshman-sophomore school record of 131 feet. Finding he had more than 110 feet to go didn't seem to faze him.

We decided that Bobby might see greater results by adding the spinning technique to his discus endeavors. We stayed after the official close of practice to review the required footwork dozens of times. I even drew footprints on the circle to show him exactly where to step. Bobby was incredibly persistent and extremely coachable. I began to wish that all my athletes shared his attitude.

The moment came to give the new technique a try. It was a sight to behold. Once Bobby got to spinning, he resembled a human centrifuge about to explode. He was still twirling when the discus flew out of his hand and landed twenty-seven feet in the opposite direction from where we'd intended. After I got Bobby to stop turning, he staggered around like a wounded water buffalo for a few minutes, looking as if he might throw up. Then he rushed to measure his latest effort—that's how I know it was exactly twenty-seven feet.

Bobby felt very encouraged by this outcome, but I didn't think the season was long enough to get his technique to the point where we weren't endangering lives— his own included. After a bit of smooth talking on my part, Bobby agreed that we should investigate another event. The long jump seemed like a possibility; the only problem was, Bobby couldn't make it to the landing pit from the takeoff board. We quickly eliminated the pole vault, high jump, hurdles and triple jump. Bobby wasn't blessed with a lot of foot speed, so sprints and relays also went by the wayside. When we ended the session, I was at a loss what to suggest for the following day's practice.

As it turned out, Bobby made his decision without me.

The next morning he informed me that he was going to be a two-miler like his brother, Mark. I knew Bobby idolized Mark, who not only was an outstanding two-miler but also an outstanding person and team leader.

I admired Bobby's enthusiasm, but to myself I questioned whether the two-mile race was a good choice. Yet Bobby was determined, and for the next two weeks, he painfully but gamely struggled through his workouts.

Our first meet was a "triangular" between St. Basil's, Notre Dame and ourselves. In those days, the two-mile race was the first running event at each meet. Because of the length of the event, both the frosh-soph and varsity teams ran at the same time; the younger runners wore their shirts inside out to identify their level. Field events all started at the same time as well.

So here we were, with the two-mile well underway. At the varsity level we were set to finish first and third. Mark Colson launched another memorable season by setting a new conference record.

Then there was Bobby. Every team has one or two very slow frosh-soph runners, but next to Bobby, they all looked like sprinters. When all the other runners had finished, Bobby still had three laps to go. The host team started putting hurdles on the track for the next event. I yelled at them to leave lane one open, so Bobby could finish the race.

As Bobby completed his first of his remaining laps, I could see tears on his cheeks. I didn't realize it, but several boys from the other squads had started calling him names and making fun of him. Only our high jumper, Pat Linden, knew what was happening. He left the high-jump area and stationed himself at the far curve to shout words of encouragement to Bobby.

Meanwhile, other athletes continued to ridicule Bobby, shouting at him to get off the track. Bobby was crying more noticeably now, but he kept going. A few more of our varsity team members noticed Pat's absence and went to join him in urging Bobby on.

During my many years of coaching since then, I've seen top athletes walk off the track when they knew they weren't going to win a race. Usually they developed a pulled hamstring or something of that nature—though often I thought the injury was more to the spirit than to the body. Bobby, in contrast, never once considered leaving that two-mile race, grueling as it plainly was for him. Once he started, quitting was not an option.

After he finished the race, Bobby went from event to event encouraging his teammates. When one of our athletes took a first place, Bobby got more excited than the winner.

A few days later, we had our second triangular meet, with Holy Cross and St. Patrick's. The scenario in the two-mile was much the same as before, except this time all our athletes left their respective areas to urge Bobby on. Imagine: Our whole team lined up around the track, clapping and cheering for Bobby as tears coursed down his face. It was really a moving sight to see.

By our third triangular meet, at Bergon High School, word had spread about Bobby. This time our team members weren't the only ones rooting for him—all the other teams were there, too, filling the straightaways as well as the curves.

At the end of the season, the varsity team purchased a large trophy for Bobby and had it inscribed: To Bobby Colson—Our Most Courageous Athlete, St. Bernard's Track Team 1968.

Bobby had been right when he told me that he felt he could make a significant contribution to our track efforts. He had joined a good team and made it into a great family. His example helped us all to understand that talent is God given, and we should be thankful, but conceit is self given, and we should be careful.

We didn't find out until late that summer, but Bobby Colson had a rare form of leukemia. He died the following fall.

Bob Hoppenstedt
Submitted by Kathy Jones

Struggle and Victory

*Brothers and sisters help each other along, first
up backyard hills, and later up life long climbs.*

William Bennett

In a small farmhouse fifteen miles from the nearest
town, my mother gave birth to her fourth child—a fragile
boy, with a fair complexion and a fretful cry.

Troy was an unusually restless baby, with a delicate
digestive system. Feedings were a struggle, as my parents
desperately tried one formula after another in an attempt
to nourish the frail child. At four months, Troy weighed
less than he had at birth.

The rural community had no sophisticated hospital, no
pediatric specialist, no support groups. Only a tiny bed in
a three-room house and a country doctor with limited
knowledge of infant disease. My parents realized something was tragically wrong with their son, but didn't
know what.

Every effort was made to make Troy comfortable; every
remedy, regardless of how bizarre, was tried. Each day the
baby grew weaker. The local doctor suggested that a

specialist in a nearby city might give my parents answers to their puzzling questions.

Arrangements were hastily made. The fifty-mile drive became a journey of hope—the only hope—for the almost lifeless baby in my mother's arms.

Upon arriving, Troy was whisked away for a series of tests. Hours seemed endless as my parents waited in silence, lost in their thoughts—and fears.

On the third day, the doctor called them into his office. His message was bleak. Their seven-month-old son was a victim of Down's syndrome. He was also suffering from an enlarged heart, thyroid disorder and serious digestive problems. He wasn't likely to live; if he did, he would be severely mentally retarded.

My parents stood rigid, listening to the doctor as he spoke of the baby's uncertain future—and of the alternatives. They moved closer together, groping for each other's hands. In their minds, there was no alternative to consider.

"I am not a perfect man," my father said. "How can I demand a perfect child?"

"We will help him do the best he can with the abilities he has," my mother added, "the same as we have helped his brothers and sister."

Medication was prescribed to relieve much of Troy's suffering. Soon parents and child were huddled together in the front seat of the car, driving home.

Troy responded well to the medication and his weight gradually increased. The crises of the first months faded.

There were no small accomplishments in Troy's development. Each achievement was recognized and celebrated by the entire family with the fanfare of the Academy Awards. As he grew, he was encouraged to explore. Colorful objects were placed within his reach. His ears were constantly entertained with simple words that were easy to pronounce. Special handles were installed on the window sills to help him stand on his unsteady legs, so that he could watch the older children at play outside. Troy rewarded the family for their care and encouragement with angelic smiles.

Shortly before his second birthday, Troy became ill with erysipelas, a dreadfully painful disease that causes the skin to become blotchy, swollen and red. He whimpered while my parents took turns bathing his feverish body. My mother sang lullabies and stroked his flushed face for hours in an effort to soothe him. He hovered near death for weeks, then months.

Gradually Troy's swollen hands returned to normal and the hours of restless wakefulness gave way to peaceful sleep. Six months of illness came to an end. The baby had bravely fought and won another crucial battle.

During this time my mother became pregnant with me. I was born in the same farmhouse as Troy, with my grandmother, a neighbor and the country doctor in attendance.

From babyhood, Troy was my constant companion. As I learned to walk, he, too, took his first faltering steps. Repeating sounds I made became a game with Troy, which thrilled my parents as they strained their ears to hear an actual word.

Occasionally we were given a treat, usually a large red apple. We would squeal with delight as my mother held the colorful fruit just beyond our grasp, patiently repeating the word "apple."

Once during this familiar ritual, Troy's eyes fixed intensely on the luscious fruit, and he pronounced his first word: "apple." Mother quickly summoned my father from the field. The older children hurried in from their chores. Troy was on stage and he knew it. Again and again he said the word, clapping his hands together, as the family cheered him on.

After that his vocabulary increased slowly and steadily. Although he was never able to speak clearly or distinctly, and his sentences were often slow and incomplete, his halting words eloquently conveyed thoughts and ideas that were uniquely his own.

For the next few years, Troy's and my life was happy and rather normal. We spent our days making mud pies, riding stick horses and cutting paper dolls out of old catalogs. We shared responsibility for simple chores around the house, and we were punished equally for our frequent mischief.

Our formal schooling started when I was five. The school board had decided Troy should attend public school. Together we walked three miles to our first day of school, stopping along the way to inspect a variety of bugs crossing our path.

The children in the community had grown up realizing Troy was different, and from most of the students he received gentle affection. I was a fierce protector of my brother and he accepted my being his keeper without complaining.

The teachers were generous with their time and attention. Troy was issued learning material along with the rest of the class, but he usually spent his time coloring in a special book. His citizenship was excellent. He was quiet and obedient in the classroom, and cheerful and cooperative on the playground. Each year he was promoted with a straight-A report card. He loved being praised for his outstanding achievements.

Soon sports and boys became big things in my life. I reveled in my new social world—a world in which my brother sadly could not belong.

My parents saw a need for change. My graduation from high school was the beginning of the transition. A week of careful planning went into a ceremony that would take place in our living room, "graduating" my brother from high school.

Mother drove fifty miles to buy a class ring at a pawn shop. Troy was delighted, sporting the ring proudly on his finger as he tried on my graduation cap and gown.

We were in a dilemma, wondering how to explain why we were having his ceremony at home, when everyone else had theirs at school. My mother was inspired to pray for rain. Sure enough the following morning rain drenched the dirt roads, making them impassable.

With a sigh of relief, Dad announced, "The graduation must go on."

Mother dressed Troy in my cap and gown. The family assembled in the living room.

I played "Amazing Grace," the only song I knew how to play on the piano. Troy marched in and stood proudly in front of my father, who was dressed in his Sunday best.

Daddy made a speech about Troy's great accomplishments and then handed him his diploma—a white sheet of paper with his name on it, rolled up and tied with a ribbon. Troy shook Daddy's hand, then quickly moved the tassel from one side of the cap to the other.

We all stood, giving thunderous applause. Mother's eyes brimmed with tears as she drew Troy into her arms. How proud he was!

No longer a student, Troy would soon be given more responsibility at home. For the rest of his life, he would relish his new role as an adult and perform any work he was asked to do with meticulous care.

Looking back on that faraway living-room graduation, I remember being filled with awe and joy at the amazing journey we had shared with Troy which had brought us to that moment: from his physically afflicted infancy when he twice almost died, to a babyhood full of challenges most families never dream of, to an education that taught many of his teachers and fellow students their greatest lessons in courage and humanity.

Through it all, Troy's capacity to love was boundless; the tenderness and kindness he demonstrated to everyone he encountered was unsurpassed; and the wide-eyed innocence with which he met the world never wavered.

Lila Jones Cathey

Mothers of Disabled Children

Most women become mothers by accident, some by choice, a few by social pressures and a couple by habit.

This year, nearly one hundred thousand women will become mothers of handicapped children. Did you ever wonder how these mothers of handicapped children are chosen?

Somehow visualize God hovering over Earth selecting his instruments for propagation with great care and deliberation. As he observes, he instructs his angels to make notes in a giant ledger.

"Armstrong, Beth: son, patron saint, Matthew. Forest, Marjorie: daughter, patron saint, Cecelia.

"Rudledge, Carrie: twins, patron saint . . . give her Gerard. He's used to profanity."

Finally, he passes a name to an angel and smiles. "Give her a blind child."

The angel is curious. "Why this one, God? She's so happy."

"Exactly," says God. "Could I give a child with a handicap to a mother who does not know laughter? That would be cruel."

"But has she patience?" asks the angel.

"I don't want her to have too much patience, or she will drown in a sea of self-pity and despair. Once the shock and resentment wear off, she'll handle it."

"But, Lord, I don't think she even believes in you."

God smiles. "No matter. I can fix that. This one is perfect. She has just enough selfishness."

The angel gasps. "Selfishness? Is that a virtue?"

God nods. "If she can't separate herself from the child occasionally, she'll never survive. Yes, here is a woman whom I will bless with a child less than perfect. She doesn't realize it yet, but she is to be envied. She will never take for granted a spoken word. She will never consider a step ordinary. When her child says 'Momma' for the first time, she will be present at a miracle and know it! When she describes a tree or a sunset to her blind child, she will see it as few people ever see my creations.

"I will permit her to see clearly the things I see—ignorance, cruelty, prejudice—and allow her to rise above them. She will never be alone. I will be at her side every minute of every day of her life, because she is doing my work as surely as she is here by my side."

"And what about her patron saint?" asks the angel, pen poised in midair.

God smiles. "A mirror will suffice."

Erma Bombeck

7

ON
ATTITUDE

My company mascot is the bumblebee.
Because of its tiny wings and heavy body,
aerodynamically the bumblebee shouldn't be
able to fly. But the bumblebee doesn't know
that, so it flies anyway.

Mary Kay Ash

Third-Place Winner

His head lowered, an exhausted but determined young man chanted over and over to himself, "You can do this. You can do it, you can do it, you can do it." These words, spoken as much for encouragement as for confirmation, found a listening heart. Without fail they drove one foot in front of the other, up into the air and then down—again and again and again. The boy watched intently as one by one, his new sneakers methodically slapped the asphalt slowly passing beneath him. It was a very tired patter. Looking up, the youth wiped his brow and searched for a glimpse of the finish line. "It's somewhere up there," he told himself matter-of-factly.

It was far off in the distance. Even so, Chris Burke had his heart set on reaching it.

With great effort, he, too, crossed the finish line. By the time he did, photographers and reporters had already gathered around the young man who had taken first place. Cameras zoomed in and flashed; microphones stretched forward to absorb the winner's words.

With a smile that stretched from ear to ear, Chris jubilantly bounded over and proudly stood next to the winner. He wrapped his arm around the young man his own age—someone he had never met prior to this event. Beaming, Chris patiently waited for the reporter to complete his interview with the victor—as patiently as he could in a moment that held so much excitement for him. When at last the reporter turned to the camera to make concluding remarks, Chris instantly stepped forward and thrust out his hand to receive a congratulatory handshake. "Oh, boy!" Chris shouted, unable to restrain his obvious joy. "I just want to tell you what a thrill this was and how happy I am to have come in third!" The reporter had little choice but to respond to the charismatic and enthusiastic athlete, wanting his turn at recognition.

"Yes . . . tell us about it," stammered the startled reporter good-naturedly.

"Wow!" said Chris. "Thank you for asking me to be interviewed. This is great! Just great. Well, I'm just very happy to be here. It's such a great honor. Of course, I finished in third place. Third place, not bad! Not bad, huh?" He didn't need an answer to his question, and he didn't wait for one. Instead, he turned his animated face for all the world to see—this was national television—and with more joy than I can remember from anyone, he said, "Thank you all for sharing in this very special time with me. It's time to celebrate!" With that, Chris turned, and ran over to line up for hugs and handshakes alongside the winner.

Chris was fourteen years old at the time. This was the Special Olympics.

There were only three runners in the entire race.

Bettie B. Youngs
Excerpted from Gifts of the Heart

[CONTRIBUTOR'S NOTE: *To appreciate the full significance of Chris's story one must recognize Chris has Down's syndrome, a condition caused by a gene malfunction. Children with Down's syndrome are born with one too many chromosomes, resulting in an uncanny similarity in appearance, thwarted development and a ceiling on potential. Since IQ peaks out at around 75, capability and ability are severely limited—or so it was once thought. When Chris was born in 1965, physicians recommended that parents place babies with Down's syndrome in institutions, the majority of which did little more than offer physical caretaking.*

Most of the world now knows Chris Burke not only from his unforgettable interview years ago, but also as the charismatic and gifted television actor and star of the television series, Life Goes On. *The show enjoyed four years of excellent ratings.*]

Challenger Baseball

Sports don't build character—they reveal it!

Heywood Hale Broun

In Little League baseball, there is a division known as the Challenger Division, for developmentally disabled youngsters. As a clinical psychologist, I had completed a postdoctoral psychology fellowship in developmental disabilities at the Neuropsychiatric Institute at UCLA. I was not aware of the Challenger division, however, until I gave a talk on positive coaching at our local Little League. A dad there asked if I would be willing to help out occasionally with the Challenger kids. I agreed.

I don't know what I expected, but when I got to the first game, it was an eye-opener. I saw a group of kids ranging in age from six to sixteen. Some had Down's syndrome, some had cerebral palsy, some had spina bifida, some had suffered oxygen deprivation at birth and some were autistic. But they all had one thing in common—they were having fun!

There is a "buddy" system in the Challenger Division, whereby each kid on the team has a helper who shadows him or her throughout the game—pushing a wheelchair, pointing out where to throw the ball or doing whatever else might be needed. Almost all of the buddies at this particular game were siblings or parents.

What I didn't see at the game were many spectators other than parents. Although the Challengers were considered part of the league, their games had been relegated to Sunday—all the other kids played on Saturday. When I saw the fun these kids were having—all the high-fives, the cheering for both sides, the atmosphere of fun and games— I couldn't help but compare it to a Little League game I had seen the day before with nine-year-olds. In that game, within a period of ten seconds, I saw a left fielder crying because he dropped a fly ball; a mother, neck veins bulging, yelling at the umpire; a coach screaming at his pitcher to "follow through" or he was going to replace him.

Suddenly it became clear to me how important it was to get Challenger games scheduled among the other Little League games—both for the exposure of the Challenger kids to the other kids, and for the lessons in sportsmanship and fun they could give the other kids and parents.

The following season I volunteered to serve as manager for the Challenger team, with the goal of integrating the Challenger Division into the rest of the organization.

First off, the kids got full uniforms, just like the rest of the league players. Next, we scheduled the Challenger games on Saturday, between the Little League games played by the eleven- and twelve-year-olds. Then we arranged the buddy system so that members of the eleven- and twelve-year-old teams could serve as buddies for our Challenger kids. The results were spectacular.

The full uniforms were a big hit. One of our players slept in his uniform the first night. Another kid, ten years old, proudly displayed his uniform and said, "Gee, Coach, now I feel like a real person!"

For the kids who were buddies, it was, in many cases, their first exposure to kids with developmental disabilities. After some initial hesitation, they took to it like ducks to water. One kid told me that when he came on to the field to be a buddy, he was "bummed out" because his team had just lost 9-4, and he had gone hitless. After being a "buddy," though, he said it put everything in the proper perspective. He wasn't alone. Kids who, in the past, may have made cruel remarks about kids who are "different" were now championing their cause, chattering about how hard these kids try and how much they enjoy playing. The Challenger kids, meanwhile, took great pride in pointing out their "buddy" to their parents and friends.

Scheduling the Challenger games amidst the other games also resulted in a significant increase in spectators. And of course, some of the Challenger kids loved playing to the crowd, bowing after sliding home, or flexing a muscle after getting a hit. Clearly, the effect of the Challenger kids on the crowd was fantastic. Everyone got into applauding, cheering, laughing and having fun. There wasn't an angry glance or a bulging neck vein to be seen. The only tears were ones of joy and laughter.

The season ended with a round-robin tournament of the six Challenger teams from neighboring leagues. Local TV and newspapers covered the event and nearly one hundred eleven- and twelve-year-old kids from our league volunteered to help as buddies for the different teams.

To see and feel the warmth of camaraderie and compassion on the baseball diamonds that day renewed everyone's faith in the goodness of the human spirit. Challenger sports created memories that whole season which will last a lifetime for those Challenger kids, those buddies, those parents, coaches and spectators.

Darrell J. Burnett

Don't Worry, Be Happy

Attitude defies limitation and exceeds expectation.

Source Unknown

"How old are you?" a stranger asked my daughter, Melissa, at a party six years ago.

"Two," she answered.

"And are you married?" the woman teased.

"No!" Melissa answered, smiling. Then she dropped her smile, and in a serious tone added, "But my mommy was, and my daddy was."

I eavesdropped from a safe distance, wondering what might follow. Would Melissa, with her advanced vocabulary, tell this stranger that her parents were divorced? Even worse, would my toddler act out and hit the woman, or start crying?

To my surprise, with glee, Melissa added, "My mommy was married to my daddy." She then toddled off.

I, meanwhile, was like a leaky faucet. A steady stream of happy tears trickled down my face as I realized my daughter seemed well-adjusted despite the divorce; her mother was the one who obviously still needed to heal.

Twenty months earlier, when Melissa was six months old, my husband discarded me like a well-worn pair of shoes and replaced me with his high-school crush. No explanation. Just a silent, seeping withdrawal that culminated in an abrupt exit from what had seemed on the surface a happy marriage.

As I'd wake at dawn to Melissa's cries, I'd find myself curled up in a corner of the huge mattress, clutching what for six years had been someone else's pillow. I'd drag myself out of bed, throw on some sweatpants—grateful that I worked at home—then feed and dress my baby.

Just before driving Melissa to day care and burying my grief in my work for eight hours, I'd dab on some make-up in a feeble attempt to cover the bags under my eyes. Somehow, I found an automatic-pilot switch that got me through the day.

But by nighttime, after I'd tucked her into the crib in a bedroom filled with rainbows and sunshine, I'd crawl next door to my lifeless room and cling to the phone, calling everyone I knew just to keep from feeling so alone.

One long day evolved into two, then two into three, and slowly, through the haze, I recognized that even though my marriage had died, I was still alive. Eventually, I propelled myself out the door and joined a divorce support group, a new-mother's network, a local social club and, eventually, dating services.

Like most new mothers, I also worked out to shed the extra pounds; but, unlike the average new mom, I had been thrust back into the dating scene with a post-childbirth body, so I ran that treadmill with urgency!

Meanwhile, Melissa grew from a crawler to a walker to a toddler to a talker. Despite knowing life with her parents as a series of good-byes and hellos, she was emerging as a precocious, happy, well-adjusted little girl.

These traits may have been planted in her genes, or they may have derived from the one-on-one attention she received from each parent.

From early on, my daughter had an extensive vocabulary and uncanny perception. When she was twenty-two months old, she saw me and her father arguing and instructed us, with finger pointing: "Don't be so angry so much, be happy." At two, she heard me complain about something and told me "not to worry."

Yet I did. I worried about competing for her affections with the woman in her father's life. I worried about whether I could ever provide us with a loving man and stepfather so she could learn about love and commitment differently than her father and I had taught her. I worried she'd forever be an only child, or, worse, that one day she'd have step- or, horrors, half-siblings who would be the children of the woman my husband had turned to when he left me.

Could I stand the emotional pain? Could I nurture my daughter in a healthy way that would teach her that not all relationships end in suffering? Could I back off enough to permit her acceptance of her father's new life, when it tore me apart?

I tried. I met new people who made my life fuller. I rebuilt my interest in my public-relations business and started making and selling jewelry as both a means to keep busy and a way to recover my self-esteem. I learned to enjoy my days off and I observed that, unlike many of my friends, I rarely took time with my daughter for granted.

With my head clearer and my body thinner from my workouts, I began dating.

After my first luscious "post-marital" kiss, I felt I'd experienced life after death!

Today, eight years after my ex-husband left, I'm

working hard to provide Melissa with a life she deserves. I help her tackle her personal goals, like writing in cursive, reading books and learning to ski, and we talk about things that matter to her, like friendships, art and animals. My heart swells with pride whenever I meet with one of her teachers, because their reports consistently paint a picture of a well-liked child demonstrating healthy self-esteem, intelligence and creativity. Just last week her third-grade teacher described Melissa as a child who is always so pleasant, she would "make lemonade if life handed her lemons." Well, life did, and she did!

As for myself, I'm doing well and have remarried. I chose a man who didn't make my heart throb at first, but who provided me with the stability I desperately desired. In time, the respect, devotion, love and attraction that has grown between us is far more solid than love sparked mainly by lust! I'm grateful not only for my new union, but for my daughter's delight over having a loving step-father and an older step-sister whom she adores.

Nonetheless, divorce is always with us. Several times each week Melissa goes off to her father's house where he lives with his new wife—fortunately not the woman he left me for. Shortly after he "dumped" her a few years ago, I panicked over whom he would choose next to be in my daughter's life; so I introduced him to a woman I hardly knew but liked, and she is now his wife! When Melissa spends time with them, I consciously remind myself I'm only temporarily "losing" her, that she'll be back, that it's quite different from losing a husband and a marriage for-ever. More important, I've learned from my daughter that these are my concerns, and she is still doing fine.

Two years ago at age six, when an audiotape of *The Little Mermaid* ended, Melissa applauded Ariel and Prince Eric's wedding. But one second later, she removed her head-phones and banged them against our coffee table.

"Please don't do that," I calmly but firmly said. "Do you think you struck the table because you were feeling angry that Ariel and Prince Eric are married, yet your parents aren't any more?" I asked, as though straight from the parenting manual on drawing out a child's feelings.

"No, Mommy," she promptly and assertively replied, looking at me as though I'd just called an apple an orange. "These headphones have been hurting my ears. Sorry." She then calmly continued with her next activity.

That day I finally learned my lesson: Lighten up, Mom! There's life after divorce! There are many wondrous new things in this little girl's world and in mine. She'll be okay. We'll all be okay. Don't worry so much; be happy.

Mindy Pollack-Fusi

CALVIN AND HOBBES By Bill Watterson

The Wake

One joy shatters a hundred griefs.

Chinese Proverb

"You want to do what?" I asked him incredulously, my voice rising to the high-pitched level it reaches when I become exasperated. "Say that again, please; I don't think I heard you!"

"Oh, you heard me, all right," Frank snapped, waving his arms in his expressive manner. "I want to have my wake now—before I'm dead! Why should everyone else enjoy it and not me?"

He stalked into the kitchen, and I could hear him muttering to himself as he rummaged in the refrigerator. He returned shortly to the deck where I had remained to watch September's twilight blanket the Blue Ridge Mountains.

He finished munching a ripe peach, and then the voice that could never remain harsh for long broke the silence. "Honey, I want to do this."

I tightened my throat and tried not to cry. I was forty-four, and the thought of being widowed—again—was a devastating one. So devastating, in fact, that denial easily became the cloak I donned each day.

"But, but, you're stronger now. You said so! And the shots, they help. . . ."

"Melva," he touched my shoulder as if pleading. "Let's have a party, and let's do it right. We could disguise it as an anniversary party. Of course, everyone who knows me so well will know."

I looked into those liquid brown eyes, their sparkle dulled now from pain, from medication, from worry. I knew what the last couple of years had taken from him. We had ceased to be the golden couple on the dance floor every weekend. Oh, we still went, he insisted; but we now spent most of the evenings sitting and chatting with friends.

His golf game, once marked by those powerful, straight drives and precision iron shots—he had four holes-in-one—had taken a downward turn.

The many enjoyable hours he once spent gardening and cutting firewood had dwindled to a precious few minutes that left him wan and spent.

The spirit never left him, though. While I seemed to constantly bemoan the changes in our life—in my life—he never complained. Suddenly, I realized that my fears and uncertainties paled in comparison to what he must be going through. The changes we had undergone appeared minuscule beside the cancer that raged within his body, vying with diabetes for the chance to determine his fate.

Swallowing my shame, I reached for his hand. "Okay. If it's a party you want, it's a party we'll have!"

The next morning, I ordered the 150 formal invitations for our "Anniversary Party." October 19, 1991, fell on a Saturday night, and we rented Frank's Shrine Club for the event.

Almost everyone we had invited came to share the

evening with us. Mid-party, Frank took center stage with microphone in hand to give a glorious rendition of singer-songwriter Mac Davis's ballad "It's Hard to Be Humble."

My husband delighted in being in the spotlight and finished to the cheers and, yes, tears, from all who loved him. He made a short speech then, thanking everyone for coming and proclaimed himself the luckiest man in the world! In so many words, he said good-bye.

And then we waltzed. Frank had begun to lose his balance and was no longer comfortable dancing with other women. But that night he danced with all.

Later, a slow number found me with one of his doctors. "How long does he have?" I asked quietly.

"That's impossible to predict, Melva, he seems stronger." "How long?" I asked again and was met by silence. We finished our dance, and he walked me back to my table. "Six months . . . maybe longer," he finally answered me.

"Thank you," I whispered.

The rest of the night flew by like a vision, with Frank passing from one group to another, talking with everyone and regaling in the many stories told at his expense. Politicking, he'd once called it. As the evening drew to a close he remained at the door to bid each and every guest good night, standing at first, then needing to take a seat—but always smiling.

Three months and three days later, I sat shivering in the cold as his lodge brothers performed Masonic rites. I clutched the neatly folded flag while the strong arms of a friend led me to the waiting limousine.

About a year later, I had lunch with a new friend. She spoke of a wake she'd attended the night before. "What an absolutely beautiful way to say good-bye!" she remarked, obviously unaccustomed to such merriment.

I listened to her recount the frivolity, and I thought

how sad that the dearly departed had missed such a fine evening. The "I should have done more" and "Why wasn't I stronger for him" guilt that had been my shroud began to slip away. My mind turned instead to Frank's joy at his last party.

"So, did you hold a wake for Frank?" my friend asked.

"Oh, yes," I replied. "It was a grand party, and he had the time of his life!"

Melva Haggar Dye

The Power of Forgiveness

If you are patient in one moment of anger, you will escape a hundred days of sorrow.

Chinese Proverb

In 1974, walking home from school the last day before Christmas vacation, I excitedly thought about the upcoming holiday as only ten-year-old boys can dream. A few doors from my home in Coral Gables, Florida, a man came up to me and asked if I would help him with the decorations for a party he was hosting for my father. Thinking that he was a friend of my dad's, I agreed to go with him.

What I didn't know was that this man held a grudge against my family. He had been employed as a nurse for an elderly relative, but he had been fired because of his drinking.

After I agreed to accompany him, he drove his motor home to an isolated area north of Miami, where he stopped by the side of the road and stabbed me in the chest several times with an ice pick. He then drove west to the Florida Everglades, walked me out among the bushes, shot me through the head and left me to die.

Fortunately, the bullet passed behind my eyes and exited my right temple without causing any brain damage. When I regained consciousness six days later, I was unaware that I had been shot. I sat by the side of the road and was found by a man who stopped to help me.

Two weeks later, I described the person who had assaulted me to a police artist, and my uncle recognized the resulting portrait as the man who attacked me. My assailant was brought in, along with other suspects. However, the trauma and stress took its toll, and I couldn't identify him. Unfortunately, the police could not obtain any physical evidence to link him to the crime, so he was never charged.

The assault left me blind in my left eye, but otherwise uninjured, and with the love and support of my family and friends, I went back to school and resumed my life.

For the next three years, I lived with tremendous anxiety. Most nights I woke up frightened, imagining I heard someone coming in the back door, and I'd wind up sleeping at the foot of my parents' bed.

Then, when I was thirteen, all that changed. One night, during a Bible study with my church youth group, I realized that God's providence and love, having miraculously kept me alive, were the basis for my life's security. In his hands, I could live without fear or anger. And so I did. I finished school, earning a bachelor's degree and a master's in divinity. I married my wonderful wife, Leslie. We have two beautiful toddlers, Amanda and Melodee.

In September of 1996, Major Charles Scherer of the Coral Gables Police Department, who had worked on the original investigation of my case, called to tell me that the seventy-seven-year-old assailant had finally confessed. Blind from glaucoma, in poor health, without family or friends, he was in a North Miami Beach nursing home. I visited him there.

The first time I went to see him, he apologized for what he had done to me, and I told him that I had forgiven him. I visited him many times after that, introducing him to my wife and girls, offering him hope and some semblance of family in the days before his death. He was always glad when I came by. I believe that our friendship eased his loneliness and was a great relief to him after twenty-two years of regrets.

I know the world might view me as the victim of a horrible tragedy, but I consider myself the "victim" of many miracles. The fact that I'm alive and have no mental deficiencies defies the odds. I've got a loving wife and a beautiful family. I've been given as much promise as anybody else—and ample opportunities. I've been blessed in a lot of ways.

And while many people can't understand how I could forgive him, from my point of view I couldn't *not* forgive him. If I'd chosen to hate him all these years, or spent my life looking for revenge, then I wouldn't be the man I am today—the man my wife and children love.

Chris Carrier
Submitted by Katy McNamara

Happy Birthday

In the game of life, heredity deals the hand, and society makes the rules; but you can still play your own cards.

Peter's Almanac

I've really been good the past four days: low-fat cottage cheese, tuna salad with lemon, broiled chicken with broccoli (no butter), grapefruit for breakfast. . . . Oh boy, I can hardly wait to step on the scale today. Slide out of bed slowly, stretch, savor the anticipated report from the scale. Slip off my robe, step lightly on the scale, look down with fragile confidence. I wonder how many pounds I've lost. Two, three, four maybe? Relishing the anticipated news, I let my eyes slip down to the mechanical device beneath my feet. . . . Disbelief! Confidence destroyed! Not only did I not lose four pounds, I gained one! I've been tricked, fooled, betrayed. The scale says I've been bad; the scale says I'm fat. Four minutes ago I didn't think so, but now I do. I'm fat. I'm bad. Devastated by the condemnation from the scale, I skulk back to bed wearing my robe like a shroud.

I am accustomed to stepping on the scale in the morning and to having the weight report determine what kind of a mood I will be in for that day. But today I am thirty-four, and I've been dieting in preparation for my birthday. I wanted to feel good today, not old and. . . But the scale has passed judgment on me: I'm fat. I'm bad. Sullenly I trudge back to bed where I feel, not think, the memories.

I remember.

I am four. My cousins romp circles around me, their loud obnoxious shrieks assaulting my ears. I suppose my quiet granddaddy loves them, too (though I don't know why), but I also know he loves me best. I don't know how I know this, but I do. Though he can hear them—they all scream so loud—and he can hardly hear me at all. My family doesn't talk loudly. We talk quietly in my house, and I talk quietest of all. But Grandpa and I don't talk much; we don't need to. *Grandpa, I want to pick pink rhubarb* I think, looking up at him. "Shall we go pick some rhubarb, Wee Ann?" he says quietly, taking my small, pudgy hand in his coarse, big one. Grandpa calls me his special version of my given name, Willanne—unlike my cousins, who call me "Pudgy." I am pudgy, as pictures thirty years later attest. But today I am four and I don't care if I'm "Pudgy," because Grandpa loves me best. I don't know how I know this, I just know, that's all.

I remember.

I am eleven. We are visiting Grandma's house and my detestable cousins have a friend over. My cousins are running around under the umbrella tree in the front yard and shrieking brainlessly. But their friend—a boy—is not running and shrieking. My cousins are gleefully teasing him, daring him to kiss me. I hate my cousins. My horrible cousins still call me "Pudgy," though I've outgrown the appropriateness of the name. I'm so embarrassed.

I remember.

I am sixteen. I pass the driving test easily, both the written and the driving portion. But the hard question comes after "Sex," "Color of eyes" and "Height." The question is: "Weight." *How much should I say,* I wonder. *What happens if I lie? Will I have to step on a scale? If I lie will an alarm go off? Will the clerk repeat my weight out loud so everyone will know? Will she question me? Will she exclaim disbelievingly, "You weigh how much?"* Filled with trepidation, I decide to lie. I wonder how much I can get away with. I take off ten pounds. I get away with it. No alarm sounds. The clerk doesn't even raise an eyebrow. She acts like she doesn't even care, though I'm sure she must.

I get away with my first ten-pound lie: Ten pounds becomes my permanent cheat number. No matter how much I weigh, from then on, I always take off ten pounds before committing my weight to paper. And I always know—no matter how much I weigh—that if I just lose ten pounds, I'll be just right. No matter how much I weigh, "just right" is always ten pounds less.

In the suburban morning quiet, I remember.

Six years ago, I was pregnant and looking like the Goodyear blimp. But today I am thirty-four, and I'm not pregnant. I'm also not fat. I'm not even pudgy. But the scale has just pronounced judgment and destroyed my mood by telling me I gained a pound.

I contemplate this: Maybe how much I weigh is not the problem; perhaps the problem is how I feel about how much I weigh.

Unhurried, I rise from the bed to which the bathroom scale has so recently sent me. I put on my robe, and go to the bathroom. I pick up the scale and carry it deliberately down the hall, past the dining room, through the kitchen, to the side yard where six empty trash cans await next week's trash. I raise the scale to the level of my shoulders, pause for just a moment and then drop the mechanical dictator into the waiting rubbish receptacle. And in so doing, I reclaim control over my own morale.

Never again will my mood be determined by the bathroom scale. A *happy* birthday belongs to me.

Willanne Ackerman

Reprinted by permission of United Feature Syndicate, Inc.

Manners

The tired ex-teacher edged closer to the counter at Kmart. Her left leg hurt and she hoped she had taken all of her pills for the day: the ones for her high blood pressure, dizziness and a host of other ills. *Thank goodness I retired years ago,* she thought to herself. *I don't have the energy to teach these days.*

Just before the line to the counter formed, she spotted a young man with four children and a pregnant wife or girlfriend in tow. The teacher couldn't miss the tattoo on his neck. *He's been to prison,* she thought. She continued checking him out. His white T-shirt, shaved hair and baggy pants led her to surmise, *He's a gang member.*

The teacher tried to let the man go ahead of her.

"You can go first," she offered.

"No, you go first," he insisted.

"No, you have more people with you," said the teacher.

"We should respect our elders," parried the man. And with that, he gestured with a sweeping motion indicating the way for the woman.

A brief smile flickered on her lips as she hobbled in front of him. The teacher in her decided she couldn't let the moment go and she turned back to him and asked "Who taught you your good manners?"

"You did Mrs. Simpson, in third grade."

Paul Karrer

Born to Live, Born to Love

Thirty years ago my friend Kelly's sister, Christine, was born into the world with several strikes against her. Her parents had split up just before she was born. Her mom had several complications with her pregnancy and Christine ended up arriving a couple of weeks early. Because she was premature, she ended up with respiratory problems that necessitated spending two weeks in the intensive-care nursery. With no insurance, her mom had to go back to work right away, and Kelly and I became Christine's chief baby-sitters. Then Christine was diagnosed with the condition known as dwarfism.

It was obvious from the time she could roll over and smile that this was one happy child. She was bright, articulate and stubborn and determined to succeed despite any of her physical limitations. Christine had no doubt that her life would turn out exactly the way she wanted it. At least that's what she would tell you if you could get her to stand still long enough to talk.

As a toddler, Christine demanded to be treated just like everyone else. Nobody could tell her she couldn't do what Kelly and I could. It didn't matter that we were six years older. When Kelly and I rode our bikes, Christine insisted on being pulled along in her wagon. If Kelly and I had to do dishes, Christine wanted to be propped on the counter and handed a dishtowel.

By the time Christine was due to start kindergarten, she was more than ready. Kelly and I had already taught her to read when she had been confined to bed following corrective surgery for one of her legs. On the first day of school, Kelly and I stood there open-mouthed as she told her teacher, "I'm just like the other kids. Don't baby me." Christine loved school and did very well. She was a natural leader, and there wasn't a single dissenting vote when she was elected class president in the seventh grade.

Other than the fact that her mom sometimes had to work double shifts to keep up with the bills, Christine had a normal, happy family.

However, during her senior year of high school, Christine's mother died. Christine then moved in with Kelly, who had gotten married two years earlier, and she soon became the favorite baby-sitter to Kelly's twins. After graduation, Christine found a job working in a bakery and moved into an apartment with me. Since I worked odd hours, we really didn't see that much of each other, and it was the first time she was truly on her own. She loved it!

Christine and our neighbor Eric really hit it off and began dating a few weeks after they met. A couple of years later, when Christine and Eric decided to marry, they had to confront the issue that Christine's physical problems would prevent her from ever having children of her own. But Christine knew without a doubt that she wanted to be a mother. Shortly after she and Eric married, they hired an attorney and tried to register with three different adoption agencies. Each agency politely but firmly told them that with her medical history and their limited funds, adoption was probably going to be impossible.

Obviously, they didn't know Christine very well.

Three weeks after the third agency rejected their application, Christine was watching the evening news and saw a program on unadoptable children. "Unadoptable" meant that these children were either too ill, too old or had too many other problems to be desirable. When the story focused on specific children, Christine heard about Illiana, a beautiful two-year-old who had been born with dwarfism and abandoned by her parents. Immediately, Christine knew she had found her ideal child.

After further investigation, though, Christine discovered that the process would take many months and cost more money than she and Eric had been able to save. Friends and relatives offered donations but it wasn't enough. Then her boss at the bakery came up with an idea: He took out a small ad in the local paper, announcing that, the following week, a percentage of sales at each of his three stores would go to help Eric and Christine adopt Illiana.

The response was unbelievable—the bakeries were mobbed. Then a local radio station ran the story and found a sponsor to match all the funds collected. At the end of the week, Eric and Christine had enough to complete the adoption process, buy clothes and toys, and even set aside a bit for their new daughter's education.

Today, Illiana is a healthy, happy seven-year-old. She is Christine's best helper and has pushed Kelly and me aside when it comes to caring for her little brother who was adopted last year.

Like mother, like daughter.

Eileen Goltz

Table Manners

Stressed is just desserts spelled backwards.

Brian Luke Seaward

The Pot-Bellied Potlucks began, unofficially, my first Christmas alone. I'd just left a marriage of twenty-two years, and I knew the days of full-family holidays, with all their rituals and comforts, were over for me. But I was determined not to feel sorry for myself, so I called up four friends and invited them to a potluck supper—nothing fancy, just a simple sharing of food and less work for everyone.

The evening was delightful, with the five of us so enchanted with its success that we decided to make the one-night gathering a monthly ritual.

Soon we had a steady roll call of nine or ten women, as new friends were introduced to the group. Some were single moms like myself, others married, some never married. All seemed to cook so well! Years of feeding families, entertaining and experimenting had resulted in well-honed recipes.

Yet outstanding meals were only part of the draw.

Friendships evolved from our potlucks, as we formed a tightly bound community. We talked about everything: work, relationships, children, pet peeves, new causes and the latest jokes. Laughter was the one constant at the table, the staple of our meals. Together we learned to melt our frustrations with a sense of humor.

Our potlucks then got an official name. One evening, a group member reported that her daughter had taken a phone message about the group's dinner plans: "Mom, someone named Marga called from your pot-bellied group. Call her back."

We howled at the aptness of her Freudian slip, and the name stuck.

The pot-bellied group had been meeting monthly for four years when I was diagnosed with breast cancer. This was not in my plans. I was facing a whole new kind of struggle. But again I was determined not to face it alone and not to become paralyzed by my fear.

Two weeks before the scheduled lumpectomy, I called Susie, a member of the group, and requested a potluck.

"I need one before surgery. Can you organize something upbeat?" I asked.

Two nights before surgery, I set the table and opened the door for the first guest, Anne. She brought the hors d' oeuvres, aka "malignant tumors." They were gorgeous little stuffed mushrooms, looking ever so innocent. Next to arrive was R.N. Rickie, dressed in green scrubs and a stethoscope, and bearing plasma in the form of red wine. With each dish, the menu dramatically spelled out my destiny.

The main course arrived—breast of chicken with lumpy gravy. Next came the vegetables—mashed potato breasts with cherry tomato nipples. The delicious green salad was served in side-by-side bowls edged in white lace with a tag that read: "Your First Wonder Bra!"

The *pièce de résistance* was the dessert. On a tray jiggled perfectly contoured, peach-colored Jell-O breasts, with two red maraschino cherries placed appropriately. Between gasps of laughter, I spied a tiny white grape, buried deep inside the left one: my tumor.

"Bring me a knife. Surgery is about to commence," I announced.

With my left hand behind my back, I used a bread knife to fish for the grape. Then, with a dramatic flick, I sent the grape flying across the table.

"The operation is a success. Sew her up, girls!"

If there was ever any doubt about my macabre sense of humor over my ordeal, that ended it.

The group then presented me with cotton bloomers— to be my surgery attire—penned with loving messages and poems. My favorite read:

> *A little nip, a little tuck.*
> *Pull one down, lift one up,*
> *The left one's wrong, the right one's right,*
> *(P.S. I prefer my rear be out of sight!)*

As each woman hugged me, I knew I was not facing my ordeal alone.

I know there are those who will not understand the irreverence shown by my potluck friends that night; some might even be offended by the seemingly flippant way I approached what is a critical health issue to women. But my life as a single woman has taught me that you can't control what life dishes out. You can only choose how you deal with it, and who stands up with you.

It's my party and I can laugh if I want to!

The women of the Pot-Bellied Potluck taught me that.

Today, I am fully recovered and have moved to New Mexico, leaving behind those strong women. The five years of evenings in which we ate and laughed and ate and became our own little family have left me with a taste for their friendship that I'll never outgrow. I have learned that divorce is not the gateway to loneliness and depression, but the open door to a life of love, healing friendships, fullness and fun—as long as there's a recipe and a joke to be shared.

Adele Frances

Mirror, Mirror on the Wall

When I look into the mirror I see a survivor.

I don't think about anything but living.

Well, that's not true because the farther I get from cancer, the more hopes and dreams I let creep in. When I looked into the mirror during my illness, I wasn't that bald person staring back at me. I didn't recognize myself.

My body had let me down, but I didn't want my soul to escape.

People responded to the way I looked.

I hated the pity I saw in their eyes as much as the fear.

The body is back to its original state, but the soul has taken on the wonderful layers of a survivor.

Now I celebrate
Bad-hair days
Bushy eyebrows
Stubbled legs with razor burn.

I celebrate
Blended flavors of peanut butter and chocolate
Sweet lemonade through a straw
Greasy hamburgers with bacon.

I celebrate
Whining children
Shouting and arguing
Pulsating music and barking dogs.

I celebrate
Making plans
Dreaming
The hoping that goes with having a future.

I celebrate life.

Karen Klosterman

8

A MATTER OF PERSPECTIVE

A kick in the rear is a step forward.

Anonymous

Big Willy

If you always keep your face to the sunshine, you'll never see the shadows!

Helen Keller

He stood six feet, nine inches tall and weighed in at 310 pounds. Rumor had it that he'd killed a man with his bare hands—just squeezed the life out of him. It was the kind of reputation that gained respect in the rough city where we grew up. At fifteen, Willy was already a legend.

Willy and I had played together since we both wore diapers, although we were the unlikeliest of pairs. He was a massive black giant and I was a pudgy little redhead. We both worked at the factory in town—I in the office, Willy on the dock. Even the hardened men who worked alongside Willy feared him.

He saw me home safely from work and I kept his secret that each night, instead of cruising the city streets, beating people up, he went home and lovingly lifted his elderly grandmother out of the chair she was confined to and placed her in bed. He would read to her until she fell asleep, and in the morning, he would comb her thin, gray hair, dress her in the beautiful nightgowns he bought with the money he made at the can company, and place her back in the chair.

Willy had lost both his parents to drugs, and it was just the two of them now. He took care of her, and she gave him a reason to stay clean. Of course, there wasn't an ounce of truth to the rumors, but Willy never said otherwise. He just let everyone believe what they believed, and although everyone wrote him off as just another street hood, no one hassled him either.

One day, in Western Civilization class, our teacher read aloud an excerpt from Machiavelli's *The Prince:* "Since love and fear cannot exist together, if we must choose between them, it is far safer to be feared than loved." I looked at Willy and winked. "That's you," I mouthed. He just smiled.

The next day, I lingered a few minutes longer than usual at school and Willy went on without me. Just around the corner from the can company, fire trucks lined the street and a thick blanket of smoke covered the sky. A small child lay wrapped in a familiar red- and black-checkered flannel shirt, held by a tearful woman. She was talking to a fireman and a reporter from the evening news.

"This big guy heard the baby crying, and came right in and got us," she said through joyful tears. "He wrapped his shirt around the baby, and when the sirens came, he ran off down the street."

"Did you get his name?" the reporter asked.

"Yes, sort of," the woman replied. "He said it was Machiavelli."

That evening, the paper ran the story offering a reward to anyone with information about the identity of the Good Samaritan. No one came forward.

Nancy Bouchard

Just Playing

When I'm building in the block room,
Please don't say I'm "just playing."
For, you see, I'm learning as I play.
About balance and shapes.

When I'm getting all dressed up,
Setting the table, caring for the babies.
Don't get the idea I'm "just playing."
For, you see, I'm learning as I play.
I may be a mother or a father someday.

When you see me up to my elbows in paint,
Or standing at an easel, or molding and shaping clay,
Please don't let me hear you say "he's just playing."
For you see, I'm learning as I play.
I'm expressing myself and being creative.
I may be an artist or an inventor someday.

When you see me sitting in a chair
"Reading" to an imaginary audience,
Please don't laugh and think I'm "just playing."
For, you see, I'm learning as I play.
I may be a teacher someday.

When you see me combing the bushes for bugs,
Or packing my pockets with choice things I find,
Don't pass it off as "just playing."
For, you see, I'm learning as I play.
I may be a scientist someday.

When you see me engrossed in a puzzle,
Or some "plaything" at my school,
Please don't feel the time is wasted in "play"
For, you see, I'm learning as I play.
I'm learning to solve problems and concentrate.
I may be in business someday.

When you see me cooking or tasting foods,
Please don't think that because I enjoy it, it is just
    "play."
I'm learning to follow directions and see differences.
I may be a chef someday.

When you see me learning to skip, hop, run and move
    my body,
Please don't say I'm "just playing."
For, you see, I'm learning as I play.
I'm learning how my body works.
I may be a doctor, nurse or athlete someday.

When you ask me what I've done at school today,
And I say, "I've played."
Please don't misunderstand me.
For, you see, I'm learning as I play.
I'm learning to enjoy and be successful in work.
I'm preparing for tomorrow.
Today, I'm a child and my work is play.

Anita Wadley

The Cracked Pot

A water bearer in India served his master by toting water from the stream to his master's home. He carried the water in two pots that hung on either end of a pole balanced across his shoulders.

One of the pots had a crack in it; the other pot was perfect. The perfect pot always delivered a full portion of water from the stream, while the cracked pot always arrived at the master's house only half full.

For a full two years this went on, every day the water bearer delivering one full and one half-full measures of water to the master's home. Naturally the full pot was proud of its service, perfect to the end for which it had been made. But the cracked pot was unhappy; ashamed of its imperfection, miserable that it was able to accomplish only half of what it had been made to do.

After an eternity of what it perceived to be a bitter failure, the cracked pot spoke to the water bearer one day. "I'm so ashamed of myself," it said. "I want to apologize to you."

"But why?" asked the water bearer.

"For the past two years," spoke the pot, "this crack in my side has let water leak out all the way to the master's house, and I have been unable to deliver but half my load. You do the work carrying me from the stream to our master's house each day, but because of my defect, you don't get full value from your effort," sighed the anguished pot.

Kindly, the water bearer told the distressed pot, "As we return to the master's house today, please notice the lovely flowers along the way."

As the trio returned up the hill, the old cracked pot noticed the winsome wild flowers—the sun glistening off their bright faces, the breeze bending their heads. But still, at the end of the trail, the faulty pot felt bad because it had again leaked out half its load, and again it apologized to the bearer for its failure.

But the bearer said to the pot, "Did you not notice that the flowers were only on your side of the path? Because I have always known about your 'flaw' I planted flower seeds on your side of the path, and every day while we wind our way walk back from the stream, you have watered them. And every day I am able to pick these beautiful flowers to adorn our master's table. Were you not just the way you are, the master would not have had this beauty to grace his house."

Willy McNamara

A Flight of Geese

*Oliver Wendell Holmes once attended a meet-
ing in which he was the shortest man present.
"Doctor Holmes," quipped a friend, "I should
think you'd feel rather small among us big fel-
lows." "I do," retorted Holmes, "I feel like a dime
among a lot of pennies."*

Source Unknown

Yesterday I watched a huge flight of geese winging
their way south through one of those panoramic sunsets
that color the entire sky for a few moments. I saw them
as I leaned against the lion statue in front of the Chicago
Art Institute, where I was watching the Christmas shop-
pers hurry along Michigan Avenue. When I lowered my
gaze, I noticed that a bag lady, standing a few feet away,
had also been watching the geese. Our eyes met and we
smiled—silently acknowledging the fact that we had
shared a marvelous sight, a symbol of the mystery of the
struggle to survive. I overheard the lady talking to herself as she shuffled away. Her words, "God spoils me,"
were startling.

Was the lady, this street derelict, being facetious? No. I believe the sight of the geese had shattered, however briefly, the harsh reality of her own struggle. I realized later that moments such as this one sustained her; it was the way she survived the indignity of the street. Her smile was real.

The sight of the geese was her Christmas present. It was proof God existed. It was all she needed.

I envy her.

Fred Lloyd Cochran

Sledding

One day in early December, we woke up to discover a perfect, freshly fallen snow. "Please Mom, can we go sledding after breakfast?" my eleven-year-old daughter Erica begged. Who could resist? So we bundled up and headed over to the dike on the Lincoln Park golf course, the only hill in our otherwise flat prairie town.

When we arrived, the hill was teeming with people. We found an open spot next to a tall, lanky man and his three-year-old son. The boy was already lying belly-down in the sled, waiting to be launched. "Come on, Daddy! Come on!" he called.

The man looked over at me. "Okay if we go first?" he asked.

"By all means," I said. "Looks like your son is ready to go."

With that, he gave the boy a huge push, and off he flew! But it wasn't only the child who soared—the father ran after him at full speed.

"He must be afraid that his son is going to run into somebody," I said to Erica. "We'd better be careful, too."

With that, we launched our own sled and whizzed down the hill at breakneck speed, the powdery snow flying in our faces. We had to bail out to avoid hitting a huge elm tree near the river, and ended up on our backs, laughing.

"Great ride!" I said.

"But what a long walk back up!" Erica noted.

Indeed it was. As we trudged our way back to the top, I noticed that the lanky man was pulling his son, who was still in the sled, back up to the summit.

"What service!" Erica said. "Would you do the same for me?"

I was already out of breath. "No way, Kiddo! Keep walking!"

By the time we reached the top, the little boy was ready to play again.

"Go, go, go, Daddy!" he called. Again, the father put all his energy into giving the boy a huge send-off, chased him down the hill, and then pulled both boy and sled back up.

This pattern went on for more than an hour. Even with Erica doing her own walking, I was exhausted. By then, the crowd on the hill had thinned as people went home for lunch. Finally, it got down to the man and his son, Erica and me and a handful of others.

He can't still be thinking the boy is going to crash into someone, I thought. *And surely, even though the child is small, he could pull his own sled up the hill once in a while.* But the man never tired, and his attitude was bright and cheery.

Finally, I could stand it no longer. I looked over at him and called, "You have tremendous energy!"

The man looked at me and smiled. "He has cerebral palsy," he said matter-of-factly. "He can't walk."

I was dumbstruck. Then I realized that I had never seen the boy get out of the sled in all the time we'd been on the hill. It had all seemed so happy, so normal, that it never occurred to me that the child might be handicapped.

Although I didn't know the man's name, I told the story in my newspaper column the following week. Either he or someone he knew must have recognized him, because shortly afterward, I received this letter:

Dear Mrs. Silverman,

The energy I expended on the hill that day is nothing compared to what my son does every day. To me, he is a true hero, and someday I hope to be half the man he has already become.

Robin L. Silverman

The Hill

We cannot direct the wind . . . but we can adjust the sails.

Source Unknown

Long past midnight, hours before dawn
I jump up from my bed, pull my longjohns on.
Peeking out the window, the snow has started to fall.
Slipping on my overalls, I race quickly down the hall.
Rushing to the closet, grasping my old wrap,
I throw it over my shoulder, give the button a snap.
Working all ten fingers, through the holes of much-worn
　　mitts,
I stick my feet into the boots that thankfully still fit.
Faster than is possible, I head straight for the door.
Behind me I am dragging a sled from years before.
The wind is loud and howling, snow is blowing all
　　around.
Already what has fallen has covered the ground.
Tramping through the deepness, only my footprints to
　　see,
I head straight for the meadow, the hill is waiting for me.

A few more steps, I reach my goal, as always in the past
I'll be the first to sled this hill, and I'll be the very last.
Breathing in the cool night air, I witness the year's first
  snow.
Perhaps this is my favorite spot, in all the sights I know.
Holding tight in a world of silence, I shove off with my
  feet.
Wind is picking up my hair, snow hits against my teeth.
Traveling faster and faster, I struggle not to tip.
Stretching out my snow-damp legs, I lean from hip to hip.
What a big delight, this morn has given thee.
As all years before have done, when it's just this hill and
  me.
Now if I do my best to hurry, I can take another run.
The sun will soon be rising, the day will have begun.
But before that can happen, I must be back in bed.
For whatever would the children think . . .
. . . if they knew Grandma used their sled!

Betty J. Reid

The Halfway Point

Don't look back unless you intend to go that way.

Marc Holm

I glance at my daughter in the rearview mirror. *What does Denise think, I wonder, when she looks at the four of us— two sets of parents, each of a different race? What does she see when she looks at us from the back seat? Does it mean anything to her that her father is white and her stepmother is Chinese-American?* In a few moments, she will see her mother, who is Filipino, and her stepfather, who is African-American.

I sense that it doesn't mean nearly as much to her as it would to a social scientist, or maybe even a politician. To her, we are just four adults who are in charge of raising her and making sure she is safe.

The highway between Monterey and Salinas is so familiar. I know every turn, every pothole and how long each red light lasts along the way. I drive it every week. I once looked at my car's odometer several years ago and wondered if our meeting point truly was exactly halfway between my ex-wife's house and mine. Am I driving a little more than I should have to?

"Denise," my second wife says, "next week when school is out, I'll bring you to my office and you can help out. I have a big mailing you can do; a lot of envelopes to stuff, okay?"

"Cool! I can't wait."

My wife could say that she needed Denise to help out with nearly anything at her office and Denise's response would be the same. The girl just wants to spend time with her stepmother. They effortlessly took to each other from day one.

"Denise, do you have your karate outfit packed? Mom will bring you to your class next Saturday, and I'll pick you up there."

"It's packed, Dad."

Her duffel bag and backpack are full for her week with her mom and stepfather. One week with one set of parents, the next week with the other. Same school. The schedule is very finely tuned. Same meeting place in the same park for the past five years.

I exit the highway. There they are. I pull alongside their car and we all get out. Denise's mother and I look at each other with more than just a look. We accept each other. We each see someone we didn't know when we were married to each other, although we thought we did. Long gone is the anger and the threats to keep one another from seeing our daughter. We see someone we have forgiven, someone we stopped being vindictive toward and someone we still have a hard time feeling comfortable with. But most importantly, we see someone we have learned to work with for our child's best interest.

I get Denise's bag while she, my wife and my ex-wife all make goo-goo ga-ga noises over Denise's half-sister, now almost two years old. I give Denise's bag to her stepfather. We nod and say "Hi." Not too much in common, but a certain respect. I respect him for being a good father and stepfather. I am fully aware that this man is in charge of my daughter's safety for exactly half the year, every year.

I finally realize that it takes more of a man to accept that than to be intimidated by it.

"Is she starting to walk yet?" my wife asks Denise's mom, speaking of the baby.

"She kind of bounces from sofa to chair to me, falling the whole way." More laughter.

I walk over, pinch the baby's cheek in an obligatory manner and then stand back and watch, wondering if I should be surprised. Denise's stepfather is African-American. Her stepmother is Chinese-American. Her mother is Filipino and I am white. This doesn't really matter, I say to myself, but I know just how much it truly matters. Four different races. Four different personalities and temperaments. The most that we have in common is that we have a child to raise.

Denise is now kissing her stepmother good-bye. They exchange "I love yous" and "See you next weeks." She comes over to me and kisses me good-bye.

I am extremely proud of my daughter. She's testimony to the resiliency of kids. She knows the schedule by heart. She's always packing a backpack or duffel bag and often forgets things in the other house—a book for school, a friend's telephone number or her clarinet. Nobody complains, least of all her. She will get what she needs the next day. One of her four parents will drive the distance to deliver it. I'm reminded of her school play, which we all attended a few weeks earlier. After the curtain call, she came out beaming, eager to see her two sets of parents who all sat at the same table. Suddenly she hesitated, wondering which set she should hug first. A look of relief then shot across her face. She knew that it didn't matter. She would hug the other set precisely a second later.

They get in their car and we get in ours. As I start the engine, I put my hand on my wife's shoulder and ask her if it's really all that hard. She fully understands what I'm asking.

"No, it isn't," she says, "it isn't at all." She's right, I think. It's not that hard if you know your priorities and know how to love.

We follow them out of the park, and I think of all the children who don't know where one or both of their parents are, who receive, at most, a card once or twice a year. I think of the many ugly custody battles and can't help but wonder what those warring parents could find if they just reached a little deeper inside themselves. I think of Denise's friend who slept over a few months ago, who hasn't seen her father in years and doesn't seem to care.

Just before reaching the highway, Denise turns around and waves at us through the back window. She blows us a kiss and we blow one back. She then turns around and talks to her mom and stepfather. I wonder if she'll think of us this coming week, although it doesn't matter, since before we know it, we'll be driving this same road again.

There's so much ahead yet: adolescence, boyfriends, failure, rejection and triumph. There are so many bumps and bruises yet to be had. So many life experiences still to come. I ask myself how long we can keep on making life secure for her. I know it's a redundant question since it's the best it can be, and we can only do our best right now. A step at a time and a day at a time.

As we reach the highway, I put my signal on to turn left towards Monterey, and they put theirs on to turn right towards Salinas. When we have gotten up to speed, I look at my odometer and wonder if it really is halfway. Am I driving more than I should be? I suddenly look back at the road, realizing it doesn't really matter.

Dennis J. Alexander

I Talk to Me

[EDITORS' NOTE: *Phil Colburn is a widow, ninety-nine years old. She writes poetry to keep her mind clear, penning a poem each month for her church newsletter.*]

I talk to me a lot these days
about the things I do.
I find that I quite often need
a serious talking-to.

"Get those shoulders back" I say to me,
as I start down the hall.
I get them back and start my trek;
and hope I will not fall.

I say to me, when I awake,
and the pain is really bad,
"Remember many have more pain
than I have ever had."

It really is annoying
not understanding what they say
and I wonder if I answered
in some stupid way.

Then I tell me to remember
stupid answers are not new.
Sometimes when I still heard well,
I made stupid answers too.

I need a reading glass these days
and so I say to me,
"Be very thankful I can read
Many cannot even see."

I tell me I should exercise
though I'd rather sit and read
but if I want to keep my strength
what I tell me I must heed.

I can still walk and see and hear
though not as it used to be.
I find it really helps a lot
the times I talk to me.

Phil Colburn

Obstacle Illusions

We enjoy warmth because we have been cold.
We appreciate light because we have been in
darkness. By the same token, we can experience
joy because we have known sorrow.

David L. Weatherford

Legs. We run, ski, climb mountains and swim without thinking much about them.

My husband Scott had used his legs to win downhill ski scholarships in college and climb to the top of the Grand Tetons in Jackson Hole, Wyoming. Then, without warning, during an unseasonably warm April, a tumor was discovered in Scott's spinal cord. We were told death or paralysis could be the end result.

Our children—Chase, Jillian and Hayden—ranged in age from seven to two. They didn't really understand all the "bad stuff" that was going on—but they were the biggest cheerleaders and the best teachers when Scott found out his life would go on but he was paralyzed from the rib cage down.

Adults sometimes get stuck looking at the things that

are gone. I would think about the camping trips we'd never take, the mountains Scott would never climb and the fresh powder he'd never ski with his children.

Chase, Jillian and Hayden were too busy with the business of life to get bogged down with what their dad couldn't do. They stood on the pedals of his wheelchair and screamed with delight as he raced them down quiet hospital corridors.

The doctors said to prepare Scott for life in a wheelchair because if he thought he'd walk again—and could not—he would be depressed. The kids didn't listen to the doctors; they urged their dad to "try to stand up." I worried that Scott would fall down; the kids laughed with him when he fell and rolled on the grass. I cried but they urged him to "try again."

In the middle of all these changes in our lives, I took a drawing class at a local college. For a week, the instructor told us we couldn't draw things, we could only draw spaces between things. One day as I sat under a giant pine tree drawing the spaces between the branches, I began to see the world as Scott and the kids saw it. I didn't see the branches as obstacles that could stop a wheelchair from traveling across the lawn, I saw all the spaces that would allow wheelchairs, people and even small animals to sneak through. When I wasn't focused on the branches—or the obstacles of life—I gained a new appreciation for all the spaces. Oddly enough, whether you draw the spaces or the branches, the picture looks pretty much the same; its just how you see it that's different.

When I joined my family in looking for the "spaces," a new world opened up. It wasn't the same—sometimes we were frustrated—but it was always rewarding because we were working together. As we tried all these new adventures, Scott began to stand up and then walk with the use of a cane. He still has no feeling in his lower body and legs, he can't run or ride a bike, but he enjoys so many new experiences.

We learned you don't need feeling in your legs to fly a kite, play a board game, plant a tree, float in a mountain lake or attend a school program. Legs aren't needed to hug, bandage a cut or talk someone through a bad dream.

Some people see roadblocks; Scott has taught us roadblocks are only detours. Some people see branches; Scott and the kids see wide-open spaces with room enough for all the love and hope a heart can bear.

Heidi Marotz

My New Set of Wheels

There you stand, and I see you stare
Thinking, poor dear, she's stuck in that chair.
But I'm not sad, I'm very happy because
I haven't forgotten the way it was.

You'd say, "How about a trip to the zoo?
A walk in the park will be good for you."
I was thinking tomorrow, I'll be a wreck,
From my aching feet, to the pain in my neck.

You'd want to go shopping, all over town,
I was thinking but there's no place to sit down.
For you it's a snap, just to go to the store,
But for me the ordeal was more of a chore.

Now I can go wherever I please
I can shop in the mall with newfound ease,
Do all the things that have to be done,
And even go out and have some fun.

So, do you want to know how it really feels,
To be sitting here between these wheels?

Can you remember back that far,
When you got your very first car?

Well, that's how these wheels feel to me.
They don't hold me down, they set me free.
So, don't think all those pitiful things:
These aren't wheels, I think they're my wings.

Darlene Uggen

What Should I Fear?

Nothing in life is to be feared. It is only to be understood.

Marie Curie

I used to live in perpetual fear of losing things I had, or never having the things I hoped to acquire.

What if I lose my hair?

What if I never get a big house?

What if I become overweight, out of shape or unattractive?

What if I lose my job?

What if I am disabled and cannot play ball with my child?

What if I get old and frail and have nothing to offer those around me?

But life teaches those who listen, and now I know:

If I lose my hair, I will be the best bald guy I can be, and I will be grateful that my head can still stimulate ideas, if not follicles.

A house does not make a person happy. The unhappy heart will not find contentment in a bigger house. The heart that is merry, however, will make any home a happy one.

If I spend more time developing my emotional, mental and spiritual dimensions, rather than focusing solely on my physical self, I will be more beautiful with each passing day.

If I cannot work for wages, I will work for the Lord—and his benefits package is unmatched.

If I am physically unable to teach my child to throw a curve ball, I will have more time to teach him to handle the curves thrown by life, and this shall serve him better.

And if aging robs my strength, mental alertness and physical stamina, I will offer those around me the strength of my convictions, the depth of my love and the spiritual stamina of a soul that has been carefully shaped by the hard edges of a long life.

No matter what losses or broken dreams may lie in my destiny, I will meet each challenge with dignity and resolve. For God has given me many gifts, and for each one that I may lose, I will find ten more that I never would have cultivated were the course of my life to always run smoothly.

And so, when I can no longer dance, I will sing joyfully; when I haven't the strength to sing, I will whistle with contentment; when my breath is shallow and weak, I will listen intently and shout love with my heart; and when the bright light approaches, I will pray silently until I cannot pray.

Then it will be time for me to go to the Lord. And what then should I fear?

David L. Weatherford

9

ECLECTIC WISDOM

I hear and I forget.
I see and I remember.
I do and I understand.

Chinese Proverb

What's Wrong with Your Dad?

Has anyone ever said, "It is important to spend less time on how we look and more time on how we see"? If not, someone should.

Carmen Richardson Rutlen

I was in high school before I realized my father had a birth defect. He had a harelip and cleft palate, but to me he looked like he had always looked since the day I was born. I can remember kissing him goodnight once when I was young and asking if my nose would go flat after a lifetime of kisses. He assured me that it would not, but I remember a twinkle in his eyes. I am sure he was marveling about a daughter who loved him so much she thought that her kisses, not thirty-three operations, had reshaped his face.

My father was kind, patient, thoughtful and loving. He was my hero and first love. He never met a person in whom he could not find good. He knew the first names of janitors, secretaries and CEOs. In truth, I think he liked the janitors the best. He always inquired about their families, who they thought would win the World Series and how life was treating them. He cared enough to listen to their responses and remember their answers.

Dad never let his disfigurement rule his life. When he was considered too unattractive for sales work, he took a bike out on deliveries and created his own route. When the army wouldn't let him enlist, he volunteered. He even once asked a Miss America contestant out for a date. "If you don't ask you'll never know," he told me later. He rarely talked on the phone, because people had a hard time understanding him. When they met him in person with his positive attitude and quick smile, people just seemed to take his disability in stride. He married a beautiful woman, and they had seven healthy children, all of whom thought the sun and moon rose in his face.

When I was a "sophisticated teen," however, I barely tolerated being in the same room with this same man who for a decade had endured me watching him shave every morning. My friends were chic, trendy and popular; my dad was old and outdated.

One night I came home with a car full of friends, and we stopped at my house for midnight snacks. My father came out of his bedroom and welcomed my friends, pouring sodas and making popcorn. One of my friends pulled me aside and asked, "What's wrong with your dad?"

Suddenly, I looked across the room and saw him for the first time with unbiased eyes. I was in shock. My dad was a freak! I made everyone leave immediately and took them home. I felt so foolish. How could I have never seen it before?

Later that night I cried, not because I realized that my dad was different, but because I realized what a pathetic, shallow person I was becoming. Here was the sweetest, most loving person you could ask for, and I had judged him on his looks.

That night I learned that when you love someone

totally and then see them through the eyes of ignorance, fear or contempt, you begin to understand the profound depths of prejudice. I had seen my dad as strangers did, as someone different, deformed and not normal. Not remembering that he was a good person who loved his wife, his children and his fellow human beings. He had joys and sorrows and had already lived a lifetime of people judging him on his appearance. I was grateful that I got to know him first, before others showed me his flaws.

Dad is gone now. Empathy, compassion and concern for fellow human beings are the legacy he left me. They are the greatest gifts a parent could leave a child—the capacity to love others without considering their social stature, race, religion or disabilities, the gifts of joyful perseverance and optimism. The lofty goal of being so loving in my life that I receive enough kisses to make my nose go flat.

Carol Darnell

Cyclops Stole Our Hearts

Beauty is in the heart of the beholder.

Al Bernstein

"Why do these cows always pick this cold weather to have their calves, anyway?" Bill's deep voice betrayed anxiety more than annoyance as Scott and I hurried along beside him toward the barn. It was midnight, and the temperature at Singing Valley had plummeted to five below zero!

Valentine was a mountainous Holstein, now a month overdue. She was far too big, weighing nearly three thousand pounds, and we were worried. For three hours, we watched the distressed animal sniffing and pawing the straw while her labor progressed. Finally she crashed to the ground, and with a little help, gave birth to a 140-pound heifer, twice the normal size and the color of butterscotch. We hurried back to our own warm beds for what was left of the night.

Before dawn I went down to the barn to make sure the calf was up and nursing. I could hear it sucking noisily in the far corner of the stall. Then my foot struck something hard buried under the straw. A piercing squeal knifed the darkness.

I hurried to let in some light. I was unprepared for what lay before me—a hideous black calf, twin to the beautiful heifer, but grotesquely deformed.

As it struggled to stand, I was appalled at its oversized head and the massive hump rising from its back. Its short, stubby legs were twisted, and its hoofs were clubbed. It trembled.

Overwhelmed with pity, I sank to my knees and reached to touch it. The calf bawled piteously and searched my fingers for milk. I turned the calf slightly so I could see its face. My heart stopped. The calf had only one eye. How could nature be so brutal?

I don't know why we didn't destroy him. His twin was afraid of him. His mother despised him. When he tried to nurse, Valentine kicked him in the face, then gored him in the sides with her horns until he fell to the ground. Every time, hurt and bleeding, the ugly little thing lurched to his feet and tried again. Determined to nurse, he watched his mother from distant corners of her stall and corral. He waited until she lay down to rest. Then he'd move in for his milk, clinging like a drowning sailor.

At first, our children thought the calf was gruesome. Their feelings changed as they watched him struggle to remain alive. "He's so friendly," said Scott. "He totters up to the gate when we come with the feed, and he won't quit being a pest until we scratch his head."

One afternoon our daughter Jennifer told us about reading Homer's *Odyssey* in her English class. "There's a story in it about a one-eyed giant named Cyclops!" she said. "Wouldn't that be a perfect name?"

So Cyclops it was. During the months that followed, the odd-looking calf became another "ranch pet." The younger children played games with him and fed him lumps of sugar or sweet feed. In gratitude, he licked a hand or a small rosy cheek. "Look, Mama," a child's voice would cry. "Cyclops loves me!"

We noticed he became a favorite of other animals wandering around the barnyard. In winter, we'd often find a cat curled up against his hump for warmth; in summer, chickens and dogs sought shade in his shadow.

His best friend was a chick named Omelette. On their first encounter, Cyclops was napping. Omelette was less than a week old. He began pecking at the beads of sweat running down the glistening black, bovine nose. Cyclops snorted loudly, blowing the chick away. Undaunted, Omelette returned again and again, finally jumping on Cyclops's face and pecking his way to where the young bull's incredible horns lay.

Instead of growing up and outward, Cyclops's horns seemed to have collapsed into a tangled mound, creating a haven for lice and horn flies, the plague of all cattle. The snarled horns formed a perfect barrier against the tree trunks and fence posts on which he scratched, desperately seeking relief from the torturous insects.

Omelette quickly discovered the banquet beneath those horns. By summer's end, it was not unusual to see Omelette, now a full-grown rooster, perched on top of Cyclops's horny crown and pecking for hours at the hidden pests.

Still, Cyclops's own kind spurned him. During the first two years of his life, not a single cow, calf or bull would tolerate his presence.

By the time Cyclops was three, he ate nearly a ton of hay a month, and had grown to weigh seventeen hundred pounds. We tried to avoid any conversation concerning how useless he was to the ranch. Bill raised pedigreed Hereford bulls. Why were we wasting time and money to keep alive this tragic mistake of nature?

Spring brought the breeding season. Bulls were turned out into designated pastures with cows of specific bloodlines. Twenty heifers that Bill planned to artificially inseminate were also set apart in their own pasture.

Detecting exactly when a cow is in heat is the most time-consuming and frustrating part of artificial breeding. Hours are wasted watching for behavior signs that tell whether the cows are ready to be inseminated.

Cyclops was no longer free to roam. The herd bulls might consider him a threat. Confined to a corral, he became frantic with loneliness. He paced. He pawed. He bawled until his squeaky voice became a whisper.

Several months passed, and Bill was getting discouraged about the insemination program. Out of twenty heifers, only two that we could be certain of had come into heat. Then we noticed Cyclops had stopped pacing. Instead, he gazed longingly over his corral fence at a young heifer. For hours, they called back and forth to one another, she in her soft alto, he in his high falsetto. "I wonder," Bill said, "if that poor thing knows something we don't?"

"Let's let him loose and find out," said Scott. Cyclops's deformities left him sterile. "After all, he can't breed. What harm can he do?"

We opened the gate.

Cyclops, nostrils flared, snorted loudly and lurched into the pasture on his short twisted legs. The heifers scattered like leaves in the wind, but he found the object of his desire. He squealed. She froze. Cautiously he approached, tilting his head upward to caress her neck with his velvet mouth. Finally she allowed him to rest his head against her shoulder. He could do no more. We knew then she was ready to breed.

For the next two years, Cyclops became our "heat-detecting" bull, finding each heifer for us when they were ready to breed. We had a 98 percent conception rate that first year and 100 percent the second. Our homely bull was no longer useless—or lonely.

Cyclops was only four and a half years old when he died. We found him beneath his favorite shade tree. His heart had simply stopped beating. As I ran my fingers along his neck, a lump rose in my throat. The children were fighting tears, too.

Suddenly I realized that our extraordinary bull had awakened something in all of us—a greater sympathy, a deeper understanding for those less fortunate than their peers.

Cyclops was different only on the outside. Inside he had the same passion for life cherished by all God's creatures. He loved us, and we loved him.

Penny Porter

An Act of Faith

*What the caterpillar thinks is the end of the world
. . . the butterfly knows is only the beginning.*

Anonymous

When my son Luke was small, he liked to sit on my lap and watch television. Sometimes he'd point out what he thought belonged to the real world—auto accidents, fires, Joe Montana, astronauts—and what did not. Big Bird, for instance, belonged to the world of make-believe. But so did dinosaurs.

Luke had trouble understanding how dinosaurs could be considered real if they were not around anymore. My explanation that they were once alive but had all died long ago perplexed and annoyed him.

One day Mawmaw, his great-grandmother, sent him a drawing of a cat with a note that suggested he color it.

He finished this project the very day it arrived and then climbed into my chair to show it to me. The cat was red, blue and green.

"I've never seen such a colorful cat," I said.

"'Course not," he said. "He's mine and Mawmaw's," as

though that somehow explained things. He nestled against me and I clicked on the TV to a retrospective of the life of John Kennedy.

As a picture of young JFK at the tiller of a small sailboat appeared, Luke asked, "Who is that man?"

"It's John Kennedy. He was president of the United States."

"Where is he?"

"He's dead now."

Luke looked at my face to see if I could be teasing. "Is he all dead?"

"Yes."

There was a short silence. Then he asked, "His feet are dead?"

"Yes."

"Is his head dead?"

"Yes."

This last question was followed by a long, thoughtful pause. Then Luke finally said, "Well, he certainly talks very well."

Though I tried not to, I laughed—partly because he did seem to speak very well, for a dead person, that is, and partly because Luke had been *so* earnest in examining the problem.

After the JFK incident, Luke seemed haunted by the problem that death presented. Thereafter, almost every walk in the woods became a search for something dead— a field mouse, a raccoon or perhaps a bird. He would squat down on his haunches over the find and sometimes make up stories about what the animal had been doing when it died. Sometimes we held small funerals.

I was concerned, of course. The concept of death was a very large one for a three-year-old to understand.

One day in the woods, we found a few tawny tufts of rabbit fur. Luke rolled it around with a sassafras twig. "This was Peter Rabbit," he said. "He was going home to his house when a fox ate him up. He is in a fox now."

"But Peter Rabbit lives in the world of make-believe," I said, "and this was a real rabbit."

"I know that," he said. "I was just seeing." I think he meant that he was making up a story that would somehow let things turn out in a way he could understand.

I explained that most people thought only your body died. That you had another part, called a spirit, which survived. We didn't know that for sure, I said. But if you believed something deep inside—even though you couldn't prove it—that was called faith and that helped you to understand many things.

This produced amazement. "You are in two parts?" he said.

"Not exactly." I now knew I was in for it. His inquiry into these new ideas lasted about a week. On another of our walks, I showed him a butterfly cocoon that had once housed a pupa. I told him a caterpillar had spun that cocoon and eventually had emerged as a totally different creature—a butterfly. He accepted that easily because he had seen it happen on a nature show.

He said, "But you can still see the real butterfly. He goes places. You can touch him. If you're dead, people can only see you on TV."

"That's true," I said. "But you can see dead people in your head—in your imagination."

He thought long about that one. Finally, he asked how that could possibly be. I told him to close his eyes and imagine someone who was not with us. His friend, Charlie, for instance. "Can you imagine Charlie?"

He squealed with delight. "No! No! But I can hear him!"

"Well, it's like that. People who aren't with you right at the moment sort of hang around with you for as long as you remember them."

"But I can play with Charlie."

"Yes."

"And I couldn't go play with the bunny. Because he's dead."

"Yes, that's right."

Luke's preoccupation continued for another few days. But soon his attention switched to his upcoming birthday party, and he did not speak of his deep concern about death again.

About a year and a half later, Mawmaw died. Our southern family's custom is to lay out our kin at home, so my father's mother had a wake. When Luke insisted he be allowed to go, my wife and I thought that might be a good idea.

Mawmaw's house overflowed with guests and food and talk. She had lived a long, rich life, so there was none of the kind of wretched grief that attends early or unexpected deaths. People remembered her joy, her amazing personal strength, her humor and her kindness.

We let Luke go about as he pleased—talking with relatives, eating, getting praised and playing with his cousins. Then, at almost the last possible moment, he asked me to take him into the room where Mawmaw lay.

I took his hand and led him to stand beside his great-grandmother's bier. He was too small to see anything but flowers, so I picked him up and held him on my hip. He took a long look and then said, "Okay, Dad."

I put him down, and we walked out of the room down the long hallway toward the kitchen. Before we got there, he pulled me into a small room where my grandmother had once pressed flowers or done needlework. Looking solemnly at me, he whispered, "Dad, that is not Mawmaw."

"What do you mean?"

"It isn't," he said. "She is not in there."

"Then where is she?" I asked.

"Talking somewhere."

"Why do you think that?" I knelt down and put my hand on his shoulder.

"I just know. That's all. I just know." There was a long pause as we looked at each other. Finally he took a deep breath and said with more seriousness than I had ever seen in him, "Is that faith?"

"Yes, Son."

"Well, then that's how I know. That's what I got."

I looked at him with awe and joy, realizing he had just found one of the most powerful resources of the heart—a guide other than his mother or me. He had found a way of understanding that would be with him for the rest of his life, even in the valley of the shadow.

I suddenly felt deeply relieved and grateful in a way I had not anticipated when that day began. I looked at Luke smiling at me, and then we walked down the hall, hand in hand, to find something to eat and perhaps tell a story of our own.

Walter W. Meade

Benny's Balloon

Benny was seventy when he died rather suddenly of cancer in Wilmette, Illinois. Because his ten-year-old granddaughter Rachel never got the chance to say good-bye, she cried for days. But after receiving a big red balloon at a birthday party, she came home with an idea —a letter to Grampa Benny, air-mailed to heaven in her balloon.

Rachel's mother didn't have the heart to say no, and she watched with tears in her eyes as the fragile balloon bumped its way over the trees that lined the yard and disappeared.

Two months later, Rachel received this letter post-marked from a town six hundred miles away in Pennsylvania:

Dear Rachel,

Your letter to Grampa Benny reached him. He really appreciated it. Please understand that material things can't be kept in heaven, so they had to send the balloon back to Earth—they just keep thoughts, memories, love and things like that in heaven.

Rachel, whenever you think about Grampa Benny, he knows, and is very close by with overwhelming love for you.

Sincerely,
Bob Anderson (also a Grampa)

Michael Cody

One, Two, Three

It was an old, old, old, old lady,
And a boy that was half past three;
And the way they played together
Was beautiful to see.

She couldn't go running and jumping,
And the boy, no more could he;
For he was a thin little fellow,
With a thin little twisted knee.

They sat in the yellow twilight,
Out under the maple tree;
And the game that they played I'll tell you,
Just as it was told to me.

It was Hide and Go Seek they were playing,
Though you'd never have known it to be—
With an old, old, old, old lady,
And a boy with a twisted knee.

The boy would bend his face down
On his one little sound knee,

And he'd guess where she was hiding,
In guesses One, Two, Three!

"You are in the china closet!"
He would cry, and laugh with glee—
It wasn't the china closet;
But he still had Two and Three.

"You are up in Papa's big bedroom,
In the chest with the queer old key!"
And she said: "You are warm and warmer;
But you're not quite right," said she.

"It can't be the little cupboard
Where Mamma's things used to be—
So it must be the clothespress, Gran'ma,"
And he found her with his Three.

Then she covered her face with her fingers,
That were wrinkled and white and wee,
And she guessed where the boy was hiding,
With a One and a Two and a Three.

And they never had stirred from their places,
Right under the maple tree—
This old, old, old, old lady,
And the boy with the lame little knee—
this dear, dear, dear, old lady,
And the boy who was half past three.

Henry Cuyler Bunner
Submitted by Laura McNamara

Mother's Hands

How far you go in life depends on your being tender with the young, compassionate with the aged, sympathetic with the striving, and tolerant of the weak and the strong. Because someday in life you will have been all of these.

George Washington Carver

As teenagers we live in a different world from our mothers, a world where mothers hang out on the peripheries. Of course, almost everyone has one; they are unavoidable annoyances.

Today, as I approach that edge, as I am the one with the teenage daughter, I look at my mother through different eyes. And I sometimes wish I could halt the years and stop her from growing older, stop her from repeating herself.

We sit at my kitchen table as the sun designs a mosaic of light on the tile floor. My daughter, Anna, sits next to my mother.

"When is Rick going to be here?" my mother asks, referring to my husband.

"I don't know, Mom," I answer patiently. "He'll be here for dinner."

I sigh and get up from the table. This is at least the tenth time she has asked that question in as many minutes.

While my mother and daughter play Monopoly, I busy myself making a salad.

"Don't put in any onions," Mom says. "You know how Daddy hates onions."

"Yes, Mom," I answer, shoving the scallions back into the fridge.

I scrub off a carrot and chop it into bite-size pieces. I thrust the knife into the carrot with more force than is necessary. A slice falls onto the floor.

"Don't put any onions in the salad," she reminds me. "You know how Daddy hates onions."

This time I can't answer.

I just keep cutting. Chopping. Tearing. If only I could chop away the years. Shred the age from my mother's face and hands. Go back to my high school days when my mother moved from room to room, leaving a trace of whatever fragrance she wore at the time.

My mother had been beautiful. She still is. In fact, my mother is still everything she has been, just a bit forgetful. I try to convince myself that's all that it is, and if she really concentrated, she would not repeat herself so much. There isn't anything wrong with her—not my mother.

I cut off the end of the cucumber and rub it against the stalk to take away the bitterness. The white juice oozes out the sides. Wouldn't it be nice if all unpleasant situations could be so easily remedied? Cut and rub. This is a trick I have learned from my mother, along with a trillion other things: cooking, sewing, dating, laughing, thinking. I learned how to grow up and when to stay young. I learned the art of sorting through emotions.

And I learned that when my mother was around, I never had to be afraid.

So why am I afraid now?

I study my mother's hands. Her nails are no longer a bright red, but painted a light pink, almost no color at all. And as I stare at them, I realize I am no longer looking at those hands but feeling them as they shaped my youth. Hands that packed a thousand lunches and wiped a million tears off my cheeks. Hands that tucked confidence into each day of my life.

I turn away and throw the cucumber into the bowl. And then it hits me. My hands have grown into those of my mother's.

Hands that have cooked uneaten meals, driven hundreds of car-pool miles, held my own daughter's frightened fingers on the first day of school and dried tears off her face.

I grow lighthearted. I can feel my mother kiss me goodnight, check to see if the window is locked, then blow another kiss from the doorway. Then I am my mother, blowing that same kiss to Anna off that same palm.

Outside everything is still. Shadows fall among the trees, shaped like pieces of a puzzle.

Someday my daughter will be standing in my place, and I will rest where my mother now sits.

Will I remember then how it felt to be both mother and daughter? Will I ask the same question one too many times?

I walk over and sit down between my mother and her granddaughter.

"Where is Rick?" my mother asks, resting her hand on the table next to mine. The space between us is smaller than when I was a teenager, barely visible at all.

And in that instant I know she remembers. She may repeat herself a little too much. But she remembers.

"He'll be here," I answer with a smile.

My mother smiles back, one of those grins where the dimple takes over the shape of her face, resembling my daughter.

Then she lets her shoulders relax, picks up the dice and rolls.

Janie Emaus

The Game

"Do you still love me?" I asked.

"I don't know." Ralph looked away.

It was a game we played again and again throughout our thirty years of married life. But today, something in his voice alarmed me. His eyes were not laughing when he said, "I don't know." This was not the way we played the game.

He was supposed to say, "Oh, I don't know" in a mocking way and then ask, "Do you still love me?"

And I would answer, with a deliberately provocative move toward him, "Mmm, let me see," then shrug regretfully and say, "I guess I don't."

Then, his brows arching mischievously he'd announce, "So what . . . I don't love you either. I guess I'll find another." And with head high and chest out he'd march away.

"Don't you dare find another!" I'd shake my fist and run after him. He'd turn with a start, and colliding he'd reclaim my lips in a most persuasive way and declare, "Mmm, I guess I was wrong. I guess I still love you after all."

That was the way we always played the game. But

today Ralph remained uncomfortably still after uttering the words "I don't know."

Suddenly feeling as hollow as my voice sounded, I drew a deep breath, and forbidding myself to tremble, I repeated the question. "Do you still love me?" The words now seemed strange on my tongue.

And after an endless moment Ralph answered in a low, raspy voice. "I guess I don't."

A crow flashed black across the sky, its shadow skimming the earth. I was frozen into limbo where decisions and actions were impossible, where feelings were impossible. A defensive mechanism I supposed, a reflex taking over. Like a nothing I stumbled through nothingness. *Pull yourself together and tell the kids*, an inner voice roused my unconscious mind. What would they say?

I stood by the window with my back to John when he came into the room. "Your father and I are getting divorced."

I felt rather than saw Johnny's shocked movement. "Why?"

"Your father doesn't love me anymore, and I can't live without love. I mean I can't live with someone who . . . I mean. . . ." Oh God, I mustn't cry. "Do you know what I mean?" I turned around.

There were lines of concern about John's eyes, masking his youth. He came toward me and put his arms around me. "I'm sorry, Mom. I'll always be here for you." His understanding and kind words barely registered on my numbed mind.

Peter masked his emotions with a deceptive calmness. He was a master at this. My defenses began to subside, puzzling over the feelings he was hiding.

Bobbie stiffened and didn't know what to say. I understood. She was very close to her dad. Yet her inability to show compassion threatened to shatter my last shreds of control.

Chris, our oldest son, seemed not surprised. After all, divorce was the norm in today's life.

But it wasn't the norm for us. We were going to grow old together, Ralph and I. It was part of the game we always played, two old hopeless fools still in love.

Severely bent over and barely able to walk or talk, Ralph would call in a quavering voice, "Schatzi, where are you? Come here, I need a woman!" With my glasses at the tip of my nose I'd cast my eyes downward in a pretense of embarrassment and cackle, "You old devil you." Then with outstretched arms we'd shuffle towards each other in excited anticipation. But almost blind, we'd pass right by and take forever to come together, two old toothless clowns afflicted with tremors, and Ralph with a twitch. But in the end we'd always succeed. We'd lie side by side exhausted and spent, and deliriously happy we'd vow, "That's how it will be in the very end."

How long had it been since we pledged our love in this way? Lately, there was never time. Could it be that my involvement with Karen, my deceased sister's runaway child, took so much effort that I had neglected to realize Ralph's needs?

Or was Ralph merely going through male menopause?

I had waited to tell Karen last of the impending divorce. What would she say? I feared how it might affect her. Even though she was almost eighteen, she still needed a stable home.

"Huh? Don't worry! I'll stay with you." Perhaps it was the tone of unexpected casualness in her words, simple and plain, that dragged me out of my cocoon.

Karen, who for so long had been our confused, lost, tormented soul, in the hour of my greatest pain was the one who hauled me out of the depth of my despair. And I began to perceive a life without Ralph as possible.

Not long after, however, on a day in October when the

valley was filled with unexpected thunder, Ralph came home early. "If you still want to see that counselor," he said, "I'll come along. Perhaps you were right. Perhaps we should give it another try."

Mystified by the unexpected, I asked, "What made you change your mind?"

And Ralph answered in a somber tone. "Yesterday, I went to look at an apartment." He paused and turned his back to me. "A very nice apartment, but all of a sudden it struck me," he turned to face me again, "you wouldn't be there when I would come home."

I gasped a sigh of relief, and while collecting the fragments of my heart I began to envision the possibility of, once again, playing the game.

Christa Holder Ocker

Hussy Sunsets

[EDITORS' NOTE: *This letter was written in 1941 by the author to her brother. She noted: "This letter sounds kind of silly—and it no doubt is. Maybe it would sound better if I could talk to you— but I can't. So you'll have to take it in a letter, and have the kindness to remember that your sister Milly was always considered a bit peculiar—tho' perfectly harmless."*]

Dear Chuck:

Letters of congratulations are hard for me to write. There are conventional and proper things to say and conventional and proper ways to say them: "Congratulations!" "Every wish for happiness," "Life's greatest adventure," etc. These things are true, but they are a bit trite, and have been said so many times that they're practically meaningless.

Other things are true. (Although it is considered very inappropriate to talk about them!) You'll rebel sometimes, and you'll hate being tied down, and you'll regret your lost freedom. Well, don't regret; never regret anything. While I can't claim an oriental fatalism, nor yet the old Puritan belief in predestination, still I think things even up pretty much in the long run. Married you'll have a lot of fun and a lot of grief; single you'd have a lot of fun and a lot of loneliness.

Sure you'll rebel sometimes—although right now you're sure you won't. One day, you'll be at work near quitting time and you're not really busy. You'll wonder how in the hell you're going to get the car payment together and the final notice on the gas bill came last night, but besides that Gretchen had made a date to play bridge with some stuffy people who bore you to tears. You light a Wing (you're smoking Wings now instead of Philip Morris) and look out the window: I always see a ship sailing into a strange wonderful unknown; you—being of a younger generation probably hear the drone of a plane, or see a flash of wings among the clouds.

The sun is setting, a brazen hussy of a sunset, beckoning you with sleeves of scarlet and gold. "Come with me—I'll show you fun and adventure and excitement. To hell with the car payment. I may burn you and starve you and lead you to a devil's life; but I promise you, you won't be bored. Come on, before you're old and stodgy and have a stomach, I shan't want you then!"

You don't answer the hussy; you're much too good a husband for that, but you mutter to yourself: "I would: by God, I would if I weren't married. I'd walk right out of this place and down to the docks and take a job on the first tramp steamer that would have me; maybe I will anyway!" You don't of course, because you're a Carr and we don't walk out on things. You go home and notice how much better your lawn looks than the one next door (he's a lazy fellow anyway); and that climbing rose that you planted to cover the gas meter—say that's doing alright: You go in and there is Gretchen, her hair all over her head and her make-up sweated off and she has flour on her cheek and she is very sweet. It's hot and she has been making peanut butter cookies—the kind you like. You kiss her with special fervor because you love her and because you feel just a bit guilty for listening to that hussy sunset.

You go into the living room and pick up the paper. You read the funnies and slip off one shoe; you read the sports and off comes the other. You're just turning to the news when Gretchen calls from the kitchen (she's peeling spuds)—"Honey, there's just enough time to water the lawn before dinner's ready. Don't you think you ought to do it now? We won't have time after," you remember that dratted bridge game and grumble, but you water the lawn.

The sunset is still there—fading now but still a hussy, no longer beckoning but jeering you with one scarlet streak of wicked merriment. And you have the wit to jeer right back because you've had your dream. And besides, the steak's about done, you can smell it and it smells pretty damned good compared to the empty promises of a hussy sunset!

And Gretchen has her dreams, too, don't forget that! She doesn't really care much about cooking, and she hates wearing sixty-nine-cent hose and doesn't like smoking Wings any better than you do. Oh yes! She, too, dreams after the sunset; why else do you think she made those cookies on such a hot day?

These dreams are good, and if you're lucky you'll always have them for when they stop—then you're old! These dreams are yours, your own private "yours," and it isn't cheating to keep a little bit of yourself to yourself. But the real fun in marriage is sharing. Sharing plans and responsibilities and memories of course, we all know that. But sharing more too, talk and little private jokes no one else thinks are funny and glances and the funnies in bed on Sunday morning. Jan Struther in *Mrs. Miniver* says "the most important thing in marriage is not a home and children or a remedy against sin, but simply there being always an eye to catch." And talk, that's important, too. It may not seem so now when kisses are so much more exciting, but believe me, it is important. Not chatter— anyone can chatter—but being able to talk—really talk— together, without embarrassment or restraint, is real and important and lasting. I've left out sex, haven't I? And although sex isn't all there is to marriage, as many young-sters seem to think, it is a very real and definite and important part of marriage. And a perfect—or even good— sexual adjustment between two people doesn't just hap-pen or come about by instinct (in spite of romantic stories and the movies), it must be learned: learned through patience and thoughtfulness and unselfishness, and it is worth the learning.

Have I shown the picture too black? It isn't really! Marriage is like all life—a background of gray highlighted by splashes of color; gay yellows and passionate red; the content and serenity of blues and greens, and occasion-ally a somber purple. And that's best. A world of contin-ual purple and red would drive the rest of us nuts.

So endeth the first lesson—ain'tcha glad!

Milly VanDerpool

Two Brothers

Once upon a time in a far away land, lived two young men, much like many young men you may know today . . .

The two brothers were likable, but undisciplined, with a wild streak in them. Their mischievous behavior turned serious when they began stealing sheep from the local farmers—a serious crime in this pastoral place, so long ago and far away. In time, the thieves were caught. The local farmers decided their fate: The two brothers would be branded on the forehead with the letters *ST* for "sheep thief." This sign they would carry with them forevermore.

One brother was so embarrassed by this branding that he ran away; he was never heard from again.

The other brother, filled with remorse and reconciled to his fate, chose to stay and try to make amends to the villagers he had wronged. At first the villagers were skeptical and would have nothing to do with him. But this brother was determined to make reparation for his offenses.

Whenever there was a sickness, the sheep thief came to care for the ill with soup and a soft touch. Whenever there was work needing to be done, the sheep thief came to help with a lending hand. It made no difference if the person were rich or poor, the sheep thief was there to help. Never accepting pay for his good deeds, he lived his life for others.

Many years later, a traveler came through the village. Sitting at a sidewalk café eating lunch, the traveler saw an old man with a strange brand on his forehead seated nearby. The stranger noticed that all the villagers who passed the old man stopped to share a kind word, to pay their respects; children stopped their play to give and receive a warm hug.

Curious, the stranger asked the café owner, "What does that strange brand on the old man's forehead stand for?"

"I don't know. It happened so long ago . . . " the café owner replied. Then, pausing briefly for a moment of reflection, he continued: ". . . but I think it stands for 'saint.'"

Willanne Ackerman

At Wit's End

Every once in a while, something happens in our lives to cause us to reshuffle our priorities. Sometimes it's a traumatic birthday or a friend facing a crisis. To me, it was the funeral of a good friend that left me vulnerable, confused and doubtful as to what I am all about.

I wanted to draw all our savings out of the bank and go to Tahiti. I wanted to put the plastic dishes in the driveway and back over them with a car. I wanted to take ballet lessons. Throw away all the imitation flowers and replace them with a jungle of vines and greenery. I wanted to take up all the carpets and let the dust fall where it wanted to.

That very night, I took a look at my life, rearranged my cards into a whole new hand and made a vow. I am not going to be like the woman on the Titanic who, as she climbed into the lifeboat facing an uncertain future, sobbed in anguish, "If I had known this was going to happen, I'd have had the chocolate mousse for dessert."

So get ready, world! Miss Practical is going to start living each day like it's her last.

Remember that big candle in the sitting room that's shaped like a rose that gathers dust and gets soft in the summer? I lit it yesterday.

And the car window—the one on my side that has a thin crack in it that we said we'd have replaced when we sell the car? Well, it's been replaced.

Guess who's coming to dinner on Sunday? Evie and Jack, whom we have seen at sixteen weddings and say the same thing every time: "We've got to get together."

And that big tin of fish that I didn't want to open because I'm the only one who eats fish and I couldn't bear to waste the rest of it? Well, so what!

As I washed my hands with a piece of pink soap shaped like a sea shell, my husband said, "I thought you were saving those. You got them wet and they don't look like a shell anymore."

I looked down at the handful of suds. A shell only holds life, I had just given it a chance to be something more.

Erma Bombeck

More Chicken Soup?

Many of the stories and poems you have read in this book were submitted by readers like you who had read earlier *Chicken Soup for the Soul* books. We are planning to publish five or six *Chicken Soup for the Soul* books every year. We invite you to contribute a story to one of these future volumes.

Stories may be up to twelve hundred words and must uplift or inspire. You may submit an original piece or something you clip out of the local newspaper, a magazine, a church bulletin or a company newsletter. It could also be your favorite quotation you've put on your refrigerator door or a personal experience that has touched you deeply.

To obtain a copy of our submission guidelines and a listing of upcoming *Chicken Soup* books, please write, fax or check one of our Web sites.

Chicken Soup for the *(Specify Which Edition)* Soul
P.O. Box 30880 • Santa Barbara, CA 93130
fax: 805-563-2945
Web site: *www.chickensoup.com*

You can also visit the *Chicken Soup for the Soul* site on America Online at keyword: chickensoup.

Just send a copy of your stories and other pieces, indicating which edition they are for, to any of the above addresses.

We will be sure that both you and the author are credited for your submission.

For information about speaking engagements, other books, audiotapes, workshops and training programs, please contact any of the authors directly.

Supporting Others

With each *Chicken Soup for the Soul* book we publish, we designate one or more charities to receive a portion of the profits. Charities we support include the National Arbor Day Foundation, the Breast Cancer Research Foundation, Habitat for Humanity and Feed the Children.

A portion of the proceeds from *Chicken Soup for the Unsinkable Soul* will be donated to the Special Olympics and The Juvenile Diabetes Foundation.

The **Special Olympics** provides sports training and competitions year-round and cost-free to all persons eight years of age and older with mental retardation. There are currently over 1 million athletes participating in Special Olympics programs throughout the world.

Special Olympics helps persons with mental retardation to find and fulfill their unique roles in the Circle of Life. Special Olympics respects the unique qualities that every life brings to this world. Their organization makes it possible for its athletes to develop their talents and abilities so that they might experience the everyday joys that many people take for granted. And isn't that really what life's all about?

Special Olympics, Inc.
1325 G Street NW, Suite 500
Washington, DC 20005
phone: 202-628-3630
fax: 202-824-0200
www.specialolympics.org

The **Juvenile Diabetes Foundation** (JDF) is a not-for-profit, voluntary health agency with chapters and affiliates throughout the world. JDF's main objective is to support and fund research to find a cure for diabetes and its complications. JDF gives more money directly to diabetes research than any other private health agency in the world.

The organization awards research grants for laboratory and clinical investigations and sponsors a variety of career development and research training programs for new and established investigators.

JDF also sponsors international workshops and conferences for biomedical researchers. Individual chapters offer support groups and other activities for families affected by diabetes.

For more information, write to:

Juvenile Diabetes Foundation International
120 Wall Street
New York, NY 10005-4001
phone: 800-JDF-CURE
fax: 212-785-9500

Who Is Jack Canfield?

Jack Canfield is a bestselling author with twenty-seven books published, including nine *New York Times* bestsellers. In 1998 *USA Today* declared that Jack Canfield and his writing partner, Mark Victor Hansen, sold more books during the previous year than any other author in the United States. Jack and Mark also have a syndicated *Chicken Soup for the Soul* newspaper column through King Features and a weekly column in *Woman's World* magazine.

Jack is the author and narrator of several bestselling audiocassette and videocassette programs, including *Self-Esteem and Peak Performance, How to Build High Self-Esteem* and *The STAR Program*. He is a regularly consulted expert for radio and television broadcasts and has published a total of twenty-seven books—all bestsellers within their categories—including twenty-two *Chicken Soup for the Soul* books, *The Aladdin Factor, Heart at Work, 100 Ways to Build Self-Concept in the Classroom* and *Dare to Win*.

Jack conducts keynote speeches for about seventy-five groups each year. His clients have included schools and school districts in all fifty states, over one hundred education associations including the American School Counselors Association and Californians for a Drug Free Youth, plus corporate clients such as AT&T, Campbell Soup, Clairol, Domino's Pizza, GE, New England Telephone, Re/Max, Sunkist, Supercuts and Virgin Records.

Jack conducts an annual seven-day Training of Trainers program in the areas of building self-esteem and achieving peak performance in all areas of your life. The program attracts educators, counselors, parenting trainers, corporate trainers, professional speakers, ministers, youth workers and interested others.

To contact Jack for further information about his books, tapes and trainings, or to schedule him for a keynote speech, please contact:

The Canfield Training Group
P.O. Box 30880 • Santa Barbara, CA 93130
phone: 805-563-2935 • fax: 805-563-2945
To send e-mail or to visit his Web site: *www.chickensoup.com*

Who Is Mark Victor Hansen?

Mark Victor Hansen is a professional speaker who, in more than two decades, has made over four thousand presentations to more than two million people in thirty-two countries. His presentations cover sales excellence and strategies; personal empowerment and development; and how to triple your income and double your time off.

Mark has spent a lifetime dedicated to his mission of making a profound and positive difference in people's lives. Throughout his career, he has inspired hundreds of thousands of people to create a more powerful and purposeful future for themselves, while stimulating the sale of billions of dollars worth of goods and services.

Mark is a prolific writer and has authored *Future Diary, How to Achieve Total Prosperity* and *The Miracle of Tithing.* He is coauthor of the *Chicken Soup for the Soul* series, *Dare to Win* and *The Aladdin Factor* (all with Jack Canfield) and *The Master Motivator* (with Joe Batten).

Mark has also produced a complete library of personal empowerment audio- and videocassette programs that have enabled his listeners to recognize and use their innate abilities in their business and personal lives. His message has made him a popular television and radio personality, with appearances on ABC, NBC, CBS, HBO, PBS, CNN, "Prime Time Country," "Crook & Chase" and TNN News. He has also appeared on the cover of numerous magazines, including *Success, Entrepreneur* and *Changes.*

Mark is a big man with a heart and spirit to match—an inspiration to all who seek to better themselves.

For further information about Mark contact:

P.O. Box 7665 • Newport Beach, CA 92658
phone: 949-759-9304 or 800-433-2314
fax: 949-722-6912
To send e-mail or to visit his Web site: *www.chickensoup.com.*

Who Is Heather McNamara?

What began for Heather as a part-time freelancing job in 1995 turned into a full-time job as editorial director for Chicken Soup for the Soul Enterprises in 1996.

"I feel so fortunate to have a job that brings joy to so many people," Heather says. Her love of literature grew from her third-grade teacher Mrs. Lutsinger, who read to the children every day after lunch.

Today Heather owns her own home in a rural outpost of the San Fernando Valley, where she enjoys the panoramic view of the valley, her garden and her four dogs—all adopted strays. Her oldest dog, an abandoned "junkyard" dog, continues to patrol her yard, despite the fact that "he is blind in one eye and doesn't hear so well. But he still has a good sniffer," Heather proclaims.

The idea for *Chicken Soup for the Unsinkable Soul* came from feedback from the many *Soup* readers whose consistently favorite chapter is Overcoming Obstacles.

"Fortunately, I've never faced the many kinds of obstacles others have," Heather says. "Compiling these stories has caused me to reflect on the blessings of my life: a father who loves me, a mother who spoils me, a grandmother who inspires me, and three siblings who make me laugh. Best of all," Heather continues, "I count my brother and sisters among my best friends.

"These stories put my own life in perspective." She recalled many conversations with William Rush, a contributor to the book, as they talked over the computer. What Heather heard was the tapping of his headstick, each delayed word spoken by his computer, until finally a sentence was strung together, again delivered in the distinctively metered voice of the computer. The day she called to tell William that his story would be published in *Chicken Soup for the Unsinkable Soul*, "I didn't hear the familiar 'tap,' 'tap,' 'tap.' I just heard this incredibly exuberant and exhilarating cry." It is the only time she heard William's voice, and it sent shivers through her.

You can reach Heather at:

Self-Esteem Seminars
P.O. Box 30880
Santa Barbara, CA 93130
phone: 818-833-1954

Contributors

Several of the stories in this book were taken from previously published sources, such as books, magazines and newspapers. These sources are acknowledged in the permissions section. However, most of the stories were written by humorists, comedians, professional speakers and workshop presenters. If you would like to contact them for information on their books, audiotapes and videotapes, seminars and workshops, you can reach them at the addresses and phone numbers provided below.

The remainder of the stories were submitted by readers of our previous *Chicken Soup for the Soul* books who responded to our requests for stories. We have also included information about them.

Willanne Ackerman, mother of four, wrote "Happy Birthday" for a writing class during her return to college after a fifteen-year hiatus. She now teaches English in a public high school in Southern California, where she encourages her students to examine their own lives and values through writing. "Often, an 'Aha!' moment comes after you see something you've written on paper. This," she says, "is when students discover important truths about life and about themselves."

Dennis J. Alexander is a high school teacher in Seaside, California, where he lives with his wife and daughter. He has traveled and taught in the Philippines, Korea, New England and California. He grew up in Milwaukee, Wisconsin, and received degrees from the University of Wisconsin and the Monterey Institute of International Studies. Dennis has written short stories and is currently at work on a family memoir and a novel. He can be contacted c/o The Millennium Publishing Group, Tenth St., Monterey, CA.

Carol Barre lives with her husband, Jim, and dachshund, Frodo, in a motorhome and migrates from work at an RV park in the Florida Keys to summer near her mother in North Carolina. Writing, bodywork and Twelve-Step programs have opened her path to self-acceptance. "I write to understand myself and sometimes it seems that may be helpful to someone else."

Karyl Chastain Beal has been a fifth-grade teacher for about twenty-five years and a hopeful writer for the last ten of them. In memory of her daughter Aryln, she is working to help parents whose children have died (from suicide or other causes) through e-mail support groups. She would like to expand this mission to include teaching others about suicide, in hopes that new awareness will produce a demand for identification of root causes and solutions to a growing problem. Visit Arlyn's memorial Web site at *www.virtual-memorials.com*. You may contact Karyl via e-mail at *103040.2452@compuserve.com* or *arlyns-mother@hotmail.com* or by mail at P.O. Box 417, Pavo, GA 31778.

Rachel Berry is a freelance writer and poet. She has an adult novel in progress and is currently circulating a juvenile novel for publication. The married mother of four is the Valentine's Day contest winner of *Byline Magazine*, and has had short stories published in *Tidewater, Parent Magazine* and *Shallow End E-zine Magazine*.

The Best of Bits & Pieces. Copyright ©1994 by Arthur F. Lenehan, editor. The Economics Press, Inc., 12 Daniel Road, Fairfield, NJ 07004. Call 800-526-2554 worldwide at 1-973-227-1224. You may fax The Economics Press at 973-227-9742 or email *info@epinc.com* or by the web at *www.epinc.com*. Please call The Economics Press, Inc., directly to purchase this book or for subscription information on, or a free sample issue of the monthly pocket magazine, *Bits & Pieces*, the magazine that motivates the world.

Deborah Tyler Blais loves playing fetch with her new kitty, Karma, relaxing at the beach, riding on the back of her husband Gary's Harley, and of course— writing! Grateful for the gifts and lessons cancer brought her, Debbie continues sharing her experiences with others as she finishes her first book, *Living Your Bliss*. Anyone touched by her story is welcome to drop her a line at: 1419 Madison St., Hollywood, FL 33020 or *debbieb688@aol.com*

Terry Boisot and her husband Bruce have two children, Michelle and Ben. The lives of her children and the support of her husband have inspired Terry to advocate on behalf of people with developmental disabilities. She has devoted her life to educating people throughout her community and the state of California as to the value of building communities that expect, welcome and support people with varying abilities. This short story, "Ben," is only one of a lifetime of stories that have and will continue to renew her spirit and keep her vision alive that the world will one day embrace all people in the mainstream of life.

Jean Bole, R.N., B.A., is restorative/rehabilitation certified, CAN instructor certified and stress management educator certified. She is currently involved with Governors State University's Wellness Conference in an effort to educate the community regarding mind-body health. She is a wife, mother and a lover of dolls. Jean is a published freelance writer/poet. You can reach her by writing to P.O. Box 512, Valparaiso, IN 46383.

Nancy Bouchard lives in New England with her husband and three children. Currently working as a public relations coordinator for a private school, she also does freelance journalism and other writing services from her home. For her self-published book of short stories and poetry, or to contact Nancy, call 978-975-1590.

Henry Cuyler Bunner (1855-1896), was an American author and editor whose literacy contributions and editorial leadership helped spark the early issues of *Puck*, America's first comic weekly. Bunner excelled in the writing of light verses, volumes of poetry and parodies. Bunner died in Nutley, New Jersey, on May 11, 1896.

Darrell J. Burnett, Ph.D., is a clinical and sport psychologist, parent, national lecturer, author, consultant, and volunteer youth league coach. He has been in private practice in southern California for over twenty years, working with troubled youth and their families, specializing in positive parenting. He can be reached at Funagain Press, P.O. Box 7223, Laguna Niguel, CA 92607-7223, 800-493-5943 or by fax at 949-495-8204. E-mail: *djburnet@pacbell.net*. Web site: *www.djburnett.com*

John Callahan. You might have first heard about him as "that paralyzed cartoonist," but this misses the point. John Callahan is a hysterically funny cartoonist, regardless of any handicaps he might have to overcome. John's autobiography, *Don't Worry, He Won't Get Far on Foot!* was a bestseller on the *New York Times* list. TriStar Pictures recently purchased the book's movie rights as a vehicle for Robin Williams. You can contact John c/o Deborah Levin at Levin Represents at 310- 92-5146.

Chris Carrier ministers to students and frequently shares about God's mercy in his life. He holds a master of divinity degree from Southwestern Baptist Theological Seminary. Chris and his wife Leslie live in San Marcos, Texas, with their children Amanda, Melodee and Preston.

Lila Jones Cathey, daughter of T.R. and May Jones of McAdoo, Texas, is owner of Hill County Leather. She is married to George Cathey and has three children, Susan Hallam, Laurie Perkins and David Cathey. Lila has had a lifetime involvement in helping the mentally retarded and became the advocate for a young man with Down's syndrome twenty years ago. Lila has written several human interest articles that have been published in newspapers in Austin, Texas and Bronwood, Texas. You may reach her at 108 Parkview Terrace, Bronwood, TX 76801, or call her at 915-643-2299.

Fred Lloyd Cochran has been a science writer and editor for the past forty years. Mixed in was a twelve-year adventure as the editor and publisher of California's oldest weekly newspaper *The Mountain Messenger* (established 1853). In his spare time he wrote documentary films. He currently lives in the San Bernardino National Forest where he is completing a historical novel about the follies of America's nuclear research programs. He can be reached at P.O. Box 2350, Crestline, CA 92325.

Michael Cody, a retired brigadier general, is an internationally recognized speaker, educator and entertainer. Mike specializes in leadership, motivation, management, communications, and Indian Wars and Medal of Honor-related historical seminars. He can be reached at 1716 Singletary NE, Albuquerque, NM 87112, by calling 505-293-3729, or e-mail at *mcabq@aol.com*.

Phil Colburn is ninety-nine years old and has lived in a senior home since the death of her husband in 1994. They shared seventy-four happy years together, as well as three children: twin sons and a daughter. Often the ideas for a poem come to Phil in the night and she must get up and write them down or they escape.

Julane DeBoer along with her husband, Mark, is currently raising six children in Zeeland, Michigan. Mark keeps busy as an assistant store director for D & W Food Center. Julane is busy being a mom and a full-time college student. They are really thankful to God for having a part in Luke's miracle.

Christopher de Vinck is a writer in Pompton Plains, New Jersey.

Melva Hagger Dye's professional involvement has encompassed newspapers, commercial printing and graphic arts for over thirty years. She remarried, lives in Houston, Texas, and works with her husband, founder and president of Print Marketing Concepts, Inc., producers of television magazine for newspapers throughout the U.S. She and her husband are avid art collectors. Melva also enjoys porcelain doll-making, pottery and golf in addition to writing. She is currently completing her first novel.

Carol Darnell was born in Lubbock, Texas, and is a wife and proud mother of three children: Nicole, Kyle and Kevin. She has been married for twenty years. She is a preschool gymnastic instructor in Corona, California. Her article was written as a loving tribute to her father, Lawrence Anderson, who passed away in 1989. Currently writing a humorous book about parenting, she also performs stand-up comedy. Carol can be reached at 909-279-9792.

Janie Emaus is a mother of two unique children, the wife of a very loving man and the daughter of the most wonderful parents in the world. Her story is dedicated to her mother, Sylvia. Her stories have appeared in numerous magazines and newspapers and she has written two novels for children, as well as educational videos. She can be reached by fax at 818-710-0353.

Mavis Burton Ferguson was born in May of 1916 in the tiny hamlet of Berlin, Georgia. She was raised in a strong Christian family amidst the backdrop of Southern racial prejudices that influenced her early views of the world. Mavis met her husband, Mac, while she was obtaining her B.A. from Stetson University. Soon after their marriage Mac was called to serve in World War II and thereafter continued to enjoy a career as an officer in the military. Mavis's story is based at one of the tours of duty that took the Ferguson family around the world. Through this experience she was able to take her racial blinders off and see the magnitude of "the Golden Rule" taught in the Bible.

Adele Frances is a career counselor who helps people find the courage to walk their true career paths and get the juice out of their lives. An aspiring freelance writer with a half-dozen published articles and essays, Adele recently relocated from New Jersey to New Mexico. She is learning to balance her career with writing on a daily basis. She offers encouragement to every novice writer with the same dream. Her advice, "Don't quit your day job yet." She can be reached at her e-mail address: *adelefran@hubwest.com.*

Mindy Pollack-Fusi is a health-care writer living in Bedford, Massachussetts, with her husband, two daughters, two dogs, a cat and a house rabbit.

Eileen Goltz was born and raised in the Chicago area. She attended Indiana University and attained her B.A. degree through the Independent Learning Program. This program allowed her to construct a major not currently listed within the university structure. During her senior year she attended the Cordon Bleu Cooking School in Paris and graduated with an elementary certificate. She recently finished a cookbook that Feldheim Publishing will publish in the fall of 1999.

Arthur Gordon attended Yale University. He was a Rhodes Scholar at Oxford, England and served as an Air Force officer in World War II. He then spent several years in New York City, on the staffs of prominent magazines. He has served as editorial director at *Guideposts,* and his articles and stories have appeared in *The Saturday Evening Post, Colliers, Redbook* and *Reader's Digest.* The author of the bestselling *A Touch of Wonder,* he is a freelance writer at his home in Savannah, Georgia.

Cynthia M. Hamond is a freelance writer whose most rewarding success have been her contributions to the *Chicken Soup* books. She and her husband, Bruce, live in a small town along the Mississippi River where they have raised five children. Her parents, whose story is in this book, live right up the street. She enjoys her school visits and answering her mail from readers. She can be reached at 1021 W. River St. Monticello, MN 55362 or at *candbh@aol.com.*

Charles A. Hart lives in Seattle with his wife of thirty-two years. They have two adult sons, the older has autism, as does the author's seventy-eight-year-old brother and two sons of his first cousin. Charles is a published author and has won awards for his writing.

Magi Hart received an R.N. degree from Mt. Saint Mary's. She has a B.A. in human services, philosophy, future policy studies and psychology. She wrote newsletters, policies, procedures and educational material. As counselor for HIV support groups in South Bay, Los Angeles, she wrote articles for the newsletter *South Bay Alive.* Between efforts to publish she visited some of the world including China, Japan, India, Tibet, Italy, Russia and Mexico. She continues to write educational materials and to experiment with "creative media."

Joyce Harvey is a motivational and inspirational speaker, trainer, facilitator and writer. She has conducted numerous training sessions on sales, leadership, empowerment and personal growth. Joyce lost her only child in October of 1995. She facilitates a local bereavement support group, FOCUS, for families who have lost children. Watch for Joyce's forthcoming books (both still in manuscript form): *Swan Lessons,* the story of her journey through grief, and *I'm Fine—I'm with the Angels,* an illustrated children's book on death and dying. Joyce can be reached at P.O. Box 196, Lambertville, MI 48144-09163, or by fax at 734-854-3942 or by e-mail at *swanlesson@aol.com.*

Deborah E. Hill has enjoyed writing since her junior high school days. "Sensory Deprivation" was written during a very difficult period in her life when she was separated from her family and those things that she holds most dear. Her greatest joy in life is her son Travis.

Margaret (Meg) Hill writes articles, short stories and young adult books. Recent titles are *Coping with Family Expectations* (Rosen, 1990) and *So What Do I Do About Me?* (Teacher Ideas Press, Libraries Unlimited, Englewood, Colorado, 1993). Kirk is the pen name used when writing from the viewpoint of a teenage boy.

Bill Holton is graciously allowed to share his home with three demanding yet adorable Siamese cats and his demanding yet adorable wife, Tara. Bill is a freelance writer from Richmond, Virginia. When not feverishly begging magazine editors for assignments, he actually dreams of retiring to the Florida Keys where he will concentrate his boundless energy on fishing. He can be reached at *bholton@reporters.net*.

Bob Hoppenstedt is the author of *Coaching from the Heart, Knights of the Sun* and coauthor of *Peak Performance*. In addition to his writing, Bob has coached over eighty teams at the high school and college levels, with over two thousand career victories. Bob was elected to Who's Who of American Teachers, was a finalist as The Most Caring Coach by *USA Today* and was inducted into the Illinois High School Tennis Coach Hall of Fame. Bob is currently teaching and coaching at Wheaton North High School and the College of DuPage in Glen Ellyn, Illinois.

Irvine Johnston is an ordained minister in the United Church of Canada. His story/messages have been a hallmark of his ministry to all ages. Irvine can be reached at R.R. 1, Napanee, Ontario, Canada K7R 3K6.

Paul Karrer has published over fifty articles and short stories. His story "The Babyflight" had over 300,000 copies published in *A 4th Course of Chicken Soup for the Soul*. He has taught in Western Samoa, Korea, England, Connecticut and currently teaches in California. He may be reached at 457 Archer St., Monterey, CA. You may contact Paul by e-mail at *pkarrer123@yahoo.com*.

Marilyn King is a two-time Olympian (Munich 1972 and Montreal 1976) in the grueling pentathlon (100-meter hurdles, shot put, high jump, long jump, 800 meters). Her twenty-year athletic career includes five national titles and a world record. Her story launched her exploration into the field of exceptional human performance. Her joint Russian-American venture called the Peace Team, prompted two invitations to speak at the United Nations. She is currently featured in numerous articles and books including *Dream Makers* by Michelle Hunt and *Spirit of Champions* by Lyle Nelson and Thorn Baclon, and appeared recently on the *News Hour* with Jim Lehrer.

Emily Perl Kingsley is a mother, lecturer and professional writer who has received thirteen Emmy awards for her work writing scripts and songs for *Sesame Street*. A frequent speaker on the subject of disability rights, she serves on a committee to improve the way disabled people are portrayed in the media. She and her son Jason, who has Down's syndrome, have appeared on *Oprah, Good Morning America* and *All My Children*.

Karen Klosterman is a wife, married twenty-five years to Pete, and mother of two daughters, Molly and Margo. She is a junior high school language arts teacher in

Piqua, Ohio, and a cancer survivor. She taught in the 1970s, was a stay-at-home mom in the 1980s and came back to the classroom in the 1990s. Karen earned her master's in education in 1996 from the University of Dayton. Her writing was submitted as part of the 1998 Ohio Writing Project for Miami University.

Paula Bachleda Koskey originally wrote "Dear Jesse" for her son when he graduated from high school, and since then she has had the privilege of witnessing his graduation from college. Paula is a freelance writer who enjoys reading, walking, dancing and chocolate but her biggest joy comes from spending time with her children, Jesse, HopeAnn and Luke. Correspondence may be sent to 1173 Cambridge, Berkley, MI 48072.

Tom Krause is a motivational speaker, teacher and coach, and the founder of Positive People Presentations. He speaks to teenagers, teaching staffs and any organization on dealing with teen issues. He also speaks with business organizations in the area of motivation and stress reduction. He can be reached at: 4355 S. National #2206, Springfield, MO 65810, by calling 417-883-6753 or by e-mail at *justmetrk@aol.com.*

Linda LaRocque has written short stories for *Guideposts* and *Signs of The Times.* Her first book is currently under review with a publisher. This award-winning author of five plays contends all writing to be a form of ministry. She writes from her home in South Haven, Michigan.

Patricia Lorenz is an internationally known inspirational, art-of-living writer and speaker. She's the author of *Stuff That Matters for Single Parents* and *A Hug a Day for Single Parents.* Patricia, a frequent contributor to the *Chicken Soup for the Soul* books, has also had over four hundred articles published in magazines such as: *Reader's Digest, Guideposts, Working Mother, Woman's World* and *Single-Parent Family.* She can be reached at 7457 S. Pennsylvania Avenue, Oak Creek, WI 53154.

Heidi Marotz lives in Idaho Falls, Idaho, with her husband, Scott, and children, Chase, Jillian and Hayden. Heidi has a graphics business, White Porch Design, and is the supervising graphic artist for the Idaho Falls School of Ballet. She delights in working in her herb and vegetable garden. Heidi believes her relationship with Jesus Christ is the light that illuminates both the challenges and celebrations of life.

John and **Edna Massimilla** wrote the poem "Heaven's Very Special Child" soon after the birth of their third daughter, Ruth, in 1952. Edna, who liked to write poetry since childhood, seemed to make her personal project to continue this talent from then on, with concern for all mentally retarded children. Her husband, Rev. John, devoted his ministry to this cause, becoming chaplain of Delaware's institution for the disabled. When columnist Ann Landers printed "Heaven's Very Special Child" in her column, the Massimillas received thousand of letters from parents and other caregivers; they answered them all. For the past several years Edna and John have opened their home to be a respite provider for the mentally retarded. John is eighty-seven and Edna is eighty-two. They are supposed to be retired but instead seem to be "refired." They received the designation "Composers Laureate" for the disabled.

Walter W. Meade started writing at the age of fourteen. His first story was published in *Colliers* magazine when he was twenty-two. He wrote short fiction for the *Saturday Evening Post, Gentlemen's Quarterly* and several others. He then turned to writing nonfiction for magazines such as *Cosmopolitan, Redbook* and the *Reader's Digest*. Later he took a position in the publishing world and became the managing editor of *Cosmopolitan* and then the managing editor of the *Reader's Digest* Book Club. His last position in publishing was president and editor in chief of Avon Books, a position he held for ten years. Today, Walter is retired and writing articles for *Reader's Digest* as well as many other magazines and periodicals. He can be reached at 4561 N.W. 67th Terr., Lauderhill, FL 33319.

Susan McElroy has been an animal lover all of her life. She has worked with animals for years as a veterinarian's assistant, Humane Society educator, dog trainer and zookeeper. She makes her home in Oregon at Bright Star Farm. She can be reached at NewSage Press, P.O. Box 607, Troutdale, OR 97060-0607.

Robert Tate Miller is an internationally published writer who has also worked as a television promotions writer/producer. He has written four screenplays and a number of essays on his early years growing up in a small North Carolina mountain town. He can be reached at 950 Hilgard Ave., Los Angeles, CA 90024.

Jason Morin works for Capitol Erectors as vice president and owns Healthy Living Enterprises. Jason and his wife Tracy borrowed $20,000 and made a video on fighting MS. The tape can be purchased on the Internet at *www.megahits.com/healthy*, or by phone at 860-628-9133. The cost of the tape is $20, which includes shipping and handling, and can be paid by check or money order. "Coping with this disease has made me a stronger person," says Morin. "At some point, we must deal with a crisis. The way you handle it is going to determine your quality of life." Jason Morin has two healthy daughters, Brooke, four, and Alexa, two. Jason says, "My wife Tracy has been with me and most likely the reason that I am doing great. Thank you so much, Tracy."

Christa Holder Ocker is her kid's mom; that has been her vocation. She is an author and a sailor; that is her present course. Currently she is working on her fifth picture book. Her poems have appeared in "Authorship" and "Concerto." "Merry Christmas, My Friend" appeared in the *Chicken Soup for the Kid's Soul*.

Diane Payne lives with her seven-year-old daughter near the Mexican border, teaching special education students at the local elementary school. She has been published in numerous magazines, and has a novel coming out from Red Hen Press.

Penny Porter is a mother of six and a grandmother of seven. She is a former teacher and school administrator. Award-winning Penny Porter is a frequent contributor to *Reader's Digest*. She has also been published in a wide range of national magazines and is the author of three books. Her inspiration is rooted in the love of family and human values which children of today need so desperately.

Betty J. Reid resides in Ellicott City, Maryland, with her husband and son. Besides writing poetry, she enjoys reading, collecting antiques and traveling with family. Her family and friends are often the inspiration behind her poetry.

Victoria Robinson lives in a small Texas town with her husband, Asa. She is a homemaker and has written poetry and short stories all of her life to get the events of her life on paper. She has two children and four grandchildren. Now that her children are grown, she has settled down to do what she loves: writing! Having her work published is a dream come true! You may contact Victoria at 235 Port Rd., Angleton, TX 77515, e-mail *victoria@computron.net* or by phone at 409-848-3530.

William L. Rush is a freelance journalist based in Lincoln, Nebraska, and a disability rights advocate. He has written a book *Journey Out of Silence* and numerous articles. Born with cerebral palsy, he can't talk, walk or use his hands. Rush enjoys fellowship at First Baptist Church, hanging out with his fiancée, Chris Robinson, going swimming, playing chess and watching movies. Chris and William will marry in October 1999. For additional information visit his Web site at: *http://www.4w.com/billrush/*.

Carmen Richardson Rutlen decided it was time to dream out loud. Writing is her dream. She is working on her first book, *Dancing Naked . . . in Fuzzy Red Slippers.* She can be reached at Richardson Rutlen Advertising, 236 N. Santa Cruz Ave., Ste. 206, Los Gatos, CA 95030 or by calling 408-658-1808.

Ruchoma Shain is the octogenarian author of *Shining Lights* (where "Tzippie" originally appeared), *Dearest Children, Reaching the Stars, All for the Best* and *All for the Boss*, all published by Feldheim Publishers. With cheer and unshakable faith in divine providence, Mrs. Shain has shared with her ever-growing devoted readership the lessons she has learned from a rich and varied life. Her books are available from Feldheim at *www.feldheim.com* or at 800-237-7149.

Alan D. Shultz lives on a rural farm in Indiana with his wife, Deb, and their three children. He is a newspaper columnist and author. Alan conducts workshops on how to preserve family stories by writing them down. He calls it the creative side to genealogy. He can be reached at 5852 W. 1000 N, Delphi, IN 46923 or by e-mail: *shultz@carlnet.org*.

Robin L. Silverman is an author, inspirational speaker and consultant specializing in human potential. She is the founder of *Creativisions* workshops and lectures, which have taught thousands of men, women and students how to use their creative power of intentional thought. She authored the award-winning children's book *A Bosnian Family,* the story of refugees from the war in the former Yugoslavia. She also authored two audiotapes: *Love from Home* and *Relaxation for Busy People*. Robin lives in Grand Forks, ND, with her husband, Steve, two daughters, and their collie, Lady.

Anne Stortz is a retired retail salesperson who lives in a retirement community in Tulsa, Oklahoma. A widow with two daughters and four grandchildren, she enjoys listening to many types of music, songwriting, reading and watching old movies.

Darlene Uggen is a fifty-three-year-old, recently retired knitter, quilter, wife and mother. "My New Set of Wheels" was a poem that came to her, fully formed, in the middle of the night. It represents the feelings of a group of people whom she got to know through an Internet chat line. They are all affected by Ehlers-Danlos Syndrome, a connective-tissue disorder which affects their joints. This positive and supportive group of people were the inspiration for this poem. Darlene's daughter, Barbara, has EDS and heads a local support group in Washington.

Milly VanDerpool was born in Los Angeles County in 1912 and has lived there all her life except for two years when she lived in Texas while her husband was building the Red River Dam. It was while living in Texas that the younger of her two daughters was born and her brother, six years her junior, was married in Southern California. Since Milly couldn't attend the wedding, she wrote a letter instead. Many years later on the occasion of her daughter's wedding, her brother sent her a copy of the letter. Much to Milly's surprise, the letter was submitted to *Chicken Soup for the Soul*.

David L. Weatherford, Ph.D., a frequent contributor to the *Chicken Soup* books, is a child psychologist and freelance writer. After thirty years of chronic health problems (fifteen years on kidney dialysis), he has learned that love and faith provide the foundation for a strong will and a joyful appreciation of life. David believes his inspiration for living and coping well come from God. He finds that much of the "divine help" he needs is sent to him through his family (Bill, Jackie, Charlie, Susan, Jason, Jared, and Joe Don) and his soul mate (Laura Kathleen). He can be reached at 1658 Doubletree Ln., Nashville, TN 37217 or by e-mail at *dwford777@aol.com*.

Erik Weihenmayer is a speaker, writer and world-class adventurer; an acrobatic skydiver and scuba diver, a long-distance biker and marathon runner; a skier and a mountaineer, an ice climber and rock climber. He has scaled Mt. McKinley (20,320 feet), Kilimanjaro (19,300 feet), Aconcagua (22,800 feet), and El Capitan, the famed 3,300-foot rock face in Yosemite Valley. What sets Erik apart, more than his adventurous spirit, is that he is blind, but he has never let this interfere with his passion for an exciting and fulfilling life. Erik's feats have earned him ESPN's ARETE Award for courage in sports, the Gene Autry Award, and introduction into the National Wrestling Hall of Fame. Erik inspires readers to reexamine their perceptions about what is possible. "Someone once told me that I would need to realize my limitations, but I've always thought it much more exciting to realize my potential."

Jeffrey Weinstein is president and chief executive officer of Certified Federal Credit Union in Los Angeles, California. He is also founder and director of the Keene Alliance Group, a management-consulting firm that puts small businesses in touch with proven professionals. In addition, Jeffrey chairs "Kidz 'n Motion," a children's medical research foundation, and spends his time traveling as an organizational-leadership and motivational speaker to schools, corporations and various other organizations. He can be reached at Keene Alliance

Group, 23312 W. Montecito Pl., Valencia, CA 91354, by calling 661-263-6589 or by e-mail at *jeffrey.weinstein@keenalliance.com.*

Nikki Willett is currently attending the University of Arizona, majoring in management information systems. She just returned from celebrating Laura's twenty-first birthday in Texas and would like to thank everyone who has made a difference. She can be reached at 602-870-7729.

Bettie B. Youngs, Ph.D., Ed.D., is an international lecturer and consultant living in Del Mar, California. She is the author of fourteen books published in twenty-eight languages including the bestseller *Values from the Heartland* and *Gifts of the Heart, Tasteberry Tales and Tasteberry Tales for Teens.* You can contact Bettie by wiriting to 3060 Racetrack View Dr., Del Mar, CA 92014.

A New Season of

Chicken Soup for the Soul

Chicken Soup for the Unsinkable Soul
Code #6986 • $12.95

Chicken Soup for the Single's Soul
Code #7060 • $12.95

Chicken Soup for the College Soul
Code #7028 • $12.95

Each one of these new heartwarming titles will bring
inspiration both to you and the loved ones in your life.

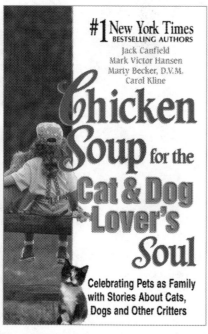

More from the *Chicken Soup for the Soul®* Series

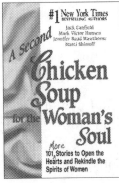

Chicken Soup for the Soul® Series

Each one of these inspiring *New York Times* bestsellers brings you exceptional stories, tales and verses guaranteed to lift your spirits, soothe your soul and warm your heart! A perfect gift for anyone you love, including yourself!

A 6th Bowl of Chicken Soup for the Soul, #6625—$12.95
A 5th Portion of Chicken Soup for the Soul, #5432—$12.95
A 4th Course of Chicken Soup for the Soul, #4592—$12.95
A 3rd Serving of Chicken Soup for the Soul, #3790—$12.95
A 2nd Helping of Chicken Soup for the Soul, #3316—$12.95
Chicken Soup for the Soul, #262X—$12.95